# PRESSURE POLITICS

# THE FOURTH OF JULY.

### UNCLE SAM IS IN BAD COMPANY.

One of the best known Anti-Saloon League cartoons. The League regarded the license system as an "unseemly partnership" between government and vice, which could be speedily destroyed by extending the suffrage to women.

# PRESSURE POLITICS

## THE STORY OF
## THE ANTI-SALOON LEAGUE

BY

PETER H. ODEGARD

1966

OCTAGON BOOKS, INC.

*New York*

*To*
MY PARENTS
THORVALD AND HULDA

# PREFACE

Democratic government implies that "the people shall rule." This means, if it means anything, that public opinion shall find expression in law. The mechanism by which this takes place seems to me one of the basic problems of popular government. Democracy without organization is inconceivable, and public opinion that is unorganized is likely to be evanescent and ineffective — a phantom. In a Greek city state or in a New England town the determination of the collective will upon a particular problem will occasion no great difficulty. But direct democracy falls down in the face of increasing numbers. The individual plain man, swallowed up in a sea of highly differentiated human beings, finds it necessary to organize with others of a like mind so that by concerted action they may bend the state to their will. Political parties are one result of this process. But political parties invariably include adherents whose wills are hopelessly at variance upon all but a very few questions. Especially is this true where, as in the United States, a two-party system and tradition exist.

It is this situation which has engendered the pressure group. Within the matrices of the major parties minor associations are formed which, without regard for party opinion on other matters, carry on agitation for or against projects deemed favorable or prejudicial to their interests. In 1921 Senator LaFollette, the elder, could point to one hundred and seventy such national organizations with permanent offices at Washington.

The Anti-Saloon League is one such pressure group. It is, I believe, one of the most powerful. The present study is an

attempt to give a closer view of the tactics which the League
employs. These methods are not peculiar to the League.
They are employed by the Association Against the Prohibition
Amendment, the League of Women Voters and innumerable
associations interested in influencing legislation.

The Anti-Saloon League, however, differs from other pressure groups in that it is an organization of Protestant churches.
This fact worries some people considerably, for if there are
those who fear that the election of a Catholic President will put
us under the iron rule of Rome, there are others no less fearful
lest we be governed by a narrow and bigoted group whose ideas
find their historic source in Geneva. Samuel Harden Church,
president of the Carnegie Institute of Pittsburgh, testifying before a Senate Committee in 1926, said:

What I am trying to call to the attention of the committee —
myself a Protestant and a church man — is the fact that some of
the Protestant Churches of our land, either by banding together, or
by working independently but reciprocally, and all of them using
prohibition as an entering wedge, are aiming by these indirect
methods to effect a union of church and state through the back door,
when the Constitution of the United States prohibits them from
accomplishing that purpose through the front door.

The evident conclusions of such people seem to be that the
church has no right to engage in politics. Individual persuasion, not legislation, should be the method employed to advance God's Kingdom. The church should confine its attention
to the future life and not meddle in mundane matters. Such a
view is of very doubtful validity. Life cannot be rigidly
categorized. Business, religion, club life, politics are not
so many distinct entities. They are parts of a full social
personality. The business man does not lay aside his economic philosophy when he considers a political problem.
Churchmen do not divest themselves of their religion when they
turn to vote. To protect the state from the influences of

church, business, labor and other such associations is to leave
it a meaningless void. To say that the members of business
organizations or religious groups shall not take an active part
in politics is to say that they shall have no voice in the determination of the legal arrangements governing their own lives.
It is not a sufficient answer to say that their influence should be
individual and not corporate. Corporate activity is the rule
of the day. Without organization, in the modern state, the
individual is lost and his influence is negligible. If he goes to
Washington or Albany as a private citizen in an effort to influence legislation, it is improbable that he will so much as be
given a hearing. If he goes as the agent of the United States
Chamber of Commerce, the Association Against the Prohibition
Amendment or the Ku Klux Klan, his influence will be considerable. Representative government is not adequately pictured when viewed as the mere selection of a number of
political servants. It embraces also the representatives of voluntary associations who advise, coerce, or cajole those servants.
To deny to the churches representation in this latter sense is
not only to defeat real representative government but to deny
our public servants the counsel of an important body of opinion.

Responsibility for what follows is entirely mine except where
otherwise indicated. For access to the material I am indebted
to Hugh Fox of the United States Brewers' Association, Joseph
Debar of the National Wholesale Liquor Dealers' Association,
Hon. George H. Tinkham of Massachusetts and the officers of
the Anti-Saloon League, particularly Arthur J. Davis, Orville
S. Poland, Ernest Cherrington, Boyd P. Doty, Miss Anne Tubbs
and the late Wayne B. Wheeler. I wish to thank Professor
Arthur Macmahon of Columbia University for suggesting that
such a book be written and for his careful reading and kindly
criticism. To Joseph McGoldrick of New York City I owe a
very great debt for his painstaking examination and criticism
of the manuscript which, in its final form, embodies many of his

suggestions   For typing, I want to thank Miss Josephine Kosky.

Above all I am sure that whatever merit the book has is due, in no small degree, to the inspiration, friendly counsel and patient persistence of my wife.

P. H. O.

New York, June, 1928.

# CONTENTS

## CHAPTER I

## THE CHURCH IN ACTION AGAINST
## THE SALOON

In November, 1832, two men of God, the Rev. John J. Shepherd and Philo P. Stewart, the latter a missionary among the Cherokee Indians, entered upon a tract of virgin forest in Lorain County, Ohio, and claimed it as the site of a new institution of learning. These men envisioned a college dedicated to "the diffusion of useful science, sound morality and pure religion, among the growing multitude of the Mississippi Valley . . . and in extending those blessings to the destitute millions which overspread the earth." The name Oberlin was chosen to commemorate the ideals of the Rev. John Frederick Oberlin, minister to the French and German population of a valley on the borders of Alsace and Lorraine. With thirty-three students, on December 3, 1833, the institution began its work. It was chartered in 1834 as the "Oberlin Collegiate Institute."

Oberlin has lived steadfastly according to the ideals of its founders. It has always been a reformist institution courageously crusading for "sound morality and pure religion." At a time when women were classed with criminals, idiots and Indians not taxed, it opened its doors to them and became the first coeducational college in America. In 1835, when Negroes had few rights which civilized men were bound to respect, the trustees of Oberlin admitted them as students. In the same year it welcomed three professors and thirty students who had left Lane Theological Seminary, in Cincinnati, because that institution would not tolerate abolitionists. The college was a center of this agitation and takes pride in the fact that it was a station on the " underground railway " from slavery to freedom.[1]

It is not surprising to find Oberlin in the vanguard of the fight against liquor. Here, in 1874, the initial organization was effected which subsequently, under the name Anti-Saloon League of America, proved the undoing of John Barleycorn. On the evening of March 20, 1874, a mass meeting was called to deal with a crisis in the local temperance situation. The Oberlin Temperance Alliance, devoted to the complete suppression of the " traffic in and the use of intoxicating liquors," was the result. James H. Fairchild, president of Oberlin College, became its first president. The Alliance differed from most of the pledge-signing temperance bodies of that day in that it sought from the outset to suppress saloons. In February, 1876, the executive committee determined to expand the activities of the Alliance. The next year, enlisting other college towns in the state, it began agitation for a college-town local option law. Professor J. M. Ellis of Oberlin, who took charge, may be regarded as the first lobbyist employed by the organization which later became the Anti-Saloon League. The Metcalf local option bill for college towns became law in 1882.

Meeting on December 8, 1887, the Alliance urged a statewide local option law for all townships. The Rev. H. H. Russell, of Berea, was employed to lead the fight for such a measure. A substitute was provided to occupy his pulpit and he devoted his entire time to the work. Headquarters were opened at Columbus and with the coöperation of the pastors and churches a Local Option League was formed. Petitions were circulated throughout the state demanding the passage of the Township Option Bill. Under this pressure the bill was put through the House and went to the Senate. Here it was vigorously contested. A preliminary poll showed a majority

[1] *A History of Honor: What Oberlin has meant and now means to American Life*, Oberlin, 1923; also, *General Catalogue of Oberlin College, 1893–1908*.

of one in its favor.  Two days before the vote was to be taken, Senator Crook of Dayton, who had promised to support the bill, announced that three committees of brewers, distillers and saloon keepers of Dayton had visited him and that he had decided to vote against it.  That afternoon, Mr. Russell went to Dayton.  Letters, telegrams and petitions from citizens of that city poured in upon the recalcitrant Crook demanding that he support the bill.  The Senator did vote for it and the measure passed by a majority of one.  A friend of the bill waggishly remarked that Isaiah's prophecy had been fulfilled: " The Crook-ed shall be made straight and the rough places plain."

Russell was now convinced of the feasibility of a permanent state-wide organization of churches and temperance societies to fight the liquor traffic.  In his final report to the Oberlin Alliance in 1888 he urged such a plan.  The following year a permanent organization for Lorain County was effected, but Russell, who now went to the Southwest Tabernacle of Kansas City, Missouri, was unable to take charge and the matter was dropped.  In Kansas City, Russell succeeded in organizing the Missouri Anti-Liquor League in 1890 and became its president.  In 1891 he was called to the Armour Mission in Chicago and the Missouri experiment languished.  Twice in 1892 Russell spoke at Oberlin advocating the formation of a state-wide organization for Ohio.  There was a disposition to act upon his plan, but only if he took charge of it.  He was unwilling to give up his work in Chicago and no action was taken.  In the spring of 1893 Russell heard that a state convention had been held in Indiana to form a state-wide, non-partisan temperance society.  He hastened to Indianapolis but the churches were unwilling to accept his plan and the whole matter was dropped.

On May 24, 1893, the executive committee of the Oberlin Alliance, meeting in the Oberlin College Library, agreed to Russell's plan for a state-wide organization.  He consented to become superintendent, and the Alliance agreed to finance the movement until it was able to stand on its own feet. Russell's salary was to be " at the rate $2000 a year until such time as that salary is fixed by the State Executive Committee." Russell outlined his plan for uniting all temperance forces in a single Anti-Saloon League. The aims of the organization were expressed as follows:

Assembled in a union mass meeting in the First Congregational Church of Oberlin, Ohio, on this 4th day of June, 1893, the friends of temperance in Oberlin adopt the following:

*Resolved,* That it is highly important, in our view, that there should be formed in the state of Ohio an organization, permanent and aggressive in character, in which all classes of the friends of temperance can unite, and led by a superintendent who shall give his entire time to the development and prosecution of the work.

*Resolved,* That this organization shall have in view the following ends: (1) The development and unification of a temperance public sentiment through the agency of local organizations, public addresses and such other methods of education and direction as may from time to time suggest themselves; (2) The enforcement of laws already on the statute books; (3) The enactment of further legislation as public sentiment may warrant in order that our people may be saved from the evils of the drink habit and delivered from the debauching curse of the drink traffic; (4) That to bring about such an organization we will undertake to raise $500 toward the expenses of the same, and hereby authorize the officers of the Oberlin Temperance Alliance to appoint temporary officers and take whatever measures may be necessary to carry this action into effect.[2]

Five hundred and thirteen dollars a year, for a period of three years, was pledged. Russell brought his activities in Chicago to a speedy close and took up the work of his new organization in Ohio. The movement caught the public imagination and spread rapidly. By September Dr. Russell was able to report subscriptions to the amount of about three thousand dollars, and to say that other temperance organizations and the press had given them " God Speed." A provisional organization was effected, and in October the Inter-denominational

[2] E. H. Cherrington, *History of the Anti-Saloon League,* Westerville, 1913.

Temperance Alliance was merged with the Anti-Saloon League by the simple expedient of adding several of its officers to the provisional board of trustees.

State headquarters for the League had opened in Columbus in September with Russell in charge. The organization developed rapidly. In November the Rev. Harry B. White of Toledo was made district manager, and in January, 1894, the Rev. E. C. Dinwiddie was chosen to assist in the legislative work. By May three hundred local committees had been formed, a state paper, *Anti-Saloon*, was being published, eight thousand dollars had been raised, and the Anti-Saloon League was a going concern.[3]

### A National Organization

The dramatic tactics and sudden success of the Ohio League attracted immediate attention in other states. Russell received numerous requests for information, and the "Ohio Idea" began to spread. Early in 1895 a call for an interstate convention was about to be issued for the middle western states, when the Anti-Saloon League of the District of Columbia invited the Ohio organization among others to join in a convention to organize a national Anti-Saloon League.

This latter move was the result of conversations between Archbishop Ireland of the Roman Catholic Church, the Rev. Luther B. Wilson, president of the District of Columbia Anti-Saloon League, and Dr. A. J. Kynett, chairman of the Permanent Committee on Temperance and Prohibition of the Methodist Episcopal Church. Dr. Kynett had suggested that the

[3] Although the Anti-Saloon League of Ohio was not the first of its kind, it proved to be the most effective and became the model for others. Its central idea of utilizing the organized churches as a political battering ram has been the secret of its success. A state-wide league of civic and religious temperance bodies had been formed in Pennsylvania May 13, 1889. This organization was merged in the Christian Temperance Alliance of Pennsylvania, April 4, 1893. In July, 1891, at the National Temperance Convention at Saratoga, resolutions favoring citizens' leagues were adopted. Perhaps the first organization specially to utilize the churches was the Massachusetts Anti-Saloon League, formed in the spring of 1892. It grew steadily in power and influence. On June 23, 1893, an Anti-Saloon League was organized in the District of Columbia.

Washington League take the initiative, and on October 18, 1895, after some correspondence, the call was given to the press.

The convention assembled on Tuesday, December 17, 1895, at the Calvary Baptist Church in Washington, with the Rev. Dr. Wilson presiding. One hundred and sixty-one delegates were present, representing more than forty-nine different temperance and religious organizations. The Rev. Hiram Price of Washington became the first president. At a second convention the following year 557 were in attendance, representing thirty-six states and territories and a total of 146 separate organizations. The third convention was held at Columbus, Ohio, in 1898. The attendance rose to 848 and the number of affiliated societies to 190. The League grew steadily.[4]

### The Weaver's Beam

Dr. Russell is by common consent regarded as the father of the Anti-Saloon League movement. He tells us that as a lad of eighteen, in 1873, he had heard Bishop Foster say, " The time will come when Lord God Almighty will take a spear like a weaver's beam, and He will drive the satanic liquor traffic down to its native hell! " In later years Russell became convinced that he was that spear. His speeches are replete with this belief. His own colorful description of how he came to see the light is worth quoting at some length. Speaking to the League's fifteenth convention at Columbus in 1913, he said:

The Anti-Saloon League movement was begun by Almighty God. . . . Often I have been asked how I came to suggest this plan of organization to my Oberlin friends and to enlist as the first organizer and leader. As often I have answered, " I could not help it. There was nothing else I could do." To the glory of Our Father, let me

[4] For the foregoing history of the Anti-Saloon League, the author has drawn upon numerous sources, including private interviews, correspondence and the following publications: *Proceedings of the Conventions of the Anti-Saloon League*, 1895–1915; G. M. Hammell, *Passing of the Saloon*, Cincinnati, 1908, pp. 183–95; E. H. Cherrington, *History of the Anti-Saloon League*, Westerville, 1913; *Evolution of Prohibition in the United States*, Westerville, 1920; *The American Patriot*, especially May, 1913.

show you in some detail today, how wondrously He moulded my life and even used untoward events in such a way as to make it His errand for me to set this League in motion. In humility we may plainly see, as in other cases in personal and national history, " God hath chosen the weak things of the earth to confound the mighty."

As a boy, I saw premature graves heaped by the drink venders over many near relatives and friends. Indeed, the saloon almost caught me, as a youth, in its jaws of destruction. My beloved brother tells in humble confession how he fought the imperious appetite a losing fight for fifteen years. Then, thank God, when I had acquired, through sympathetic ministry to my brother and by many other similar sorrows, so clear a title to hate this despoiler, and when I had dedicated my life to help its destruction, one of the first blessings my Father in Heaven gave for my sacrifice was the restoration of the soul of my dear brother, and for twenty years he has been a Christian conqueror! A year on a newspaper in 1876 was very instructive to me about drink. Then later, as a lawyer, during the years from 1878 to 1883, I prosecuted these lawbreakers, and learned the stony-hearted treason and perjury of the rumsellers. Two experiences also during my practice at the bar, taught me how to bring things to pass in such a cause as this — my work for the passage of a bill through the Iowa legislature, and again for the pardon by the governor of a convict in the penitentiary. In both cases the private letters and telegrams of legislative and executive constituents brought the desired result. Then came to me that mysterious change when the human will, despite its stubbornness, was subdued by the mighty power of God, and I gladly laid aside personal aims and political ambitions to devote my life to the gospel ministry. For the period of preparation I found myself at Oberlin. It is very plain now that it was the hand of the Most High that turned my course toward that historic seat of reform. There for five years, God held me under the benign influences of that militant college center where I could be trained as a reformer and just where His guiding star would hang above the future cradle of reform.

Two other preliminary facts laid emphasis upon my call. Under my seminary ministry, and because of my appeals, at Berea, a suburb of Cleveland, six saloons were closed. During this campaign a vicious grog-seller sneaked upon me and knocked me down in the street. This changed at least fifty votes, and we carried the election by a majority of six. I enforced the Prohibition against them, trying the cases myself as prosecuting attorney. God had sent me, mean-

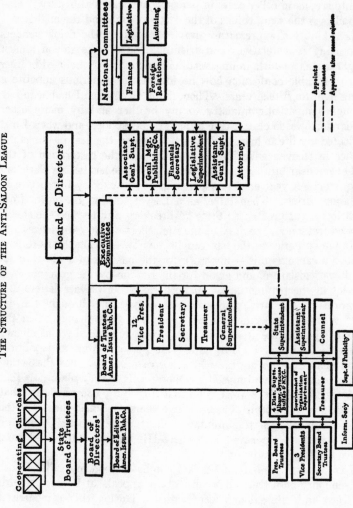

THE STRUCTURE OF THE ANTI-SALOON LEAGUE

Appoints
Nominates
Appoints after second rejection

1. In states where the League is not incorporated "Board of Directors" would read "Headquarters Committee."

while, to see the hell-sent tragedies in the lives of those to whom I ministered at Kansas City and Chicago, and I was over and over shocked and indignant by the agony of what I saw as well as what I remembered. At Kansas City I daily passed the Rochester Brewery, located between my home and the church. Always when I passed this devil's-broth factory I prayed God to stay the tide of sin and shame flowing therefrom. During my ministry in those cities whenever I passed a saloon I sent up a prayer, " O, God, stop this! " At length God plainly said to me, " You know how to do it; go and help answer your own prayers! " At last, as I have told many thousands of people, in the presence of an orphaned boy and girl, their father drunk upon the floor, by the coffin-side of their mother dead from drink, I pledged the boy that he would never drink and that he would teach his little sister to abstain, and then and there I registered my vow before Almighty God to go out to my brethren in the churches and to plead with them to lay aside their differences upon other questions and come together in a never-ending war on behalf of suffering humanity until the cause of such tragedies as this shall be put away forever. At a Conneaut, Ohio, church in the winter of 1893 a pastor, introducing me to his congregation, said: " There was a man sent from God whose name was John; it is equally true there was a man sent from God whose name was Russell! " In the awed silence of my heart, I was compelled to believe the statement was true.[5]

## The Framework

Although the call for the national league came from the Anti-Saloon League of the District of Columbia, the form of the organization and the methods which have been consistently followed were the result of the experience in Ohio and came to be known as the " Ohio Idea." [6] Stated briefly, the pillars upon which the structure rests are: (1) paid professional officers and workers giving their entire time to League activity; (2) a financial system based upon monthly subscriptions; (3) political agitation directed toward the defeat of wet and the

[5] *Proceedings of the Fifteenth Anti-Saloon League Convention,* pp. 89 ff.

[6] Ohio not only furnished the idea, but also the men; more than forty state superintendents of the League have come from that state.

election of dry candidates; (4) concentration upon the liquor question — refusal to be sidetracked by other issues.

### Board of Directors

An examination of the League's existing constitution (adopted in 1914) and its by-laws will give some idea of the nature of this organization. The real ruling power centers in the board of directors and the executive committee. The former comprises two representatives from each state league. Every state having over a million population, however, is entitled to an additional member for each million of population or major portion thereof. To prevent the populous urban states from gaining control, it is provided that no single state may have more than five representatives. The board has power to make all by-laws. It appoints the following national officers: president, twelve vice-presidents, secretary, treasurer, and general superintendent. In addition the board selects an executive committee which in fact becomes the active governing body. The board of directors also chooses, upon nomination by the executive committee, an associate general superintendent, a general manager of its publishing interests, a financial secretary, a legislative superintendent, an assistant general superintendent, and an attorney. As the executive committee is appointed by a board of directors, it may be conjectured that the nominations will be satisfactory. The powers of these bodies may be further indicated by the fact that amendments to the constitution are made by a two-thirds vote of the board upon recommendation by two-thirds of the executive committee; in the absence of such recommendation, a three-fourths vote of the board suffices.

### Executive Committee

The national executive committee consists of nineteen members chosen biennially by the board of directors. They are usually members of the board. There is one member for each of sixteen districts into which the country is divided, and three chosen at large, of whom not more than one may come from any one of the districts. These districts are determined roughly on the basis of population; New York constitutes a single district; the New England states taken together comprise another. Not more than one-third of the members may be salaried employees of the League. The executive committee fixes the time and place of League conventions. These meet every two years unless the executive committee by a two-thirds vote calls a special convention in the interim. At these conventions all persons are recognized as delegates who are appointed by local churches and other affiliated organizations.[7]

The executive committee acts in all matters for the board of directors when the latter is not in session. Its duties include direction and control of the movements and expenditures of the active officers of the League; the provision of assistance wherever necessary; the preparation of a budget; the fixing of salaries for all active officers. It has power to fill all vacancies occurring in the interim between meetings of the board of directors. It determines all questions of policy or procedure, investigates the financial condition of the League, and makes assessments upon the state leagues for the support of the national league. These powers make the executive committee the most important organ in the League's government.

*General Superintendent*

The by-laws define the powers and duties of the various boards and officers. Only the more important of these need be mentioned. The general superintendent supervises League activities throughout the United States. He has authority to nominate state superintendents, and under the provisions of the

---

[7] No machinery is provided in the constitution for taking or making effective the votes of delegates. The real control in the convention, as outside, resides in the board of directors, central executive committee and voting officials. The convention serves as little more than a dry ballyhoo.

constitution this amounts to virtual selection. The state superintendents are required to report to him each month, and tech-
nically at least his power over the state branches is enormous.

The financial secretary supervises the work of securing
funds. Upon authorization from the executive committee and
the local organization, he conducts subscription campaigns
within the states and sees that the percentage due the national
league is forthcoming.

### The Publishing Company

The Anti-Saloon League owns the American Issue Publishing Company [8] at Westerville, Ohio. This is the League's right
arm of propaganda. The manager of the company, who is appointed by the board of directors of the League, is in some respects the most important of all the officials, for upon the quality and quantity of the literature circulated depends much of
the League's influence. Although theoretically under the direction of the executive committee and the board of directors,
the editorial and business management is quite largely in his
hands.

### A National Lobbyist

The legislative superintendent is the congressional lobbyist.
His influence with the state leagues is also considerable, since
it is from him, in large measure, that they learn of the conduct
of their representatives in Congress. Nominally under the direction of the executive committee and the general superintendent, he has, in fact, become the outstanding figure of
the League's structure. Under the efficient management of
the late Wayne B. Wheeler, this office assumed an importance

---

[8] The American Issue Publishing Company is incorporated under the laws of
Ohio. The board of directors of the League chooses five trustee-directors of
the corporation, for a term of one year, who hold all property in the printing
establishment. They receive no salary and do not have power to convey any
of the property except under authority of the national board of directors. The
profits go to the League.

in the public mind comparable to that of a national political boss.

## State Structure

Within each state there is a state board of trustees (called a board of directors in the few states where the League is incorporated) made up of representatives from the various churches coöperating with the League. It operates through a headquarters committee of at least five members chosen biennially. The board has power to determine questions of policy for the state league in harmony with the policies of the national organization. It also chooses the state's representatives on the national board of directors.

The state superintendents are elected by the state leagues, annually, upon nomination by the general superintendent. If the state league does not approve the first nomination, it may ask the general superintendent to name a second. A rejection must be made in writing, for cause, within forty days of the nomination. Should the second nomination prove unsatisfactory, the national executive committee elects the state superintendent. His salary is fixed by the state board, subject to the approval of the national executive committee. State superintendents supervise the work in their respective areas, subject to the direction of the state headquarters committee, the general superintendent and the national executive committee.

Notwithstanding the apparently close supervision by the national officers, there is much leeway for the state superintendent to act as he sees fit. His familiarity with the local situation renders his opinion especially valuable and usually decisive. There is extensive room for experimentation, and few superintendents complain of undue interference. In this connection the value of the federal character of the League is apparent, for an experiment which has proved successful in one state may be copied by another and may, if consistently effective, be laid down by the national executive committee as the policy for all states to pursue. Successful superintendents are rewarded by transfer to a larger and more important state or promotion to a national office.[9]

Local organization within each state, apart from that above described, varies greatly according to its wealth, population, and political importance. Ohio is divided into several districts with a deputy superintendent for each; there are also county superintendents. Generally speaking, except for state and district organization, local committees have been *ad hoc;* they are formed anew for each campaign. After the New York league had aided in defeating Senator Wadsworth in 1926, the headquarters committee adopted the following plan of organization: " (1) County conferences as the initial step in a comprehensive system of organization reaching down to the community. (2) The selection with great care of a man and woman in each election district of the state as local representatives of the various interests of the League. . . . (3) The organization of these representatives into county committees to serve as the connecting links between the state and district offices of the League and the local communities of the state." [10]

The form of organization here outlined lends itself to highly

[9] William H. Anderson successively filled the positions of state superintendent in Illinois, Maryland and New York, and acted as national legislative superintendent for a time. E. H. Cherrington had demonstrated his abilities as superintendent of the Anti-Saloon League in the State of Washington and was called to Westerville to take charge of the American Issue Publishing Company when it was organized, a position he continues to fill very ably. Arthur Davis, former superintendent of the League in Massachusetts, was transferred to New York after the Anderson scandal, because it was felt that the situation required the services of a level-headed, straight-forward and courageous man. Wayne Wheeler served in the ranks as a speaker while he was studying law, later as attorney for the Ohio league, then as its superintendent, from which office he was sent to Washington as national attorney. Upon the resignation of Mr. Dinwiddie, he became general counsel and national legislative superintendent. Numerous other instances could be cited to illustrate the skillful manner in which the Anti-Saloon League has made the most of the services of its able men.

[10] *American Issue,* New York Edition, Jan. 22, 1927.

centralized control. Federal in theory, in practice it has all the advantages of unitary control. It is true that the state boards of trustees are selected by the various organizations affiliated with the League, but it is doubtful whether the rank and file have any real power. The actual government has always centered in the hands of a few men. Purley Baker, Wayne Wheeler, E. C. Dinwiddie, Howard Russell, Ernest Cherrington, F. Scott McBride, Bishop Luther B. Wilson, S. E. Nicholson, Arthur J. Davis, the Rev. James Cannon, Jr., the Rev. A. J. Barton, Filmore Condit, William F. Cochran, and a few others, have really constituted the directive power of the League.

## The Machine

By working through the organized churches, the League can reach every part of the state, and its power and influence vary directly with the influence of certain coöperating Protestant churches. The plan of organization as described by Dr. A. J. Kynett, one of its founders, is " a company in every church; a regiment in every city; an army corps in every state; a conquering army in the nation." [11]

" The scheme of organization might well excite the envious approval of an oriental despot," said the brewers. " Its distinguishing feature was the absence of any membership except the official personnel. No machinery was provided in the constitution for taking or making effectual the votes of delegates to conventions and it is apparent that their function was to be entirely ornamental, the determination of all matters of policy . . . being absolutely in the hands of the all-powerful junto at national headquarters." [12] Whether this characterization is held to be justified may well depend on one's point of view. It is certain that any real influence from the rank and file is not within the contemplation of the League. To allow complete

[11] *Proceedings of the Sixteenth Anti-Saloon League Convention,* 1915, p. 110.
[12] *Year Book of the United States Brewers' Association,* 1919, p. 7.

democracy would destroy the unity of purpose necessary, dissipate leadership and prevent quick, effective action.  Much fruitless dissension is avoided by centralized control, and the League sacrifices democracy for effective leadership.

Charged with being a political machine, the League has answered, " The church is a machine and the League is a machine within a machine." But they continue, " The ordinary political machine is built and maintained for the personal advantage of the biggest cogs in the machine.  The Anti-Saloon League is so constructed that all personal advantage is submerged to the one task of establishing sobriety in the nation." [13]  The League was organized to give church people an effective political organization to fight the liquor traffic.[14]  The existing political parties, it was felt, left to their own devices, were hand and glove with the saloon.

Independent action was essential.  It was out of the question for the various churches to enter the field of politics directly, and the Anti-Saloon League was the solution.[15]  Temperance societies in or outside of the churches were asked to coöperate. The W. C. T. U., Good Templars, Sons of Temperance, National Temperance Council, Scientific Temperance Federation, Catholic Abstinence League, besides a host of others, have given consistent support.  Prior to 1915 the Civic League had been regarded as the official spokesman of the allied temperance organizations in New York.  By 1915 the Anti-Saloon League had so demonstrated its effectiveness that the Civic League " gladly yielded the leadership in the temperance campaign to

---

[13] H. M. Chalfant, " The Anti-Saloon League — Why and What ? " *Annals of the American Academy of Political and Social Science,* Sept., 1923, pp. 279 ff.

[14] *American Issue,* Maryland Edition, July 8, 1911.

[15] For example, when, in 1905, the legislative committee of the newly formed Temperance Society of the Methodist Episcopal Church addressed inquiries to Senator J. H. Gallinger and Representative C. E. Littlefield, the recognized temperance leaders in Congress, as to the best tactics, they unequivocally replied that the best plan was to work through the Anti-Saloon League.  This advice was promptly acted upon and the Methodists constituted the League as their agency for national legislative work.  See W. H. Anderson, *The Church in Action against the Saloon* (pamphlet), Westerville, 1910, p. 35.

the Anti-Saloon League." [16]   Church societies, it is felt, are
often too narrow and " exclude thousands of citizens who are
opposed to the saloon and who have no interest in the churches
as such." [17]

Nevertheless the churches constitute the backbone of the
organization.  Outside the League, say the leaders, the church
is politically powerless on the liquor question.  " The church
that refuses to open its doors to the Anti-Saloon League is not
hurting the League as such.  It is only crippling the agency for
accomplishing what that church and every other church wants
done." [18]   There is no cause for jealousy.  " The League is not
another temperance society.  It is not the rival of any organization, but, as its name implies, a League of organizations.  It is
a clearing house for church and temperance societies.  Its
primary purpose is not the creation of anti-saloon sentiment
but the direction of existing sentiment to secure immediate results. . . .  It is supported by Catholics, Protestants and
' Liberals.'  Democrats, Republicans, Prohibitionists and Socialists work harmoniously together through it." [19]

## A Protestant Oligarchy

Critics insist that the League does not represent the churches
but rather a powerful political group using part of the Protestant church population to further its schemes for political
domination.  " While the League claimed to represent the
churches, the latter were without voice in the management and
were calculated to furnish the votes and pay the expenses of
the autocracy purporting to act in their name." [20]   Behind the
mask of Prohibition, they assert, it seeks Protestant political
supremacy.  " Prohibition is merely the title of the movement.

---

[16] *Proceedings of the Sixteenth Convention of the Anti-Saloon League*, 1915.
[17] *American Issue*, New York Edition, April, 1909.
[18] *American Issue*, Maryland Edition, Jan. 8, 1910.
[19] Anderson, *The Church in Action*, p. 10.
[20] *Year Book of the United States Brewers' Association*, 1919, p. 8.

Its real purpose is of a religious, sectarian character. . . .
How many Roman Catholics are prohibitionists? How many
Jews? . . . Are Lutherans? Are German Protestants generally? What is the proportion of Episcopalians . . . to that
of the Methodists, Baptists, and Presbyterians? . . . The answers to these questions will, I venture to say, prove conclu-
sively the assertion that the fight is for the supremacy of its
[the Protestant church's] ideas," said the brewers' star orator.[21]
    Certainly the Anti-Saloon League has received no appreci-
able support from the Catholics or Jews. The fact that the
Episcopal and Lutheran churches do not as a rule admit the
League speakers seems to justify the statement that it is a
league of Methodist, Baptist, Presbyterian, and Congregational
churches, although it is not, by any means, limited to these denominations. In New Jersey fifteen distinct denominations
are represented on the board of trustees, while in most states
there are more than the four last mentioned.[22]
    The Anti-Saloon League did not find coöperation with the
churches a primrose path. If the League was in politics, there
was also much politics in the League. The Baptists, Methodists, Presbyterians and Congregationalists were quite willing
to endorse, but this endorsement did not always imply coöperation. Efforts of the League to secure the official coöperation
of church councils have generally failed. The question of
actually admitting League speakers to the pulpit has always
been left to the decision of individual congregations. In Indiana it had long been urged that the Presbyterian State Synod,
in addition to endorsing the League, elect two of its trustees.
In 1908 the judicial commission of the national synod, which is
the supreme court of the Presbyterian Church, had decided in

[21] Percy Andreae, *Prohibition Movement*, Chicago, 1915, p. 12.
[22] *Proceedings of the General Assembly of the Presbyterian Church*, 1914,
p. 70; *American Issue*, National Edition, May 17, 1912. In final analysis, the
question of coöperation is left to the officers and congregations of the separate churches.

a case from North Dakota that the synods had no authority to appoint such representatives, in that their confession of faith limited them to strictly ecclesiastical matters. None the less, several states, among them Indiana, continued to nominate trustees. In 1911 an appeal was taken to the general assembly, which referred the matter to its judicial committee. This committee held that the action of the Indiana synod was invalid, but the general assembly expressed its sympathy with the League and pledged coöperation so far as the church constitution would permit.[23] Such a ruling did not, it should be noted, interfere with the right of local churches to coöperate. In 1914 sixty cities petitioned the general assembly to amend the constitution to permit state synods to be represented on the League board. The amendment was rejected but the assembly declared: " The General Assembly rejoices in the good work of the various denominational temperance agencies, the Anti-Saloon League, National Temperance Society, the Women's Christian Temperance Union and all other organizations coöperating for the destruction of the liquor traffic." [24]

The League's efforts to secure church coöperation were resented and on occasion impeded by certain Prohibition Party leaders. In 1912, the *American Issue* declared that there was a determined effort being made on the part of that organization to break the Anti-Saloon League in Indiana by fighting it in the councils of the churches.[25] The *American Advance,* a Prohibi-

[23] *American Issue,* Indiana Edition, June 11, 1912; Ohio Edition, June 1, 1912.
[24] *Proceedings of the General Assembly of the Presbyterian Church,* 1914, pp. 70 and 99.
[25] *American Issue,* Indiana Edition, June 11, 1912.
" I have had a wild-eyed Prohibition Party preacher," said Baker, " whose church compelled him to open up for a League service, introduce me with these words: ' Mr. Baker, the Superintendent of the Anti-Saloon League, is present and will speak to us. I do not believe in the League nor in the work that Mr. Baker is doing but we will try to hear him patiently.' . . . Preachers and laymen who could not distinguish between a ' fighting chance and a chance to fight ' wrote me when we were struggling for a piece of advance legislation, and would be compelled to yield some point in order to secure it, asking, ' How

tion Party paper, declared that the Anti-Saloon League was a Methodist political machine which " wants to shove every other church temperance society off the earth." [26]

Statistics showing the total number of churches coöperating with the League are nowhere available. Eleven state superintendents responded to inquiries for such information; their figures cover the period 1911–25. The others either do not know or will not tell. The proportion which the affiliated churches bear to the total number of Protestant churches is given for eight states.

TABLE I

CHURCHES COÖPERATING WITH STATE LEAGUES

| STATE | NUMBER OF CHURCHES | PERCENT OF TOTAL | MEMBERSHIP |
|---|---|---|---|
| Arkansas............ | 1,000 | ... | ........ |
| Connecticut........ | 389 [27] | ... | ........ |
| Louisiana.......... | 100 | 60 | 75,000 |
| Nevada............ | about 25 [28] | 100 | 1,000 |
| New York.......... | 3,000 | ... | ........ |
| New Jersey......... | 650 | about 50 | ........ |
| North Carolina...... | 1,000 | " 50 | ........ |
| Pennsylvania........ | 5,000 | " 50 | about 1,500,000 |
| South Carolina...... | 300 | " 25 | 6,000 |
| South Dakota....... | 953 | 98 | 22,000 |
| Virginia............ | 2,000 | 57 | ........ |

The national League estimates that during the above period approximately 15,000 churches coöperated. Since the national

much money did you receive for selling out to the breweries?'"—*Proceedings of the Nineteenth Convention of the Anti-Saloon League*, 1919, p. 31.

The brewers were alert to detect disharmony. For example, in 1911, their agent at the Fourteenth Anti-Saloon League Convention reported, "The League is torn by dissensions and has offered to appoint Dinwiddie as legislative superintendent in the hope that he will bring Presbyterians and dissenting Baptists and others back into line."—From files of the United States Brewers' Association at New York City.

[26] *American Advance*, June 1, 1912.

[27] These churches had altogether 604 pastors.

[28] All Protestant churches except the First Baptist of Reno.

League deals only with the larger churches, it is probable that the average number of affiliated churches throughout the United States between 1911 and 1925 was not far short of 30,000. Mr. Frank R. Kent estimated that the League had the support of 60,000 agencies.[29] At the height of its success, this estimate is perhaps not too high. Certainly the number is much below that now.

But we must examine this machine more closely. In 1908 Superintendent Nicholson in Pennsylvania, through the co-operation of some 4500 churches, had on file the names, addresses and party affiliations of 50,000 to 75,000 voters. The fact that a voter was willing to give his name indicated a certain degree of sympathy. " Philadelphia is really mobilized," said a Pennsylvania spokesman. " The forces are ready for action. . . . It is no idle boast or empty dream. I can dictate twenty letters to twenty men in twenty parts of the city and thereby set 50,000 men in action . . . especially for temperance propaganda. . . . I can name 100 churches that can marshall 20,-000 men in Bible classes alone. . . . Governor Brumbaugh, a few months ago, said that no politician or political party . . . could afford to turn a deaf ear to the demands of such an organized body of men. They must surely hold the balance of power on any great moral issue." [30]

On a single Sunday the pastors in more than 2000 churches in Illinois discussed a pending temperance measure.[31] In 1917, the Rev. E. F. Jones, Superintendent in Nevada, reported that he had access to all of the Protestant churches; that more than 600 people had been personally interviewed and that they had agreed to coöperate in the organization of 125 precincts. At the same convention Anderson reported that the New York

---

[29] " The Anti-Saloon League as Seen by Frank R. Kent of the *Baltimore Sun.*" — Anti-Saloon League reprint, no date (about 1918).
[30] *Proceedings of the Sixteenth Convention of the Anti-Saloon League,* 1915, p. 218.
[31] Anderson, *The Church in Action,* p. 25.

League had access to 3000 churches; that its staff numbered twenty-seven, exclusive of a clerical force of thirty; and that on the last Sunday in January, 1917, more than 3000 pastors had engaged in a concerted discussion " of the issues then pending before the legislature." He boasted that some Jews and Catholics had participated.[32] Hundreds of meetings were held each year in every state. In the eight years from 1914 to 1923, the subscription department of the national league held 19,799 meetings in forty-one states and the District of Columbia, exclusive of special campaign meetings.[33] This total does not include meetings held by the state leagues.

Supplementing the churches and temperance organizations local committees of voters were formed after the most approved fashion of machine politics. States were divided into districts, districts were organized by counties, counties by wards, precincts and townships. There was a paid superintendent for each district, a paid manager for each county, while volunteer captains and lieutenants served in the smaller units. If possible there was a key-man for every ten voters. An active man might be able to look after as many as thirty; but where the number was smaller, the results were more satisfactory.[34]

### Recognition

This politico-ecclesiastical machine was not long in making itself felt. T. M. Gilmore, president of the National Model License League, said of it in 1908:

I want to say that the Anti-Saloon League which is today directing this prohibition wave, is the most remarkable movement that this country has ever known. . . . In its incipiency it was the personification of modesty, the personification of humility. I say today

[32] *Proceedings of the Eighteenth Convention of the Anti-Saloon League*, 1917, pp. 220, 225.

[33] E. H. Cherrington, *Report to the Executive Committee and National Board of Directors*, 1923.

[34] *Proceedings* of the Fifteenth, Sixteenth, Seventeenth and Nineteenth Conventions of the Anti-Saloon League, especially in state reports.

it is the most autocratic, the most dictatorial, as well as the most
dangerous power ever known in the politics of this country, and that
no man can run for any office, in the majority of our southern and
western states, without being catechized by some men connected with
it. And when he is asked the questions, the answers are given to
him, and he is told to respond favorably or be retired to private life.
. . . I say without the slightest hesitation that the Anti-Saloon
League is the most dangerous political movement that this country
has ever known.[35]

President Schaefer of the New York State Brewers' Association said, " In our controversies with the Anti-Saloon League,
we are not dealing with a theory which is the delusion of the
fanatic alone, but with a real condition which is in the hands
of a well-organized force, led by aggressive, experienced and
untiring leaders." [36]

An Alabama politician poured out vials of wrath upon the
League thus: " I was run over by the Anti-Saloon League
steam-roller. . . . They won over the churches and the army
controlled by them. . . . The good but gullible people of the
churches permitted themselves to be humored and hoodwinked
by the professional promoters of the Anti-Saloon League. The
politicians who surrendered, saved themselves from slaughter.
Those like myself were just swept aside to make room for the
more susceptible. . . . They [the Anti-Saloon League] fig-
uratively hit us politicians over the head with a steeple." [37]

The churches boasted of their new Excalibur against booze.
" The Anti-Saloon League has always been cautious and deliberate, and so when it now throws down the gauge of battle for

[35] Speech delivered at the Model License League Convention, Louisville,
Kentucky, Jan. 21, 1908.

[36] Quoted from *Leslie's Weekly* in the *American Patriot*, May, 1913.

[37] Quoted by Louis Seibold, in a reprint of a series of articles which appeared
in the *New York World* in May, 1919. Mr. Seibold appraised the League's
machine thus: " The leaders of the Anti-Saloon League, discarding partisan lines,
organized the churches, through which they worked for or against candidates according to their stand on the prohibition issue. It was not long before local
candidates for office began to feel the effect of this unusual system of censor-
ship — and to surrender."

a fight to a finish with the saloons, we do well to take notice." [38]
A prominent church paper said: " This organization is the instrument of the churches. They have supported it. They have
opened their pulpits for the presentation of its interests. They
have, by money pledges, enabled it to live. They have manned
it with their ministry and said to them, ' Go; this is the work of
your Lord; cease not until you have driven the enemy from
the field.' Now we have every evidence that they have fought
a good fight. They have met the foeman and made him taste
the keenness of their steel. They have brought the enemy to
bay." [39]

### Intolerance and Bigotry

A struggle so intensely emotional as that for prohibition produced its own fanaticism. People who refused to coöperate
with the League were sometimes regarded as friends of all iniquity. The attitude toward the Catholic Church is in point.
Although the leaders insisted that their criticism was due solely
to the Church's stand on prohibition, there were extremists who
desired a vigorous anti-Catholic campaign. This fact has enabled critics of the League to brand it as a spiritual confrere
of the Ku Klux Klan and the heir of the A. P. A.

The Anti-Saloon League sought to meet this criticism by insisting that prohibition was not a peculiarly Protestant nos-
trum.[40] It has long been able to point to Father J. J. Curran,
who for twenty-five years has been a vice-president of the National Anti-Saloon League. When in 1913 Father Patrick J.
Murphy of Texas addressed the Anti-Saloon League Convention on " Why Should We Do Away with the Saloon Business,"
copies of his speech were widely distributed. The South Dakota League, about 1915, issued a pamphlet, *Catholic Clergy*

[38] *Baptist World*, April 10, 1913.
[39] *Western Christian Advocate*, Feb. 5, 1913; also, *Proceedings of the Methodist General Conference*, Minneapolis, 1912.
[40] *Christian Science Monitor*, June 26, 1918.

*and the Saloon,* with quotations from Pope Leo XIII, Archbishop Keane, Bishop Conaty, Bishop Canevin, Bishop Monaghan, Father P. S. McKenna and Father J. M. Cleary, advocating prohibition. Thousands of reprints of an article by United States Senator Ransdell of Louisiana, a Catholic prohibitionist, on *Catholics and Prohibition* were circulated. The Catholic Clergy Prohibition League was also cited. Mayor Dever, of Chicago, a Catholic, was praised for his ardent advocacy of strict enforcement.[41]

None the less, certain extremists within the League had difficulty in restraining themselves when confronted with the indifference or active opposition of Catholics.[42] In 1919, William H. Anderson, superintendent in New York, in a public letter denounced the views of Joseph P. Tumulty, President Wilson's secretary, thus: "There is a pro-brewery and reactionary element within the Catholic Church which is violently anti-prohibition and it is this element that has been able to reach the President with the impression that the Catholic Church is opposed to prohibition, when the truth is that a large portion of the membership of the Catholic Church is just as strong for prohibition as the majority of the members of Protestant Churches. . . . It is time for someone to say, so the public will know, that a certain element of the Catholic Church in New York last fall, deliberately and stealthily went out to put

[41] The following favorite quotations from Catholic sources are of some interest:

Archbishop Glennon of St. Louis: "Violations of the prohibition law today are dishonorable, illegal, disgraceful and altogether unworthy of Catholics and Christians."

Bishop Lenihan of Montana: "Nothing ever happened in America that will make for the spiritual progress of the Catholic Church as prohibition. Fifty years hence the greatest wonderment will be, why all Catholics did not work tooth and nail for prohibition."

Cardinal Mercier of Belgium: "I am a great believer in the repression of all intoxicating drinks such as alcohol and absinthe. If general prohibition were introduced, more human lives would be saved than by general disarmament."

See various publicity releases of the New York Anti-Saloon League — for example, those of June 23, 1919; July 21, 1922; Feb. 15, 1924.

[42] *American Issue,* New York Edition, Jan. 19, 1923.

over a Catholic governor by arousing religious prejudice through the systematic circulation of the mendacious falsehood that the success of the opposing candidate (a prohibition Protestant) would interfere with religious liberty and prevent the securing of wine for sacramental purposes. . . . The Anti-Saloon League is not anti-Catholic . . . but when certain wet elements in the Catholic Church . . . attempt to use the prohibition issue as a stalking horse behind which to put over some Catholic project, then it is the duty of the Anti-Saloon League to turn on the light and expose the proposition. . . . The talk of running the New York Governor for President looks like these wet Catholics . . . having played the game successfully once, with respect to the governorship . . . now intend . . . to capture the presidency in 1920 by a secret coalition between the German brewers and certain ecclesiastics. . . ." He concludes by calling upon all " Christian, right-thinking, patriotic, American-minded, sincere, God-fearing, man-loving Catholics " to repudiate the scheme.[43]

Commenting upon this and similar effusions of the League's stormy petrel, Archbishop Hayes called Anderson " This sinister figure in American politics, a sower of strife, who sinks so low as to play the un-American role of a brewer of bigotry. He seems but little concerned about protection against unlawful search and seizure, religious freedom, free speech, free press and free legislatures. Fomenter of distrust and breeder of mischief! Better for America that he had never been born! "[44]

To this Anderson replied: " . . . if . . . it makes me a sinister figure, a sower of strife, a brewer of bigotry, to state the truth about the attitude of some leaders of the Catholic Church with respect to the enforcement of the prohibition amendment, then . . . so much the worse for these leaders. . . . Not even the Archbishop of New York can obscure an issue by talk-

---

[43] *American Issue*, New York Edition, June 14, 1919.
[44] *Current Opinion*, May, 1920; *New York Evening Post*, March 9, 1920.

ing about something else. . . . What I did say is that most of the officiary of the Roman Catholic Church in this state are in sympathy with the Tammany efforts to destroy the prohibition victory." [45]

Even more violent was a letter to the Archbishop from the Rev. W. M. Hess of Trinity Congregational Church, New York City, defending Anderson. Portions of this letter would certainly warm the heart of the Grand Dragon of the Klan. After criticizing the Archbishop for evading the issue, Dr. Hess says: "Should not a representative of the most bigoted church in America, the Roman Catholic, make a better reply than to merely call him a 'bigot' and 'fanatic'? . . . Will you tell me what else Tammany Hall has been during the past forty years, but a combination of Rum and Romanism? . . . Why so sensitive now when William H. Anderson tells a simple truth that every intelligent person knows? Is it not about time for the real Americans to drive the low-down, grafting, Irish-Catholic rum-sellers and 'rummies' out of city politics?" [46]

Catholics who feared such outbursts advised against doing anything that would justify the charge that they were defending law violation. On June 7, 1923, Father George Zucher of St. Vincent's Church, North Evans, New York, wrote "as a Catholic and a priest" requesting Governor Smith not to sign the bill repealing the state enforcement law. "Your signing the repeal would revive, not without some shadow of truth, Burchard's slander, of Rum, Romanism and Rebellion." [47]

Generally speaking, Catholic leaders have been a bit lukewarm toward prohibition and many have actively opposed it. In February, 1918, before Maryland had ratified, Cardinal Gibbons declared his opposition to the Eighteenth Amendment.

[45] *New York World,* March 10, 1920; *New York Daily News,* March 10, 1920.
[46] Reprint dated March 20, 1920.
[47] Letter in New York Anti-Saloon League files. Father Zurcher was the organizer of the Catholic Clergy Prohibition League in New York. See *Pioneer,* Nov. 24, 1922.

His purpose is reflected in the assertion that " the Cardinal's statement would have had telling effect with the people at the polls had they been permitted to vote on the measure. Those behind the amendment realized this and pushed it through an anti-Catholic legislature without consulting the people." [48]

Archbishop Messmer of Milwaukee issued in 1918 an order forbidding any priests who visit in the archdiocese to deliver addresses in favor of prohibition or under the auspices of the Anti-Saloon League.[49]   The Catholic Clergy of Brooklyn declared that they would oppose " any candidate for public office who is endorsed by the Anti-Saloon League or who endorses the League." [50]   The Rev. Dr. J. J. Cloonan, President of St. John's College, also of Brooklyn, denounced the Volstead Act as immoral and unjust.[51]   It is safe to say that, with a few exceptions, all Catholic editors repudiate prohibition.[52]

Aside from a few individuals of the type represented by Anderson, the League officials frown on anti-Catholic propaganda. They feel that Catholics are not friendly toward the amendment, but they know that the least effective method for securing their coöperation is slander and abuse.   The League is interested in making a success of prohibition. Leaders of moral crusades are often intolerant of opposition.   The remarkable thing is not outbursts like those quoted, but the surprising fairness and restraint of the League leaders.

In supporting a candidate for public office the League does not inquire as to his religion.   His stand on the liquor question alone determines its attitude.   The Anti-Saloon League supported Senator Ransdell of Louisiana, a Catholic.   One of its

---

[48] I. T. Martin in *America*, May 25, 1918.   The article denounces the Methodists and the Anti-Saloon League, calling the Methodist Church, the Anti-Saloon League, and Prohibition, a Trinity of Tyranny.   It asserts that prohibition is but the first of a series of anti-Catholic measures.

[49] *Liberal Advocate*, May 22, 1918.

[50] *New York Times*, March 12, 1920.

[51] *New York Times*, Feb. 28, 1926.

[52] William C. Murphy, Jr., " The Catholic Press," *American Mercury*, Dec., 1926.

outstanding friends in the United States Senate is Walsh of Montana, a well-known Catholic. Others who come to mind are Senator Ashurst of Arizona and Congressman Sinnott of Oregon.

During the latter weeks of the Senatorial fight in New York in 1926, Arthur J. Davis, superintendent of the League, received a letter from the Women's Republican Club of New York City. This letter appealed to Davis to " throw all your weight and influence with your League . . . to induce them [*i.e.*, League supporters] to vote the Republican ticket." Among the arguments presented was a reference to " events during the Eucharistic Congress . . . [which make it] seem little short of treason for Republicans not to stand together for Mills and Wadsworth." Here then was a direct attempt on the part of a responsible Republican organization to inject a nasty religious controversy into the campaign. Davis replied: " With all courtesy, I must decline to discuss the Eucharistic Congress in its relation to Mr. Wadsworth's campaign."

Prohibition has produced its fanatics on both sides. If some of the drys seem willing to institute a Holy Protestant Inquisition for wets, there are wets who advocate the tar barrel for drys. It is difficult to say just who, on this issue, should cast the first stone. It may be that the membership of the Ku Klux Klan sympathizes with the aims of the Anti-Saloon League, but it is certain that few League leaders have anything but contempt for the Klan.

### Main Street Morality

It is true that the Anti-Saloon League, being a league of Protestant churches, appeals to essentially the same constituency as the Ku Klux Klan.[53] The Protestant Church in America is overwhelmingly rural. This is true even in cities. " The Protestant Church in American cities is largely the property and

[53] See J. M. Mecklin, *The Ku Klux Klan*, New York, 1924, pp. 95–125.

product of rural immigrants. In the larger cities it has sur-
vived from the earlier rural period of the state's development.
Counts made of those attending city churches indicate that they
are largely made up of rural immigrants; seventy-five percent
of those present are frequently found to have been born in the
country." [54] The rural church tends to be a center of intel-
lectual and social life. The city church competes with movies,
theaters, clubs, music halls, libraries and lectures. The rural
church, particularly the Protestant Church, is ideally adapted
to crusading. It is more than a place of worship; it is a meeting-
house, a forum.

The rural Protestant seems to be a natural-born reformer.
To him the city is a place of vice and corruption, a fleshpot to
be feared. It is the home of the " foreign element " which he
abhors. In the city, on the other hand, strange persons, strange
ideas, and strange customs meet and mingle. A live and let-
live philosophy prevails; there is less demand for conformity.
The interstimulation of a variety of sects and creeds works
for tolerance bordering on indifference. Any other attitude
would make city life unendurable. Villagers and the inhabitants of Main Street live in glass houses; every man is his
brother's keeper. The village dweller, his own life drab and
uneventful, is an ideal soldier for a moral crusade.[55] He takes
literally the admonition of St. Paul, " It is good neither to eat
flesh, nor drink wine, nor anything whereby thy brother
stumbleth, or is offended, or is made weak." Reformist movements in cities emphasize the social and economic rather than
the moral; prohibition has been essentially a moral movement.
Its leaders used economic and political arguments, but to the
rank and file it was at bottom a moral problem. Drink was not

[54] *World Survey of the Inter-Church Movement*, American Volume, p. 26.
[55] J. G. Thompson, *Urbanization*, New York, 1927, particularly Chapters
III, XX, XXI; Brunner, Hughes and Patten, *American Agricultural Villages*,
New York, 1927, pp. 64 ff., 190–225; S. A. Rice, *Farmers and Workers in
American Politics*, New York, 1924, pp. 108–27.

only the cause of disease, destitution and depravity; it was above all "the Great Destroyer of the Temple of the Soul," the inciter of base passions and the arch enemy of Christian virtue.

Where Protestants are in the majority, as in the rural South, prohibition sentiment is strong. There were nine Southern states which adopted prohibition prior to 1916. Table II shows them to be overwhelmingly Protestant, rural and native.

Contrast this with Connecticut and Rhode Island, the two states which failed to ratify the Eighteenth Amendment: the Catholic percentage of the total church population was 67 and 76 respectively. Without concluding too much from these figures, they help to explain the League's attitude. The League, being a league of Protestant churches, could look for small influence in the cities where the Catholics generally predominated. Sixty-five percent of the church-goers in cities of 350,-000 or more are Catholics. Three-fourths of the Catholics in the United States live in cities of 25,000 or more. In these cities they constitute one-half to two-thirds of the church-going population.

Lastly, the constituency to which the Anti-Saloon League appeals is suspicious of aliens. When the Arbeiter Bund of Michigan declared its opposition to prohibition, the *American Issue* said: " Really, is not the country growing rather tired of having a lot of swill-fattened, blowsy half-foreigners getting together and between hiccoughs laying down definitions to Americans regarding the motive of our constitution and laws. But then we suppose that to intimate anything of this sort is A. P. A.-ism and 'attempting to excite odium against foreigners.' " [56] This charge was in fact made. " This whole Anti-Saloon movement," said an opponent, "is in reality a thinly veiled warfare on everything foreign — an outbreak of envy and jealousy, directed against the hard-fisted, hard working,

[56] *American Issue,* Maryland Edition, Aug. 1, 1908.

TABLE II

POPULATION OF SOUTHERN PROHIBITION STATES

| STATE | ADOPTED PROHIBITION | POPULATION, 1910 [57] | | | NATIVE BORN, 1910 [57] | | CHURCH POPULATION, 1910 [58] | | |
|---|---|---|---|---|---|---|---|---|---|
| | | Total | Rural | Percent Rural | Total | Percent | Total | Protestant [59] | Percent Protestant |
| Georgia......... | 1907 | 2,609,121 | 2,070,471 | 79 | 2,593,644 | 99 | 1,234,132 | 1,140,215 | 92 |
| Oklahoma....... | 1907 | 1,657,155 | 1,337,000 | 80 + | 1,616,713 | 97 + | 424,492 | 269,775 | 63 |
| Mississippi...... | 1908 | 1,797,114 | 1,589,803 | 88 | 1,787,344 | 99 + | 762,977 | 687,778 | 90 |
| North Carolina.. | 1908 | 2,206,287 | 1,887,813 | 85 | 2,200,195 | 99 + | 1,080,723 | 947,301 | 86 |
| Tennessee....... | 1909 | 2,184,789 | 1,743,744 | 79 | 2,166,182 | 99 | 840,133 | 680,591 | 81 |
| West Virginia.... | 1912 | 1,221,119 | 992,877 | 81 | 1,163,901 | 95 | 427,865 | 262,863 | 60 |
| Virginia......... | 1914 | 2,061,612 | 1,585,083 | 76 + | 2,034,555 | 98 + | 949,136 | 653,595 | 69 |
| Alabama......... | 1915 | 2,138,093 | 1,767,662 | 82 | 2,118,807 | 99 | 1,009,465 | 867,356 | 85 |
| South Carolina... | 1915 | 1,515,400 | 1,290,568 | 85 | 1,509,221 | 99 + | 794,126 | 731,346 | 92 |

[57] Abstract of the Fourteenth Census of U. S., 1920, pp. 75, 103.
[58] U. S. Census of Religious Bodies, 1916, Part II, pp. 108–13.
[59] Includes Methodists, Baptists, Presbyterians and Congregationalists only.

TABLE III

RELIGIOUS GROUPS IN PRINCIPAL CITIES

| CITY | ALL DENOMINATIONS | ROMAN CATHOLIC | PERCENT CATHOLIC | METHODIST | BAPTIST | PRESBYTERIAN | CONGREGATIONALIST |
|---|---|---|---|---|---|---|---|
| Baltimore | 296,599 | 137,730 | 46 | 41,784 | 33,511 | 9,105 | ..... |
| Boston | 401,498 | 298,914 | 73 + | 9,053 | 15,959 | ..... | 15,458 |
| Buffalo | 277,045 | 193,220 | 69 + | 10,333 | 6,029 | 8,441 | ..... |
| Chicago | 1,058,785 | 718,114 | 67 + | 33,676 | 36,309 | 27,408 | 15,448 |
| Cincinnati | 167,028 | 101,931 | 61 | 12,268 | 10,648 | 9,269 | ..... |
| Cleveland | 357,261 | 261,427 | 73 | 16,725 | 12,374 | 8,286 | 7,808 |
| Denver | 71,847 | 28,772 | 40 | 10,038 | 5,694 | 5,741 | 3,768 |
| Detroit | 330,600 | 294,796 | 62 | 19,789 | 9,690 | 14,113 | 3,658 |
| Jersey City | 146,490 | 109,436 | 74 + | 4,612 | 2,865 | 2,774 | ..... |
| Kansas City | 103,905 | 32,311 | 31 | 18,063 | 17,533 | 7,993 | 2,350 |
| Los Angeles | 122,697 | 49,107 | 40 | 16,598 | 8,362 | 9,763 | 5,643 |
| Louisville | 129,529 | 53,474 | 41 | 10,789 | 29,536 | 7,057 | ..... |
| Milwaukee | 201,682 | 126,921 | 63 | 4,592 | 2,465 | 3,198 | 6,327 |
| Minneapolis | 122,259 | 51,776 | 42 | 9,778 | 8,016 | 7,205 | ..... |
| New Orleans | 195,617 | 147,695 | 75 + | 6,695 | 11,369 | 3,828 | ..... |
| New York City | 2,101,233 | 1,545,562 | 73 + | 50,745 | 45,954 | 61,707 | 25,230 |
| Philadelphia | 776,422 | 436,700 | 52 | 55,848 | 63,958 | 62,929 | ..... |
| Pittsburg | 377,703 | 225,562 | 59 + | 25,678 | 18,652 | 41,169 | ..... |
| Richmond | 82,944 | 10,776 | 29 | 12,621 | 41,234 | 4,498 | ..... |
| San Francisco | 174,745 | 139,676 | 80 | 3,889 | ..... | 3,377 | 1,885 |
| Seattle | 72,986 | 29,862 | 41 | 5,876 | 3,810 | 10,428 | 4,207 |
| Washington | 164,413 | 51,421 | 31 | 20,836 | 39,978 | 9,338 | 3,255 |
| St. Louis | 392,435 | 281,627 | 71 + | 17,827 | 17,425 | 9,864 | ..... |
| Total | 7,924,741 | 5,231,611 | 66 | 417,313 | 442,372 | 327,441 | 155,037 |

From *U. S. Census of Religious Bodies*, Part II, 1916, pp. 123–27.

money saving, child-rearing foreigner and his descendants, who in the struggle for existence are gradually crowding out the effete, bloodless, anaemic, self-righteous remnant of puritan stock which is physically too feeble to do anything but cavil and denounce." [60]  The League's attitude is reflected in resolutions adopted in 1925 demanding the deportation of aliens convicted of violating the liquor laws.[61]

Whatever anti-Catholic or anti-alien sentiments the Anti-Saloon League may have should not be attributed to a dislike for Catholics or aliens as such.  If these groups suddenly mounted the water wagon, there is reason to believe that the League leaders would be the first to sing their praises, though the rank and file of their supporters might not do likewise.

### Pulpit Politics

The idea of the church engaging in politics filled many with alarm.  "There will be few," said a writer for the German-American Alliance, " who will not agree with me when I say that a political propaganda carried on by or under the auspices of a religious body is extremely dangerous, let the ostensible purpose for which the propaganda is made be ever so noble or meritorious. . . . [The church] cannot mix in these affairs itself, without thus eventually losing that hold on the faith and reverence of mankind which alone enables it to successfully do God's work on earth." [62]

The League met the charge head on:

The cry of politics in the pulpit has grown old and stale. . . . The mission of the church is to right wrongs and to establish the Kingdom of Heaven among men.  Whatever will tend to these ends, it is the business of the church to promote, and the part which the pastor should play is that of leadership.  If that leadership compels

[60] Joseph Debar, ed., *Prohibition, Its Relation to Good Government,* Cincinnati [no date, about 1910], p. 249.
[61] *Proceedings of the Twenty-second Convention of the Anti-Saloon League,* 1925; *New York Times,* Nov. 10, 1925.
[62] Andreae, *Prohibition Movement,* p. 67.

him to take an active part in movements of civic reform, his duty may be in the political arena as well as in the pulpit.[63]

Assistant Attorney General Trickett of Kansas declared: " The Christian pulpit might properly be called the upper house in the parliament of world politics." [64]

" Occasionally some poor specimen of humanity," said the *American Issue,* " leaning over a saloon bar and looking through the bottom of a beer glass, condemns the Anti-Saloon League for its activity in politics. . . . Of course the Anti-Saloon League is in politics. That is part of its business. It is not playing either the elephant or the donkey as a favorite, but it is in politics to help elect good men to office and to keep bad men out of office. . . . It is in politics to keep the brewers and liquor dealers from filling offices with their tools and from hanging a beer sign above the doors of legislative halls.[65]

In general the League's answer has been that it would get out of politics when the liquor interests did.[66]

[63] *American Issue,* Maryland Edition, Oct. 2, 1909.
[64] *American Issue,* Ohio and Maryland Editions, Feb. 22, 1908.
[65] *American Issue,* Ohio Edition, April, 1912.
[66] *American Issue,* Maryland Edition, Jan. 20, 1912.

# CHAPTER II
## FROM CONVICTION TO PERSUASION

The temperance movement in the United States began with appeals to the individual to abstain from alcoholic drink. These appeals were made not only on the ground of increased health and longevity, but also because abstinence would save the drinker's children from being tainted with alcoholic cravings which early temperance enthusiasts readily asserted were hereditary. As in the early agitation against slavery, it was believed that in a democratic country an appeal to the individual conscience was the surest and best way to counteract social evils. Notwithstanding the widespread consumption of liquor in the early days of the republic, little scientific knowledge was available concerning the effects of alcohol upon the human organism. The observable results of excess consumption, however, were too patently evil to admit of much argument. There was a well defined opinion in many quarters that something should be done to mitigate the evil of drunkenness and the unfortunate demonstrations of crime and debauchery associated with it. A frontier population, just emerged from a seven years' struggle for political independence and educated by the propaganda of that period to regard with suspicion all governmental interference, would have looked askance at a prohibitory policy. The only alternative was an appeal to the individual.[1]

[1] J. A. Krout, *The Origins of Prohibition*, New York, 1925, particularly Chapters I and V.

Dr. Benjamin Rush published, in 1785, his *Inquiry into the Effects of Ardent Spirits upon the Human Body and Mind*. He was particularly interested in portraying the dangers of excessive consumption of distilled liquors. He urged light wines and beers. As a substitute for distilled liquors he advised opium and laudanum.

The first temperance society in America, that of Dr. Billy J. Clark in 1808, was a pledge-signing movement.[2] The prevailing attitude is reflected in the pledge of the members of the Maine Temperance Society, organized a few years later: " We will be at all times sparing and cautious in the use of spirituous liquors at home; in the social visits, decline them so far as possible; avoid them totally in retail stores and in general set our faces against the intemperate use of them, conceiving as we do that, except in a very few cases as of medicinal use, spirituous liquors are the bane of morals and a drain on health, piety and happiness." [3] These pledges did not brand liquor as bad *per se,* nor seek to inculcate a feeling of abhorrence for alcoholic beverages in themselves. Used in moderation they had their legitimate uses.

With the organization of the American Temperance Society in 1826 the pledges changed from moderation to complete abstinence from spirituous liquors. In 1840 the Washington Society [4] was ready to extend the ban to wine, beer and cider:

We, whose names are annexed, desirous of forming a society for our mutual benefit to guard against a practice, a pernicious practice — which is injurious to our health and the standing of our families, do pledge ourselves as gentlemen that we will not drink any spirits, malt liquors, wine or cider.

From this time forward the temperance movement came to stand for total abstinence. Its theory was that alcohol as a beverage was not merely injurious when used in excess, but

---

[2] *Encyclopedia of Temperance,* p. 22. See also Krout, *op. cit.,* p. 78.
[3] Wilson and Pickett, *The Case for Prohibition,* New York, 1923, p. 21.
[4] The few previous organizations of this kind, such as the Virginia Total Abstinence Society, 1804; the Total Abstinence Society of Greenfield, Saratoga, N. Y., 1809; the Tee-Totaler Society of Hector, N. Y., 1818, were of small consequence.

The term " tee-total " is said to have originated in the latter society. There were two kinds of pledges. The secretary placed before each member's name on the roll the initials " O. P." or " T." — the former meaning " Old Pledge " against the use of ardent spirits, and the latter " Total," or " New pledge against the use of all intoxicating liquors."

was bad physically, mentally and socially, in any quantity.  It
was but a step from personal tee-totalism to legal prohibition.
The Women's Christian Temperance Union was organized in
1874, and the very next year declared this its object:

> *Resolved,* That whereas, the object of just government is to con-
> serve the best interests of the governed: and whereas the liquor
> traffic is not only a crime against God, but subversive of every in-
> terest of society; therefore, in behalf of humanity, we call for such
> legislation as shall secure this end: and while we will continue to
> employ all moral agencies as indispensable, we hold prohibition to
> be essential to the full triumph of this reform.[5]

When in the nineties the Anti-Saloon League entered the field
the groundwork had been laid.  The League set out to turn the
flood light of publicity upon the saloon and the liquor traffic.
Its object was not so much to form opinion as to mobilize for
political action an already existing opinion.  A widespread conviction as to the baneful effects of alcohol had been produced
by over three-quarters of a century of temperance agitation.
It was the League's purpose to mould this into a battering-ram
of public opinion which would destroy the entire traffic.  The
League went a step further than the W. C. T. U. by concentrating attention on the saloon.  The very name Anti-Saloon
League was chosen to focus interest on the institution which
was the fountain of the poisonous product which the " Pledg-
ers " shunned and the W. C. T. U. would outlaw.  Moderate
drinkers and total abstainers, who balked at the idea of absolute prohibition, were willing to admit that the American saloon
had become a noisome thing.[6]

[5] *Encyclopedia of Temperance,* p. 651.  See also Duff Gilfond, " The White
Ribboners," *American Mercury,* March, 1928.

[6] " It is not a prohibition wave but an anti-saloon wave, a protest against
the conduct of the liquor business as it has developed in this country." — William Allen White in the *Chicago Tribune,* March 10, 1908.

" Let it be clearly perceived, that this present war is not a total abstinence
propaganda, it is an anti-saloon campaign, because the saloon has proved itself
a chief public enemy." — *American Issue,* Maryland Edition, March 3, 1908.

*Beyond Reform*

The need for some reform of the saloon was recognized by the trade itself.[7] Reform, however, would not satisfy the League. The propaganda with which it proceeded to arouse the public conscience leaves little room for doubt that it regarded the institution as hopelessly beyond reform or repair.

" The saloon is the storm center of crime; the devil's headquarters on earth; the school-master of a broken decalogue; the defiler of youth; the enemy of the home; the foe of peace; the deceiver of nations; the beast of sensuality; the past master of intrigue; the vagabond of poverty; the social vulture; the rendezvous of demagogues; the enlisting office of sin; the serpent of Eden; a ponderous second edition of hell, revised, enlarged and illuminated." [8]

If there be such a thing as black-washing, this is what the League did to the saloon. Its violent language could not have been calculated to appeal to the critical faculties of even the most abstemious. The League set itself the task of creating, through the instrumentality of a powerful propaganda, an emotional abhorrence of the saloon and the liquor traffic. To the sincere dry crusader a licensed system of selling liquor or a state-conducted saloon, such as was attempted in the South and is being successfully operated in England today, would be as intolerable as a licensed system of vice.[9] To him, it was a

---

An editorial in the Ohio Edition of the *American Issue* for April 25, 1908, severely criticizes an article by Arthur Brisbane in the *Cosmopolitan* of March, 1908. The editorial claimed that it was unfair to present the issue as between prohibition and license, instead of between the "saloon and social order."

[7] *Year Book of the United States Brewers' Association*, 1909, pp. 147 ff.

Joseph Debar, president of the National Association of Distillers and Wholesale Dealers, in a letter to the author says: " The American people did not want to be deprived of liquor. They objected to the American method of dispensing it and to the American abuse of it."

[8] *American Issue*, Kentucky Edition, April, 1912.

[9] " There is no more reason for the legalization of the sale of liquor for beverage purposes than for the legalization for the same purpose of the sale of morphine or cocaine." *Proceedings of the Eleventh Convention of the Anti-Saloon League*, 1906.

moral issue, admittedly with two sides — a right and a wrong side.

To have admitted that there was one decent saloon would have seemed like giving the whole case away. The saloon must be made to appear as the epitome of all that was vicious in modern social life; the enemy of society, of the home, the individual, the church, law, order and humanity. To it must be assigned the blame for all vice and misery extant. The American saloon was compared with the lupanars of Rome. Fear of disease destroyed them — fear of moral and social degradation must likewise destroy the saloon. This tower of sin and corruption was erected to create a fear psychology which, in the name of civic and moral righteousness, would rise and destroy it.

### The Saloon as the Enemy of the Child

Propaganda designed to frightened parents into the Anti-Saloon ranks told how millions of lives were annually sacrificed to this modern Moloch:

> The saloons of New Jersey are annually sending thousands of our youths to destruction. We boast of our great industrial enterprises, railroad facilities, our excellent oyster beds, and mammoth fisheries; but what shall it profit us if we gain the whole world and lose our boys. . . . Dr. Hitchcock, president of the Michigan State Board of Health, says that ten percent of the deaths, annually, in the United States are due to alcohol. . . . That means there must be over 100,000 new recruits to take the places of these, if the liquor business is to prosper.[10]

The saloon keepers were charged with creating a desire for liquor among the youngsters for the purpose of replacing those customers who should fall by the wayside through death or abstinence. The following remarks made before the Retail

[10] *American Issue,* New Jersey Edition, May 17, 1912.

Liquor Dealers' Association of Ohio, in 1912, were given wide
publicity by the League:

> We must create the appetite for liquor in the growing boys.  Men
> who drink . . . will die, and if there is no new appetite created, our
> counters will be empty as well as our coffers.  The open field for
> the creation of appetite is among the boys.  Nickels expended in
> treats to boys now, will return in dollars to your tills after the appe-
> tite has been formed.[11]

It was further alleged that a Chicago school-teacher discovered cards in the possession of her scholars which had been
given them by a saloon keeper near the school. " The cards
were punched for every drink taken by the boys — one punch
for beer, two punches for straight drinks and three punches for
mixed drinks. At the end of each month prizes were given.
The boy having the largest number of punches in his card was
given a revolver; the second, a life of Jesse James; and the
third, a pipe." [12]

A League writer summed up the case in a proposed " ad "
for the saloons:

### WANTED — BOYS FOR CUSTOMERS

Most of our old customers are rapidly
dropping out.
Ten committed suicide last week.
Twenty are in jail — eight in the chain
gang.
Fifteen were sent to the poorhouse.  One
was hanged.
Three were sent to the insane asylum.
Most of the rest are not worth fooling
with; they have no money.

### WE NEED FRESH YOUNG BLOOD [13]

[11] *American Issue,* Maryland Edition, May, 1912.  The author has in his
possession copies of affidavits testifying to the truth of the foregoing statement.
  Another ingenious method imputed to the liquor dealers was: " Small bottles
of whisky with a rubber tube like a nursing bottle have been distributed among
the schoolboys by the saloon keepers in Ohio towns. . . ." (*American Issue,*
Ohio Edition, May, 1912.)  Such stories were broadcast wherever League literature was circulated.
[12] *American Issue,* Ohio Edition, June 8, 1912.
[13] *Ibid.,* Jan. 11, 1908.

## The Saloon as the Enemy of the Home

The liquor traffic as the enemy of the home was a favorite theme for League propaganda. If divorce threatens the home, then drink must be sought as the cause. It was freely asserted that " from sixty to one hundred percent of the divorces are due to liquor." [14]

*The Home Against the Saloon,* a pamphlet of the South Dakota League, says:

> The liquor traffic is in the crisis of a death struggle for supremacy over the American Home. God is silently but surely sifting the American people into two classes — Home Defenders . . . and Saloon Defenders . . . Protect the Home from the Saloon or the Saloon will destroy the Home.

A pamphlet of the national league, called *The Nation's Foe,* declared: " Our children are in danger while the saloon stands. . . . When a man's tracks point toward the saloon, his back is toward heaven." Another, entitled *Is the Saloon a Good Thing?* answers: " Yes, for the saloon keeper, the brewer, the distiller, the gambler, the confidence man, the hold-up man, the ward boss . . . for the trapper, who lives by snaring young men and girls at the wine-room supper. But Eternally No!!! for the man who drinks up his wages there, for the wife whose home is bare of comfort because of the wages her husband lost there, for the children who go to bed supperless, . . . for the butcher, the baker, the shoe dealer. . . ." Other leaflets and pamphlets bear the suggestive titles, *The Saloon, An Enemy of the Home, Better Babies, Unborn Children, Why Babies Die, My Boys,* and *Boys Worth More Than Taxes.* Poetic appeals to the chivalry of drinkers were made:

> Women and Children First, 'tis the law of the sea,
> But why not make it the rule wherever a man may be?
> Let it become the law where roisterers quench their thirst,
> Emblazon it over the bar — " Women and Children First." [15]

[14] *Home and State,* organ of the Texas League, Oct. 15, 1917.
[15] *American Issue,* Oklahoma Edition, June, 1912.

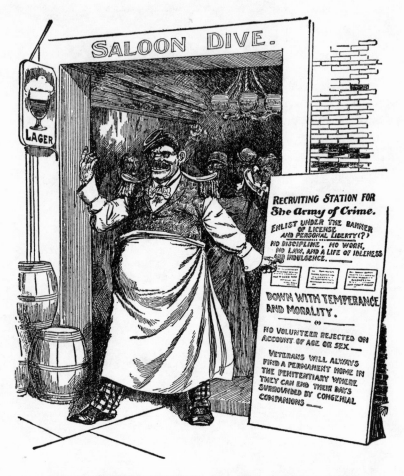

**THE RECRUITING SERGEANT FOR THE ARMY OF CRIME**

This cartoon, depicting the saloon as a natural center for vice and crime, was widely used in Anti-Saloon League publications.

*The Saloon and Its Allies*

The saloon was represented as the rendezvous of the criminal, as the office of the political manipulator and purveyor of drugs. " The saloon is the resort of the underworld. There the inhabitants swarm like maggots and an awful cry goes up, ' Give us drink and you can have us body and soul.' The saloon with its unholy alliances is Hell on earth. Yet the saloon is not only tolerated by a Christian civilization, but authorized in fact and protected. A day of vengeance draweth nigh. An institution so unholy cannot hope for a permanent existence." [16] It was called " The Recruiting Sergeant for the Army of Crime." A pamphlet entitled *The Texas Roundup on the Saloon*, by George Stewart, lists as " industries " associated with the saloon:

The wine and liquor dealers, brewers and distillers, wholesale liquor dealers, saloon keepers and bartenders, gamblers, prize fighters, horse racers and reckless sports, houses of ill fame, highway robbers, burglars and counterfeiters, drunken bums, corrupt politicians, vote sellers and vote buyers, toughs and thugs, anarchists, low-class foreigners . . . that is to say, All Persons who are Opposed to Decent Government . . . Standing opposed to these are the Church, Philanthropists, Masons, Odd Fellows, Knights of Pythias, Foresters, Locomotive Engineers, All the Higher Class Order of Brotherhoods, Clean Statesmen, Manufacturers and Merchants, Railroads, Mothers, Wives and Daughters . . . All Men and Women who stand for Sobriety and Good Citizenship.

League pamphlets described the saloon as a training school for crime and immorality:

The saloon produces 80% of the criminals in this country.

The saloon is responsible for most of the 60,000 girls who go astray into immoral lives every year.

The saloon and the brothel are twin evils, and every man who votes for the liquor traffic is indirectly voting to create conditions which feed the social evil. . . .

[16] *American Issue*, National Edition, Oct. 25, 1912. The Maryland Edition for Jan. 18, 1908, calls the saloon, " The Headquarters for Murderers."

The saloon is responsible for more vice, degradation, sorrow, misery, tears, heartaches and deaths than any other cause tolerated by Government.

Summing up a long enumeration of social abuses for which the saloon was responsible, the national edition of the *American Issue* said, " The American People has been hysterically trying to mop up the deluge of paupers, blind, epileptics, criminals, etc., . . . which have flowed from the faucet of the liquor business, the saloon. Better to stop the faucet." [17]

At the door of the saloon was laid the blame for political corruption. It was represented as the *sine qua non* of such political machines as Tammany Hall and the Cox Machine of Cincinnati, " none of which could continue in existence for a day but for the liquor traffic." [18] " If we wish to purify politics," said the League, " the saloon must be destroyed; we can never get the saloon out of politics so long as we get our politics out of the saloon." [19] Levying petty tribute upon disreputable dives, saloon politicians were bound to protect the forces of organized vice from the penalties of law enforcement. As an instance of this relationship, the Maryland League published the program for a ball given by a Democratic Club in Baltimore. The program contained the advertising cards of eight houses of ill fame. Just opposite the advertisements appeared the slogan: " Patronize Our Advertisers." It was further alleged that several of these " ladies of the evening " were present.[20]

The attempts of the brewers and liquor dealers to disguise their organizations as " Manufacturers and Merchants Associations " were unmasked by the League. A startling description of one such association appeared as an advertisement in the *American Issue*:

[17] *American Issue*, National Edition, Nov., 1912.
[18] *American Issue*, Ohio Edition, April 2, 1910.
[19] *Proceedings of the Thirteenth Convention of the Anti-Saloon League*, 1909. Speech of J. C. Jackson.
[20] *American Issue*, Maryland Edition, March 25, 1911.

ALCOHOL, ASSIGNATION, ANARCHY
& CO., UNLIMITED

NEWARK, NEW JERSEY
(More widely known as Manufacturers and
Merchants Association)

1400 Main Stores, 1000 Speak Easies,
Brothels, Gambling Houses. Never Closed.
We Threw the Keys Away When the Good
People Became Discouraged.

AS WE SUCCEED, OUR CUSTOMERS FAIL
Our Raw Material: The Blue-Eyed Boy
of the Home Circle. Our Finished Product:
The Diseased Bum of the Slimy Gutter.

OUR GUARANTEE
To Good Customers: Lost Hopes and
Character. To Regular Trade: Blasted
Homes and Broken Hearts, with Choice of
Asylum, Poor House or Jail.

EVERY DEPARTMENT COMPLETE
Fashionable Society to Dens of Unspeakable Vice.

EXCHANGE DEPARTMENT
Bestiality for Innocence. Dinner Pails for
School Books.

DELIVERY SERVICE
Of Our Finished Products Day and Night
Paid For by the City.[21]

## The Poor Man's Club

Much was made, by the defenders of the saloon, of its services to the workers. They called it the poor man's bank. The
League used this with quite different implications. " Out of
3600 checks paid out in wages by one manufacturer in Joliet,
Illinois, on a recent pay day, all but one were returned with
the endorsement of some saloon. The single one had been endorsed by a man running both a saloon and a grocery store." [22]

[21] Suggested advertisement for Newark's " Leading Industry " at the Industrial Exposition. — *American Issue*, New Jersey Edition, May 17, 1912.

[22] *American Issue*, Maryland Edition, June 19, 1908. The saloon keeper
was by no means altruistic in the services he rendered as a banker. The *Detroit
Journal* of November 7, 1907, quotes a saloon keeper as follows: " If the person
wanting the check cashed is not a patron of the suds parlor, he will have to

There is evidence that a considerable portion of the worker's pay check was permanently deposited in the saloon. " Mc-Keesport was a city of about 40,000 population and there were 69 saloons.  On the Thursday preceding the semi-monthly pay days . . . the three leading saloon keepers of the city drew from their bank accounts from $1200 to $1500 each in dollar bills and small denominations to be used as change.  Other saloon keepers drew varying amounts, and the total thus drawn each fortnight was over $60,000.  On the Mondays after pay days the saloon keepers usually deposited double the amount drawn.  These periodic leaps in deposits never failed to coincide with pay days, and the inevitable conclusion is that about $60,000 of the steel workers' wages are regularly expended in the saloons within the next two days." [23]

The saloon was the poor man's club, said its defenders.[24] A widely circulated poem expressed the League's attitude:

### THE POOR MAN'S CLUB

*What It Does*

The poor man's club, the poor man's club!
The man who says that deserves a rub.
The club that takes the Saturday pay,
The club that chases all hope away,
The club that empties the workman's bag
And leaves the wife a bone and a rag;
That takes the schoolbook from the boy,
And leaves him naught that he might enjoy;
Takes the price of toil from the laboring man,
That empties the stomach and fills the can.
. . . . . . . . . . . . . . . . . . . . . . . . . . . . . . . .
That makes the home where peace might dwell,
Instead of a heaven a raging hell.

---

buy the round of drinks for the house before his request will be granted.  Others require the same." — See also *American Issue,* Maryland Edition, Jan. 11, 1908.
[23] *American Magazine,* March, 1919.
[24] John Koren, *Alcohol and Society,* New York, 1916, p. 244.

With the wife out washing, her rub, rub, rub,
Beats time for the songs of the poor man's club.
If you don't need clothes and can live without grub,
Why, just go and join the Poor Man's Club.
                              — AN ENLIGHTENED EX-MEMBER

## The Great Destroyer

Notwithstanding the fact that the League insisted that its campaign was against the saloon and not for prohibition, its propaganda made little effort to keep the issues distinct. The thing that made the saloon a hellish thing was liquor, and it was this that the League was " gunning for." It made little difference how it was sold or served, it would wreak its ruin. The voters were asked to stop the flood at its source. Drink was the " Great Destroyer." It was dangerous to life, health and happiness; it was economically wasteful and morally vicious. Not the saloon alone, but the whole traffic in intoxicating beverages, was the enemy of law and order:

The liquor traffic has never obeyed the law and it never will. The first organized rebellion against the laws and authority of this nation was made by the anarchist saloon in the Pennsylvania Whisky Rebellion which cost the Washington administration an army of 15,000 men and the largest single expenditure of the infant government to suppress. The nation was not twenty years old when the liquor traffic rose in rebellion against the law, and it has been in rebellion ever since. It has never obeyed the law and it never will.[25]

This version of the whisky rebellion is more valuable as propaganda than as history.[26] It is needless to point out that it was not a rebellion of an organized liquor traffic but the resistance of Pennsylvania farmers to the collection of a Federal tax on whisky. The League's version, however, served its purpose well and is still used.

[25] *American Issue*, Maryland Edition, Sept. 21, 1912.
[26] Fish, *Development of American Nationality*, New York, 1918, p. 55; Bowers, *Jefferson and Hamilton*, New York, 1926, pp. 250-56; Krout, *op. cit.*, p. 62. See W. B. Wheeler, " Rum Rebellions, Past and Present," *Forum*, May, 1921.

Saloon keepers and liquor dealers were pictured as a vile tribe dehumanized by the business in which they engaged. When the local option wave was at its crest, they were accused of fighting the temperance forces with ruthless savagery. Every crime in the calendar was chalked up against them by the League — assault, arson, bombing, robbery, even murder.[27]

## The Economics of Liquor

In America, with our Puritan tradition, to call a thing immoral is to damn it. Since the advent of industrialism, to question its dollars and cents value is to doubly damn it. The Anti-Saloon League damned and doubly damned the liquor business. Much energy was spent in showing that dry states were economically better off than wet states. The alleged superiority of dry Kansas over wet Missouri was demonstrated thus: " Missouri with a total population of 3,300,000 had assessed property worth $1,650,000,000. Kansas with a population of only 1,600,000 had assessed property worth $2,750,000,-000." [28] Just what relation these figures have to the fact that one state was dry and the other wet is obscure. Tax rolls are certainly not the most reliable source for comparative figures as to actual wealth. The proportion of negro population, the ratio of urban to rural population, the quality of the soil, and a host of other factors must be considered in a fair comparison. Prohibition may well have been a contributory influence in the superior prosperity of Kansas, but it was not the sole element, nor even the most important.

Continuing its analysis, the *Issue* claimed that prohibition was responsible for the fact that Kansas had one motor car for every five farmers, to one for every one hundred in Missouri. Missouri paid laborers an average of less than four

[27] *American Issue*, Indiana Edition, April 11, 1916, Maryland Edition, Feb. 29, March 21, and April 11, 1908.
[28] *American Issue*, Ohio Edition, Sept. 21, 1912.

dollars a week; Kansas paid fourteen dollars. Kansas spent twice as much for education as Missouri, but Missouri spent three times as much for liquor. It is needless to point out the exaggeration in such figures.

The national edition of the *American Issue* summarized the economic status of the liquor trade, basing its figures on the Census Bureau's *Bulletin of Manufactures* for 1910. For instance, it appears that the average wage of workers in all industries was about $518 per annum, while that of workers in the liquor business was $720. It is difficult to see just what the League is driving at in this case. Such figures were scarcely calculated to appeal to the wage earners, unless to excite their envy. Perhaps it was intended as a warning to employers that, unless the liquor trade was destroyed, a general increase of wages would ensue. Statistics more definitely designed to appeal to the working classes showed that the liquor business employed only 77 workers for every $1,000,000 invested, as compared with 587 in the textile industry, 579 in the lumber industry, 469 in leather goods, 367 in the paper industry and 284 in the iron industry. It was also pointed out that the portion of product-value going to the worker in wages was less in the liquor trades than in other industries, the actual percentage being: liquor, 7.3; textiles, 19.8; lumber, 26.8; leather, 15.8; paper, 20.5. Such arguments would appeal to workers, but there is some question whether investors would be similarly impressed. Every effort was made to minimize the economic importance of that moral monster, the liquor trade:

According to the census figures the brewery industry ranks only twenty-fifth among the industries of the country, and the distilling industry only forty-third. Furthermore, the tonnage on the railroads utilized by the liquor business was only .003 of the total tonnage carried. Of the total grain crop, only three percent went into the manufacture of liquor.[29]

[29] *American Issue*, National Edition, Nov., 1912.

During the war the League made a complete about face so far as this type of propaganda was concerned, as did the liquor dealers. Instead of continuing to show the inconsequential nature of the business, it bent every effort to prove that the manufacture and sale of alcoholic drink constituted a serious drain on the country's resources. It is interesting to note that in doing this they had but to quote the figures of the liquor trade itself.

To allay the fear of the workers and to meet the argument of the trade that prohibition would cause serious unemployment, it was pointed out :

In 1900 there were, according to census reports, 20,962 brewers and maltsters and 3,144 distillers and rectifiers in the United States. If the liquor industry were destroyed, those so employed would be compelled to learn a new trade or apply their skill to other lines of endeavor — only those maltsters, etc., whose work is of a highly specialized character would be forced into an entirely new way of living — the majority, including many skilled workers such as carpenters would be forced to find other employment in industries into which the released capital would go.[30]

After all, it was shown that, of the 6,615,046 workers in all manufacturing industries in 1910, the liquor business employed but 62,920.

Estimating the annual retail drink bill of America at $1,800,000,-000 and the amount spent for bread and clothing at about the same, on the basis of the cost of raw material [and] wages of workers employed . . . if the money spent for intoxicating liquor were spent for bread and clothing it would employ seven times as many workers who would collectively receive about five and one-half times as much wages, or nearly $200,000,000.[31]

Such arguments would appeal to the worker to favor the suppression of the liquor business and the transfer of its capital to other industries. In addition to enlarging the market for his

[30] *American Issue*, National Edition, Nov., 1912.      [31] *Ibid.*

labor, the change would, by increasing the supply of necessities, tend to lower the cost of living. "For every man put out of business by the elimination of the ruinous gin mill, work is provided for two in legitimate occupations, and the general level of real wages is bound to rise." [32]  In a pamphlet, *Brewery vs. Labor*, appears this table:

| WET | EMPLOYED | DRY | EMPLOYED |
|---|---|---|---|
| Ranier Brewery.......... | 156 | Now a Tannery......... | 1,600 |
| Portland Brewery........ | 100 | Now a Furniture Factory. | 600 |
| Pacific Coast Brewing Co... | 123 | Now a Shoe Factory..... | 2,500 |
| | 379 | | 4,700 |

The Anti-Saloon League had to meet the charge that prohibition would mean a loss to the community in increased taxes, falling real estate values and general depression.

Nobody who knows anything . . . believes that it pays financially to have our children transformed into drunkards or even into drinking men and women. . . . Nor should anyone need to believe that if 17,500 persons should be retired from the manufacture and sale of ardent spirits that it would produce an economic void. . . . For if the people of Ohio intend to inaugurate a new departure whereby they will purchase $10,000,000 less of liquor, they will be enabled to purchase $10,000,000 worth more of other commodities.[33]

Even the brewers were quoted: "The secretary of the Ohio Brewers' Association admits that there is no record of a town in Ohio or in the United States which shows an increased tax rate or a decreased volume of business to be due to banishing the saloon." [34]  It was pointed out to the worker that he, and not

[32] *California Liberator*, Dec., 1917.
[33] *American Issue*, Ohio Edition, Feb. 8, 1908.
[34] H. G. Furbay, field secretary of the Anti-Saloon League, in the *North American Review*, 1903, Vol. 177, pp. 43 ff. Commenting upon an article in the *Baltimore Sun* of August 8, 1909, calling for a concerted campaign for the de-

the liquor dealer, was the real taxpayer: "Ordinarily he does not pay his taxes direct and so he does not see in exact figures just how much the saloon is actually costing him. . . . How long will the workingman be the 'goat' of the liquor business? . . . the interests of the saloon are always opposed to the interests of the workingman." [35]    Other examples of this form of propaganda are to be found in pamphlets. *Prohibition in Kansas*, an address by Hon. W. R. Stubbs, Governor of Kansas, 1910, and *Ten Years of Prohibition in Oklahoma*, by W. E. (Pussyfoot) Johnson, are two of the best known.

The League did not scruple at times to edit reports from dry communities as to the effect of prohibition.  A letter from a member of the Memphis, Tennessee, Chamber of Commerce, in answer to an inquiry from the League as to the effects of prohibition, expressed unqualified satisfaction with the policy. Yet so fearful was the League of admitting anything which might be construed as derogatory, that in the published copy the following passages were omitted: " We do not know how it is affecting the balance of the State but presume it is favorable. . . .   Our tax rate has not been reduced.  In fact it has been slightly raised.  This is accounted for in a measure by the loss of revenue from the saloons and in a large measure by the demand for up-to-date civic conditions, good streets, roads and schools. . . .  We think the condition of the poor is better. . . ." [36]

---

struction of rats, the *American Issue* said: "We suppose that if each rat could steal enough grain or get enough soap grease fat out of the garbage can over and above the amount required for its own consumption to enable it to pay a license amounting to 10 to 25 cents a year, so as to make a total revenue of something over a million dollars a year, that the *Sun* would consider the rat was a beneficent institution and ' made business ' and saved taxes, and it would have editorial spasms over the insolence of any 'Anti-Rat Society' that might be started."

[35] *The Workingman Pays the Bill*, an anonymous pamphlet.

[36] Original letter and reprint in the files of the Anti-Saloon League of New York, undated, about 1912.

*Wasted Wages*

To bring home to the worker-drinker the extent of the waste involved in spending his money on liquor, a committee of grocers in Delaware County, Maryland, made a striking offer which was broadcast by the League:

Anyone who drinks three glasses of whisky a day for a year and pays ten cents a drink for it can have in exchange at any of the firms whose names appear here —

|   |   |
|---|---|
| 3 bbls. of flour | 10 lbs. candy |
| 20 bushels of potatoes | 3 doz. cans tomatoes |
| 200 lbs. granulated sugar | 10 doz. pickles |
| 1 bbl. crackers | 10 doz. oranges |
| 1 lb. pepper | 10 doz. bananas |
| 2 lbs. tea | 2 doz. cans corn |
| 50 lbs. salt | 18 boxes matches |
| 20 lbs. rice | ½ bushel beans |
| 50 lbs. butter | 100 cakes soap |
| 10 lbs. cheese | 12 pkgs. rolled oats |
| 25 lbs. coffee |   |

. . . for the same money and get a $15.30 premium for making the change in his expenditures.[37]

Such propaganda is very effective, since it translates the issue into terms easily understood. " The great sink-hole for the workers' wages is the saloon. When that abomination is destroyed, labor is freed from its greatest curse." [38] The worker was reminded that it was he who supported the saloon: " John P. Lennon, treasurer of the American Federation of Labor, says that seventy percent of the drink bill of the United States is contributed by the American laboring man. . . . This means that . . . liquor money is usually bread money, meat money, shoe money and money that ought to go for clothing." [39]

[37] *American Issue*, Maryland Edition, Sept. 19, 1908.
[38] *California Liberator*, Dec., 1917.
[39] Dan Poling, *High Cost of Living*, a League pamphlet. See also *American Issue*, Maryland Edition, June 12, 1909.

The League played upon the prejudices of the organized workers:

There is no Union-Made Whisky . . . *The Teamster,* for February, 1910, organ of the Brotherhood of Teamsters, says also that every barrel or case of beer delivered in Chicago is delivered by non-union men. . . . Mother Jones, in the *Appeal to Reason,* April 9, 1910, describes conditions in Milwaukee breweries, where girls are paid only 75 or 85 cents a day for three or four days' work a week.[40]

C. H. Durand, an Illinois labor leader was quoted:

Here is a Trust that ignores unionism, pays starvation wages to its employees, and carries on a continual agitation to create and foster class strife, by contending that the warfare to destroy the saloon is directed against the liberties of the laboring man. Laboring men should resent this insult of the liquor interests, the declaration that they are the beneficiaries of the saloon, the dispensaries for non-union-made goods.[41]

Carroll D. Wright, former United States commissioner of labor, was cited:

I have looked into a thousand homes of the working people of Europe and I do not know how many in this country. In every case, so far as my observation goes, drunkenness was at the bottom of the misery, and not the industrial surroundings of the men and their families.[42]

Emphasis was laid upon the fact that abstaining workers were usually in a better position to secure employment than those who drank: " The United States Department of Labor figures show that 90 percent of the railways, 79 percent of the manufacturers, 88 percent of the trades, 72 percent of the agriculturists, discriminate against employees addicted to the use of intoxicating liquor as a beverage." [43]

[40] *American Issue,* Illinois Edition, May 20, 1911.
[41] *Ibid.,* May 31, 1912.
[42] *American Issue,* National Edition, Nov. 16, 1912.
[43] *American Issue,* Maryland and Ohio Editions, Jan. 14, 1911.

The baneful effects of the liquor traffic upon the economic life of the community were painted in lurid colors. It was called " the Czolgosz of trade and commerce." [44] Consider the plight of Wheeling, West Virginia, after seventy-six years of license:

The city is run as a brewery game preserve. The city is bankrupt. Last edition of the Census Bureau's Statistics of Cities shows the value of all city property in Wheeling as $1,138,362,000. To offset this there is a funded debt of $1,138,700,000, leaving Wheeling worth less than nothing. At a meeting of the city council, councilman Grogan introduced a resolution requesting the board of control to permit the homeless people to sleep in the city hall corridors. According to census reports the city received during the year $26,059 in liquor licenses and paid $47,877 for police protection. State prohibition showed the people of Wheeling the way out. Business interests are looking forward to the November election in the hope of deliverance.[45]

The League did not hesitate to lay all the ills under heaven at the door of the saloon and brewery. *The Facts about the Liquor Traffic in New York,* by Abner B. Brown, attorney for the Anti-Saloon League of New York, published in 1917, gives a somewhat similar description of conditions in New York State:

The cost of the liquor traffic in New York every year is equal to the assessed valuation of all the realty in 17 representative counties . . . 24,339 places (liquor stores, etc.) employ an average of three men each, all of them being non-producers. Counting the production of a man at $600 a year, we therefore compute the loss as follows — $24,339 \times 3 \times \$600 = \$43,810,000$. To each bar should be credited two drunks who are entirely non-producers . . . making a further loss of $29,206,000.

The sum of Mr. Brown's estimated cost, including the land used in raising products for making liquor, amounted to $612,-

44 *Proceedings of the Fifth Convention of the Anti-Saloon League,* 1904.
45 *American Issue,* Vermont Edition, March, 1912.

555,000. A similar survey for New Jersey was published in 1917 — *Liquor and Labor,* by Charles Stelzle. In 1914 the League published *Alcohol's Ledger in Industry,* by Cora Stoddard. These latter surveys are carefully documented and persuasively written.

## Liquor and Social Ills

The relation of drink to insanity, tuberculosis, mortality, crime, divorce and school attendance was iterated and reiterated. "The report of the superintendent of state hospitals of Kansas declares that the decrease in the number of commitments for insanity has been due to prohibition."[46] Dr. T. S. Clouston of Morningside Asylum, Vermont, asserts that "alcoholic insanity steadily increases with the increased use of alcohol," which is very much like saying that hunger is due to the lack of food. However, such truisms are useful enough as propaganda.

The license states of New York, Delaware, California, Wisconsin, Nevada, Maryland, Massachusetts, New Jersey and Connecticut showed 26.9 percent of their insane as due to alcohol. In Maine, Kansas, Mississippi, North Carolina and Texas, where the sale of liquor is prohibited or severely restricted, only 5.9 percent of the insanity was due to alcohol. The states having prohibition — Maine, North Dakota, Alabama, Georgia, Oklahoma and North Carolina — had one insane person to every 873 persons. The average for the United States as a whole was one insane person for every 490 persons.[47]

"Dr. Bertillon, the famous statistician, says that from the ages of 35–45 he finds that tuberculosis is twice as prevalent among drinkers of alcohol as it is among abstainers."[48] The

---

[46] *American Issue,* Vermont Edition, March, 1912.

[47] Filmore Condit in *Proceedings of the Fourteenth Convention of the Anti-Saloon League,* 1911. This address was published by the League and widely circulated.

[48] *American Issue,* National Edition, Nov., 1912, quoting from *Wichita Daily Eagle.*

national edition of the *American Issue* for October, 1912, quoted Mr. Edward B. Phelps, editor of *The American Underwriter*, as saying that 66,000 — or about 5 percent — of all the deaths in 1908 were due directly to alcohol, not including those in which alcohol was a contributory factor. It was said that 20 percent of these were women.[49]

Perhaps the greatest of all the League's propaganda "scoops" was a letter addressed to the Keeley Institute, a sanitarium for inebriates:

KENTUCKY DISTILLERS' & DISTRIBUTING COMPANY

Kansas City, Mo.
Keeley Institute                Dec. 3, 1913.
Dwight, Illinois.

GENTLEMEN: Our customers are your prospective patients. We can put on your desk a mailing list of over 50,000 individual consumers of liquor. The list is the result of thousands of dollars of advertising.

Each individual on the list is a regular user of liquor. The list of names is new, live and active. We know this because we have circularized it regularly. We furnish this list in quantities at the prices listed below. Remittances to accompany each order.

40,000 to 50,000  $400
20,000  . . . . . . .    300
10,000  . . . . . . . .  200

We will not furnish this list in lots less than 10,000. Discontinuance of business January 1, is the occasion for selling our mailing list.

Yours truly,
KENTUCKY DISTILLERS' CO.,
W. Franklin, President.

[49] This is not a completely accurate quotation. In *The Mortality of Alcohol* Phelps wrote (p. 73): "In default of positive truth to the contrary, it would . . . seem entirely safe to assume that the total annual mortality of the continental United States in which alcohol directly or *even remotely* figures as a causative or *contributory factor* at last reports, *did not exceed* 66,000." Phelps says that of this number about 16.6% were women. The national edition for November 16, 1912, acknowledged the mistake and made the correction. (Italics mine.)

This letter, convicting them out of their own mouths, was used with great success in meetings, in the public press and distibuted in leaflet form. It did its bit in writing the Eighteenth Amendment into the Constitution.[50]

Liquor, it was insisted, was a major cause of crime. A Missouri lawyer was quoted: " I have defended 41 men and women for murder, and 19 out of 20 of the crimes were caused by whisky. I have defended lots of other criminals, and I am safe in saying that 19 out of 20 of them were caused by liquor." [51]   The League's statistics sometimes strain one's credulity. For instance: " In Bell County, Kentucky, 68 murders in 27 months are traceable to the use of intoxicating liquors." [52]

The fact that liquor was a source of crime was proved by citing the decrease of crime in prohibition states.   " As a result of the abolition of the saloons in Berkeley, California, a city of 40,000, only four persons were arrested for drunkenness in the year ending June 30, 1912." [53]   No figures are given to enable a comparison with conditions before. Muskogee, Oklahoma, served as an example of what a dry régime would do in solving the crime problem. It was shown that although the population of the city had increased by more than 12,000 from 1912 to 1917, crime had so declined that the police force had been actu-

---

[50] Innumerable pamphlets and leaflets of a scientific or semi-scientific nature, showing the evil effects of liquor, were published by the League. A few titles are indicative of what some of them contained: *The University Man and the Alcohol Question,* by Professor E. Kraeplin, University of Munich; *The Causes of Alcoholism,* by Dr. A. Cramer, Göttingen; *An Ally of Tuberculosis,* by Emma L. Tansreau; *Alcohol and the Next Generation* and *The Live Baby That Counts,* by Cora Stoddard; *Effects of Alcohol on the Brain, Effects of Alcohol on Heredity* and *Effects of Alcohol on Sex Life,* by W. S. Hall of Chicago; *Effect of Alcohol on Disease* and *Alcohol and Crime,* by J. Gosner. Some of these pamphlets are deserving of careful reading and represent sound investigation and scholarship. Many might be read with especial profit at the present time.

[51] *American Issue,* Maryland Edition, Jan. 11, 1908, quoting Col. I. W. Boulware of Fulton, Missouri.

[52] *American Issue,* Ohio Edition, Sept. 21, 1912.

[53] *American Issue,* Indiana Edition, Oct. 22, 1912.

ally reduced from forty policemen in 1912 to twenty-four in 1917.[54]

" When the saloon is banished, the school takes its place," said the drys. " Prohibition is the best friend of education. . . . During the last nine years the enrollment of the State University has risen from 1150 to 2063; the Normal from 1630 to 2860, and the Agricultural College from 870 to 2192. Besides that, 9000 young men and women are attending denominational institutions and 4548 attending business colleges. The value of public school property has advanced from $10,-000,000 to $16,000,000 . . . during the first twenty years of prohibition illiteracy was reduced 49 percent . . . and the next census reports will give the state first place in education."[55] The school enrollment of wet Rhode Island is contrasted with that of Mississippi, a dry state. In Rhode Island 14.9 percent of the population were enrolled in schools, in Mississippi 26 percent were so enrolled.[56] The League compared the high school population of two Nebraska towns significantly:

Norfolk — *wet*, with a population of 6025, had 158 high school students.

York — *dry*, with a population of 6235, had 315 high school students.

Superintendent Carson, of the Nebraska Anti-Saloon League, declared that " when the saloon comes to town the children are forced to stay out of school to work in support of a drinking father."[57]

Further evidence that the abolition of the liquor traffic meant less crime, insanity and pauperism is contained in a League pamphlet reprinting an editorial from the Philadelphia *North*

[54] W. E. Johnson, *Ten years of Prohibition in Oklahoma*, p. 26.
[55] Hon. W. R. Stubbs, governor of Kansas, *Prohibition in Kansas,* an address delivered in the Great Northern Theatre, Chicago, March 27, 1910, reprinted by the Anti-Saloon League.
[56] *American Issue*, Illinois Edition, May 31, 1912.
[57] *American Issue*, Kentucky Edition, Apr., 1912.

*American* of August 21, 1913, entitled *Something's the Matter with Kansas.* " In 87 of her 105 counties there are no insane. In 54 of this number there are no feeble-minded. Ninety-six counties have no inebriates, and in the other nine they are as scarce as hen's teeth. Twenty-eight county poorhouses are as empty as a last year's locust shell. . . . The pauper population of the state falls a little short of 600. . . . At one time not long ago the jails in 53 counties were empty and 65 counties were on the roll as having no prisoners serving sentence in the penitentiary. Some counties have not called a jury to try a criminal case in ten years. . . . Something is the matter with Kansas. That something, we believe, can be boiled down into these fourteen words constituting an amendment made to her constitution in 1881: ' The manufacture and sale of intoxicating liquor shall forever be prohibited in this state.' "

A League poster summed up the charges against the liquor traffic as follows: " Liquor is responsible for 19 percent of the divorces, 25 percent of the poverty, 25 percent of the insanity, 37 percent of the pauperism, 45 percent of child desertion and 50 percent of the crime in this country. And this is a very conservative estimate."

### The Magic of Great Names

Luther, Goethe, Moltke, Bismarck, Kaiser Wilhelm, even Lincoln and Grant were cited as enemies of booze.[58] The wets laid considerable emphasis on the fact that Abraham Lincoln had on March 6, 1833, taken out a license to sell liquor in his store at New Salem.[59] The Anti-Saloon League insisted that, notwithstanding this, Lincoln was an ardent prohibitionist. The Total Abstinence organization sponsored by the League was called the Lincoln-Lee Legion.

Lincoln has been so frequently claimed by both wets and drys

[58] *American Issue,* Ohio Edition, Aug. 1, 1908. See also Kentucky Edition, April, 1912.
[59] See *Anti-Prohibition Manual,* 1915, p. 56.

that a brief statement of his views would not be out of place. Speaking in 1842, Lincoln, after discussing the revolution of 1776, said, " Turn now to the temperance revolution. In it we shall find a stronger bondage broken, a viler slavery manumitted, a greater tyrant deposed; in it, more of want supplied, more disease healed, more sorrow assuaged. By it no orphans starving, no widows weeping. By it none wounded in feeling, none injured in interest; even the dram maker and the dram seller will have glided into other occupations so gradually as never to have felt the change, and will stand ready to join all in the universal song of gladness." [60]

The same speech continues even more forcefully: " Whether or not the world would be vastly benefited by a total and final banishment from it of all intoxicating drinks seems to me not now an open question. Three-fourths of mankind confess it with their tongues and, I believe, all the rest acknowledge it in their hearts."

Certainly Lincoln was no friend of intoxicating drink. There is considerable doubt as to his views on prohibition. He deplored the over-much blaming of both the dram dealers and dram drinkers as " impolitic and unjust." " It is not much in the nature of man to be driven to anything; still less to be driven about that which is exclusively his own business; and least of all where such driving is to be submitted to at the expense of pecuniary interest or burning appetite. When the dram seller and drinker are incessantly told, not in accents of entreaty and persuasion, diffidently addressed by erring man to an erring brother, but in the thundering tones of anathema and denunciation . . . that they were the authors of all vice and crime in the land; that they were the manufacturers and material of all the thieves and robbers and murderers that infest the land, that their houses were the workshops of the devil; . . .

[60] Ida Tarbell, *In the Footsteps of the Lincolns*, New York, 1924, pp. 192 ff. Nicolay and Hay, *Abraham Lincoln*, Vol. I, Chapter IV.

I say, when they are told all this, and in this way, it is not wonderful that they were slow, very slow to acknowledge the truth of such denunciations." He advised the prohibitionists that " A drop of honey catches more flies than a gallon of gall." [61]

Nor was the ' great ' man always dead. Contemporary politicians, congressmen, senators and others were called upon to testify to their opposition to the liquor traffic. Seventeen governors announced themselves as against the saloon.[62]

### Liquor the Killer

In the South the Anti-Saloon League did not hesitate to use the menace of the drunken negro as propaganda.

Is it plain now? the secret of many a lynching and burning in the South? The primitive negro field hand, a web of strong, sudden impulses, good and bad, comes to town or settlement on Saturday afternoon and pays his fifty cents for a pint of Mr. Levy's gin. He absorbs not only its toxic heat, but absorbs also the suggestion subtly conveyed that it contains aphrodisiacs. He sits in the road or in the alley at the height of his debauch, looking at the obscene picture of a white woman on the label, drinking in the invitation it carries. And then comes . . . opportunity. . . . Then follows the hideous episode of the rope or the stake.[63]

Terrible stories were told of upright young men metamorphosed into murdering beasts by alcoholic drink.

Malcolm Patterson, son of ex-Governor M. R. Patterson of Tennessee, was arrested a few months ago at Port Orchard, Washington, for the attempted murder of Robert T. Seal, a liveryman of that place. He was adjudged insane by a lunacy commission. Patterson stated that he had been a hard drinker since he was sixteen years of age

[61] Carl Sandburg, *Abraham Lincoln: The Prairie Years,* New York, 1926, Vol. I, p. 272.

[62] *American Issue,* Maryland Edition, Jan. 9 and 11 and Aug. 8, 1908. Even such a thing as a prize fight was made to point a moral. The *Issue* attributes the defeat of Jeffries in his battle with Johnson to the fact that Jeffries was a heavy drinker. *American Issue,* National Edition, Nov., 1912.

[63] Quoted from *Collier's* in *American Issue,* Maryland Edition, June 6, 1908. The reference here is to gin sold by Lee, Levy & Co., of St. Louis, whose bottles bore labels with gaudy pictures of nude white women in various seductive poses.

. . . that he had been in a sanitarium five times for treatment of the drink habit but that it had done him no good. Ex-Governor Patterson has been for some years the most able and persistent defender of the liquor traffic in Tennessee, even going so far as to veto legislation to drive the saloon out of the state.

It was only last summer that the son of Henry Watterson of Kentucky, the southern journalist, and leading advocate of the saloon, shot a bartender in a fit of drunken frenzy.[64]

For sheer terrorism the following story is difficult to match. Grayville, Illinois, had voted dry. The saloons were about to close.

Two negroes who worked on the section here, Paul Thomas and James Burress, got the section boss' speeder and went down to Grayville last night. . . . Their bodies were found on the track this morning. Burress lay close to the demolished speeder surrounded by beer bottles, some of which were broken and others filled with the liquid devil. Burress' skull was crushed and both his legs broken. Thomas was carried some distance down the track before he was ground under the wheels. His body was cut in two just above the hips, and one arm was cut off. Bits of flesh and his entrails were strung along the track. He had been a hard working fellow and but for drink would have made a good living for his wife and five little children who mourn his loss. . . . Another fellow from Griffin, Indiana, was also at Grayville and was killed by an Illinois Central train. . . . This makes eight for the Grayville saloons in twelve months . . . "But we must have the revenue ! ! ! " Therefore Hell hath enlarged herself and opened her mouth without measure. . . . Hell and destruction are never full, the purse of the brewer is not satisfied.[65]

### The Stainless Flag

The League was not unmindful of the need for planting the fear of alcohol firmly in the minds of the growing generation. It heartily approved of compulsory instruction in so-called

[64] *American Issue,* New Jersey Edition, May 17, 1912. Patterson, whose son is here portrayed in such sorry straits, later became one of the most effective of the League orators. *A Modern Miracle,* a League pamphlet, is devoted to the story of his conversion.
[65] *American Issue,* Illinois Edition, May 10, 1912.

scientific temperance in the public schools. Through the Lincoln-Lee Legion the League reached the children directly in the Sunday schools. A tremendous amount of literature for children was published and distributed. The flag was frequently pictured with a huge black blot upon it. This stain could only be removed by the obliteration of the saloon and its allies. " The coming generation, bearing that purged and purified banner, will, with enraptured vision, view a destiny more exhalted and glorious than earth has ever known." [66]

Stories, plays, poems, pageants were distributed in leaflet form with other Sunday school literature. The moral in each story is always printed in boldface type. Space will not permit a full description of this literature; only its general character can be indicated. *Bessie's Mothers* is the story of a little girl whose father had died of drink and who was saved from the poor farm only through the generosity of a kind, childless, temperance lady who becomes Bessie's second mother. *Poor Bennie* was the child of drunken parents and as a consequence " he never had a fair show in the world. Just as children may inherit from father or mother the color of their eyes or hair . . . so they may inherit weak and nervous bodies from parents who have poisoned their own bodies by alcohol taken in whisky, beer or wine. . . ." Bennie's father soon died of drink, and he went with his mother to the poorhouse. The little lad resolved to spend his life driving the Demon Drink from the world. Due to his weak constitution, inherited from his drunken parents, Bennie falls in his first venture and freezes to death in a blizzard.

Hundreds of these stories, equally touching and appealing to children, could be cited. *The Outcast* tells of a little boy ostracized by his playfellows because he wanted to build a saloon when they were playing city. They informed him that their city was dry and promptly ran him and his saloon out. *Esther's*

---

[66] E. S. Chapman, *A Stainless Flag*, a League pamphlet.

*First Party* is the story of the conversion of a drinking father by his little daughter. It serves as a vehicle for telling children that moderate drinkers always become drunkards and lose their jobs for "people do not like to employ drinking men." *Peter's Experiment* relates how a little colored boy made his dog very sick by feeding him meal with whisky in it to warm him up. By this he was able to convince his uncle that "whisky is not necessary for medicine," and that "alcohol is poison and injures the body instead of healing it." *The Order of Freedom* shows the dangers of disobedience to law. *At the End of the Line, A Grand and Glorious Time, Nina's Dream, Wendell's Reward,* are a few other titles.

*The Young Mother's Convention, Grandma's Visit, The Good Citizenship Class* and *The Sick Girl* were plays in which liquor was always the scheming villain and prohibition and temperance were the heroes. There were recitations without number, of which the following is typical:

### REFORMED

I've thrown my bottle out the door,
I don't need it any more . . .
Whisky's not the thing for me
When I'm sick. Don't you see
That a dose of castor oil
Is better far than alcohol?

Course I know as well as you,
Oil's not good, but this is true:
It can't hurt you, not at all
Like that Poison Alcohol.
Alcohol in whisky's found;
I don't want that stuff around.

*Verse*

League writers moved inevitably into the poetic. What the poems lacked in quality was made up in quantity. A few examples must suffice.

### THE PRICE OF AN OHIO LICENSE

What's the price of a license?   How much did you say?
The price of men's souls in the market today?
A license to sell, to deform, to destroy,
From the gray hairs of age to the innocent boy.
        How much did you say?

How much is to pay?   How compare with your gold?
A license to poison . . . a crime oft retold —
Fix a price on the years and the manhood of man —
        What's the price, did you say?

### THE LIQUOR SELLER'S PSALM OF LIFE

Tell me not in wild orations
That the business I am in,
Is of all men's occupations,
Most depraved and full of sin.

What if women, broken hearted,
Pray that God may let them die?
What if Mothers weep, and Children —
Drunkard's children, moan and cry?

What if beer and rum and whiskey
Crowd men into prison cells,
Robbing them of all their manhood,
Sending them to drunkards' hells?

As to all your moral questions
I have only this to say: —
There's my license, bought and paid for,
Stamped with Uncle Sam's O. K.

### IF YOU KNEW

If you knew the dreadful story of that sparkling cup you're draining,
How it drags a man from virtue, down to dark perdition's brink,
Yes, and wrecks his brain and body, leaves no trace of good
        remaining —
You would never dare to touch a drop of the Accursed Drink.

Other suggestive titles are, *The Drunkard's Dream, The Drunkard's Advice, The March of Truth, King Alcohol, The Battle Is the Lord's, Slay the Wolves.* Perhaps the most famous was Hugh D'Arcy's *The Face on the Barroom Floor.*[67]

## Charts of Victory

On the theory that "nothing succeeds like success," the League made extensive use of maps showing the rapid spread of prohibition. The wet territory was always black and the dry area white, and local option territory was checked, a suggestive color scheme. In 1893 the map was almost wholly black; by 1917, white and checked. Needless to say, the League did not always bother to point out that much of the dry territory was very sparsely inhabited save by jack rabbits and sage hens.[68]

Other charts and posters were employed widely and with much success. "The investment in and display of charts constituted one of the most valuable assets of the Anti-Saloon League." [69] These charts were displayed on public bulletin boards, in churches and meeting halls, on the main streets of cities, at county fairs, conventions and public gatherings generally, wherever the League could gain admittance.

## War Propaganda

The war gave the League a rare opportunity to deal the liquor traffic a mortal blow. The extraordinary demand for men and

[67] This poem appeared first in the *New York Despatch* in 1887 and had done good work for the W. C. T. U. before the League appropriated it. It is amusing to find that D'Arcy himself never intended his poem as anti-liquor literature. Its original title was simply *The Face Upon the Floor.* It portrayed the sufferings of an artist driven to drink and death by the loss of his sweetheart. "If I thought that my poem had done anything to help prohibition I would jump in the Hudson," declared D'Arcy a short time before his death. *New York Herald Tribune*, Nov. 12, 1925.

[68] These maps may be found in any of the Year Books of the League. See *American Issue*, Maryland and Ohio Editions, March, 1909, for excellent examples. See pp. 164, 165.

[69] *American Patriot*, Nov., 1914: "A Practical Demonstration of the Value of Temperance Charts in Wet and Dry Campaigns."

material, and the frantic appeals to sacrifice everything to winning the war, were contrasted with what seemed to the League the criminal waste of the nation's substance in the manufacture and sale of intoxicating drink.  The reader will recall that when the brewers and liquor dealers had predicted that prohibition would involve a serious disturbance in the national economy, the League had emphatically denied it and had insisted that the liquor business was economically insignificant.  Now, however, this industry was depicted as a yawning gap in the armor of our national defense.[70]

The lessons learned in twenty years of propaganda were applied with added zeal.  The country was deluged with literature depicting the brewers and licensed trade as treacherously stabbing our soldiers in the back.  Raw materials and labor were being used in the manufacture of a useless and harmful product which not only did nothing to help win the war but actually rendered us less able to do so.

The brewery was depicted as a *monstrum horrendum* pillaging the country's resources.  *Eliminate the Waste, Liquor the Traitor, Food Wasted by the Liquor Industries,* are a few of the captions appearing in the League publications.[71]  " If food will win the war," said one pamphlet, " the cessation of brewing, according to Mr. Hoover, would effect a saving in grain of approximately 3,150,000 bushels a month from the nutritive point of view.  War prohibition means saving by the ton in a

[70] " When in April, 1917, the United States declared war upon Germany, the professional prohibitionists of the country, marshaled by the Anti-Saloon League, were quick to seize an exceptional opportunity.  By playing upon the patriotism . . . the doubts and the prejudices of the population, and by utilizing every crisis to enforce their argument, they found a way to take toll, as it were, out of the very blood and agony of the world and to advance their cause exceedingly.  The columns of the press were filled with highly colored propaganda, and though their misstatements were repeatedly refuted, they were as often reiterated with unblushing effrontery." — *Year Book of the United States Brewers' Association*, 1919, p. 113.  See above, p. 50.

[71] *American Issue*, Illinois, Ohio, Maryland and New York Editions, April to Dec., 1917.

world where things are so serious that women are asked to save by the crumb. We read that potatoes last year rotted on the ground for lack of car space, industries and schools closed because cars were lacking to move coal — and yet all the time at least 100,000 of these cars were carrying that worse than non-essential, beer." [72] " Food, Labor, Life. These are the chief factors in winning the war, and the liquor men are wasting all three," said another pamphlet. " Suppose the booze makers should turn shipbuilders? The result would be in Pennsylvania alone the transfer of $94,135,000 into the building of ships. This would then employ over 22,000 workers who would receive over $19,000,000 in wages, whereas now the breweries employ only 7,234 and pay only $5,435,000 in wages." [73]

The League also republished the three most famous of the English pamphlets, *Defeat or Victory, The Fiddlers* and *The Parasite*. These publications contained very much the same kind of propaganda as that used in the United States and gave added force to the arguments against the American trade. Even the Kaiser was quoted to the effect that " in the next war victory will be with that nation which uses the smallest amount of alcohol." A League pamphlet quoted General O'Ryan of the 27th Division as saying, " Our experience on the border burned into the minds of all, that customs which justified the use of liquor were improper, unmilitary and subversive of discipline, and should be abandoned." The League then drew the moral, " If prohibition is good for our soldiers, why not the rest of us? " [74]

The chief reasons for war prohibition were summarized in a pamphlet issued in 1918 by the Committee for a Dry Binghamton:

[72] *If*, a pamphlet of the Massachusetts League.
[73] *American Issue*, National Edition, Feb. 2, 1918.
[74] *American Issue*, New York Edition, Aug., 1917.

## TEN REASONS FOR WAR PROHIBITION

1. It would save in one year more than $2,000,000,000 now spent for liquors; enough money to pay interest on our seven billion dollar loan for eight years. . . .

2. It would put out of commission a traffic that has been denounced by the British Premier as a more dangerous foe than Germany or Austria. . . . A traffic that has been absolutely prohibited in Germany. . . .

3. It would disarm an enemy that every year kills and wounds and renders inefficient hundreds of thousands of men who ought to be enlisted in the army or navy or ranks of industry. . . .

4. It would release for the protection and conservation of our national strength an army of men who are at present manufacturing a habit-forming drug that eats away the physical and moral fiber of our people.

5. It would stop what is now an almost utter waste of not less than 110 million bushels of grain, and 152 million gallons of molasses; enough . . . to feed seven million men for a year.

6. It would remove from the workers of the nation their greatest handicap to efficiency and place them on a par with soldiers and sailors to whom liquor cannot lawfully be sold.

7. It would remove from the nation the reproach of depending for revenue upon the debauching of its citizens.

8. It would save the nation from the inanity of trying to make legally right what is morally, socially, politically and economically wrong.

9. It would speed the End of the War and of All War.

10. It would result, as has everywhere proven true when tried, in a great moral, physical, social and economic uplift.

The German names of many of the brewers were too tempting a target to miss:

German brewers in this country have rendered thousands of men inefficient and are thus crippling the Republic in its war on Prussian militarism. . . . The brewers who are helping the enemy by cutting down America's fighting force are threatening to strangle the Government at Washington if it legislates against the beer industry.[75]

[75] *American Issue*, Ohio Edition, Aug. 3, 1917.

President Hexamer of the German-American Alliance, a brewery financed organization, was quoted as saying: " We have suffered long the preachment that ' you Germans must allow yourselves to be assimilated, you must merge in the American people '; but no one will ever find us prepared to descend to an inferior level. . . . Many are giving our German culture to this land of their children, but that is possible only if we stand together and conquer that dark spirit of muckerdom and Prohibition. Let us stand up for our good rights and hold together. Be Strong; Be Strong and German." [76] Hexamer was catalogued as an agent of the Kaiser as well as of the brewers. " The Kaiser said in 1908, ' If ever a man was worthy of high decoration of my hand, it is Herr Dr. Hexamer, the president of the Alliance, who may be justly termed to be, by my grace, the acting ruler of all the Germans in the United States.' " [77]

" Kaiserism abroad and booze at Home must go. . . . Liquor is a menace to patriotism because it puts beer before country. . . . The brewery advocates in the Senate threatened to talk the bill [food control] to death unless beer was saved," declared Wayne Wheeler in an address at Provincetown, R. I. " Recent investigations of brewery and liquor lawlessness and corruption in politics should arouse every patriot. . . ." [78]

The challenge to loyal patriots of America today is to demand the absolute prohibition of the liquor traffic. In this way only, can Democracy be made safe and the forces which aid disloyalty be eliminated. . . . The shot and shell and poison gas of the Germans at the front are more easily met than insidious attacks in camp of the devils of lust, of gambling and of drink.[79]

Early in 1917 E. Lowry Humes, United States District Attorney for the western district of Pennsylvania, began to investigate brewery corruption in Pennsylvania politics. The

[76] *American Issue,* Ohio Edition, Aug. 3, 1917.
[77] *If,* a pamphlet of the Massachusetts League.
[78] *Milwaukee Journal,* Oct. 3, 1917.
[79] *Home and State,* organ of the Texas League, Oct. 15, 1917.

result was a grand jury investigation which culminated in the return of indictments against the United States Brewers' Association, the Pennsylvania Brewers' Association and approximately one hundred corporations for violation of Section 37 of the Federal Criminal Code (the conspiracy section). These associations and practically all of the corporations entered pleas and were sentenced.

In July, 1918, Congress, by unanimous vote, revoked the charter of the German-American Alliance, after a thorough investigation by a subcommittee of the Judiciary Committee in the Senate. The Anti-Saloon League published a summary of the evidence that, under the circumstances, would have damned a saint.[80] Here the League found official corroboration of its own charges and used it without stint. " Everything in this country that is pro-German is anti-American. Everything that is pro-German must go . . . German Alliances and the whole German propaganda must be abolished. . . . The Brewers and Allied Liquor Trades that back such an Alliance should suffer the same penalty." [81]

It may well be that the revelations of the Senate committee and the Pittsburgh grand jury together became the final straws that broke the back of the American liquor business. The Anti-Saloon League was fully aware of the special advantage which the war conditions afforded. " The spirit of service and self-sacrifice exemplified in an efficient and loyal staff made it possible to take advantage of the war situation and of the confusion which He whom we serve has wrought among our enemies." [82]

[80] See pamphlet, *The National German-American Alliance and Its Allies, Pro-German Brewers and Liquor Dealers, a Disloyal Combination.*

[81] *Ibid.*, p. 8. The more extensive investigation by the subcommittee of the Judiciary Committee of the Senate which began in September, 1918, largely through League influence, was not completed until the Armistice had been signed. It heaped mountain high the evidence taken in the first investigation and covered all phases of the activities of the brewers. It should be borne in mind that most of the pro-German activity with which the brewers were charged had been carried on before the United States entered the war.

[82] *American Issue*, New York Edition, May 14, 1919.

## How the League's Message Was Spread

The League was primarily concerned with the voters. Its propaganda was not so much an educational as a political weapon. Its purpose was to spur into action those voters who believed the liquor traffic to be an evil. To accomplish this it was necessary to produce enough literature to reach a substantial portion of the voting population. At first the literature was printed and circulated by the local organizations with some small financial and ideational assistance from the national league. But this was soon found to be ineffective.

### The League's Own Printing Plant

The idea of a national organ and a publishing department from which the state organizations might be supplied had long been in the minds of the national officers. It was thought that greater unity and effectiveness could be secured through a centralized editorial control, but nothing was done in this direction until 1907. In that year the *American Issue,* which had been published by the Ohio League, was taken over as the official national organ and moved from Columbus to Chicago. Under the editorship of Dr. J. C. Jackson an effort was made to secure closer coöperation between the national and state leagues in the matter of publications. The project included state editions of the *American Issue.* In 1908, Dr. E. H. Cherrington, state superintendent in Washington, was called to act as associate editor with Jackson and as general manager of the League's publishing interests. Within two years fifteen states adopted the new arrangement. The national officers were now convinced of the feasibility of a League-owned publishing plant, and in 1909 the American Issue Publishing Company was established. The people of Westerville, Ohio, a small town near Columbus, offered to donate a plot valued at $10,000 for the erection of a printing plant. The building was completed in 1909 and no time was lost in transferring the publishing interests there.  About that time Jackson died and Cherrington became editor-in-chief of all the League's publications, a position he has ever since held.[83]

Since the establishment of the American Issue Publishing Company the literary output of the League has assumed Gargantuan proportions.  By 1912, its eight presses were printing more than forty tons of temperance literature each month, including thirty-one state editions of the *American Issue,* with an aggregate monthly circulation of more than 500,000.[84]

A new monthly periodical, *The American Patriot,* began a feeble career in 1913.  The next year, a second and more successful monthly was started, the *New Republic,* under the editorship of W. E. (Pussyfoot) Johnson.  This became the most important of the League monthlies.  It attained an average monthly circulation during the four years of its existence, 1913–1916, of about 300,000.  *The Scientific Temperance Journal,* edited by Cora Stoddard, was added the next year.  Its circulation, never very large, is now almost negligible.  In 1915, two papers, *The Worker* and *The National Daily,* were started.[85]

Thus by 1916, the Westerville plant was printing six different temperance journals, including four monthlies with an aggregate circulation of about 420,000, one weekly with a circulation of over 130,000 each week, and a daily with a circulation

[83] As related to the author by E. H. Cherrington.  See his *History of the Anti-Saloon League,* pp. 123 ff.

[84] In 1922 the number of separate editions of the *American Issue* had been reduced to twenty-three.  Of these, seven were weeklies, six were published bi-weekly and ten monthly.  Copies of the *American Issue,* both state and national editions, are sent directly to subscribers from Westerville.  The price of the national edition is $1.50 per year for the bi-weekly edition and $1.00 per year for the monthly edition.

[85] In 1914, J. T. Breece and Pearl Selby of Portsmouth offered to contribute what was equivalent to $40,000 to the American Issue Publishing Company to found a national daily, provided additional subscriptions could be secured to maintain the paper for at least three years.  Subscriptions raised by personal solicitation amounted to $60,195, making a total of $100,195 for this National Daily Fund.  On January 1, 1917, it was decided to merge *The National Daily* into the enlarged national weekly edition of the *American Issue.* — *Report of Committee on Financial Management as of January 1, 1919, to the Executive Committee of the Board of Directors of the Anti-Saloon League of America.*

of approximately 15,000. The war forced the League to completely reorganize its publishing work. Four publications were discontinued in 1917, leaving only the *American Issue,* national and state, and *The Scientific Temperance Journal.* Although the circulation of the *American Issue* increased markedly, the aggregate circulation showed a decrease of over twenty-five percent. This was recovered in 1918 and there was a considerable increase in 1919 when the circulation of the *American Issue* rose to approximately sixteen million for the year. The banner year came appropriately enough in 1920, when a total of 18,386,400 copies of the *American Issue* were printed. In 1921 the *Intercollegiate Statesman,* to promote the observance of the Eighteenth Amendment among college men, and the *Ohio Messenger* were established. By 1922 popular indifference had set in and that year shows the smallest literary output since 1915 — 14,651,423 copies of League publications.

One might almost say that the liquor business was drowned in a deluge of temperance literature. From October, 1909, to January, 1923, the American Issue Company turned out 157,-314,642 copies of temperance papers. The periodical literature so far discussed comprised only part of the League propaganda. The record of the job department at Westerville follows. The figures cover the period from 1909 to 1923.[86]

| | |
|---|---:|
| Books | 1,925,463 |
| Pamphlets | 5,271,715 |
| Leaflets | 114,675,431 |
| Window Cards | 2,322,053 |
| Other cards, tickets, etc. | 18,522,471 |
| Miscellaneous | 21,553,032 |
| General printing, not strictly propaganda — letterheads, forms, etc. | 80,512,132 |
| Total | 244,782,296 |

[86] The books included more than one hundred titles, the posters were of over seventy varieties; there were more than two hundred pamphlets and as many different leaflets. — *Report of the General Manager of the American Issue Publishing Company, January 1, 1923, to the Executive Committee of the Board of Directors of the Anti-Saloon League of America.*

That such a gigantic outpouring should have profoundly modified the behavior of the American people toward the liquor traffic is not surprising.  Never before, perhaps, has a moral suasion organization, maintained by voluntary contributions and directed to a non-profit-making end, been able to conduct a campaign of education and agitation on such a scale.

### *Distribution of Literature*

The problem of distribution was an important one.  To send the literature through the mails required a regular subscription list, and the postage bill was considerable.  The American Issue Publishing Company had special clerks of the postal department at its Westerville plant, for the purpose of stamping, weighing and sending out its publications.  They were mailed, for the most part, from Westerville directly to the individual.  The League had in 1920 upwards of half a million addresses upon its lists.[87]  Distribution through the churches was also effective.  Here the literature reached the child as well as the adult.  With League literature in his hands and with the imprecations hurled from the pulpit resounding in his ears, the churchman was not likely to be unaffected.  The League also furnished corporations and labor unions with leaflets and posters.  These were posted in conspicuous places in the plant and put into the pay envelopes of the employees.[88]

On the distribution and use of propaganda there were frequently detailed instructions.  A letter sent out by Superintendent Holsaple of the South Dakota League, in 1914, illustrates this:

[87] *American Issue*, Maryland and Ohio Editions, Sept., 1912.

[88] *Brewing and Liquor Interests and German Propaganda*, Senate Document 62, 66th Congress, 1st Session, Vol. 1, pp. 164–83.  In the plants of the United States Steel Corporation the leaflets were first edited by an official of the corporation and then struck off by the American Issue Publishing Company.  They were almost entirely of a nonmoral character, appealing to the worker from the economic point of view.  *Drink Makes One More Liable to Accident; Ninety-five Percent of Accidents Occur to Drinking Men; Drink, the Largest Cause of Unhappy Homes; Abstainers Have Less Sickness; Small Death Rate; The Better Chances of the Sober Workman*, are a few characteristic titles.

DEAR CO-WORKER:

Is your town going to vote on the saloon question this Spring? . . .
We wish to urge the greatest CAMPAIGN OF PUBLICITY it is
possible to make. . . . Our only hope lies in TURNING ON THE
LIGHT and making a noise.

Look over the enclosed leaflets (33 in all) and pick out what you
want and let us supply you. They are FREE to those towns in
which the League work is allowed to be presented during the year.
. . . FLOOD YOUR TOWN with these leaflets.

FILL THE BILL BOARDS and store windows of your town
with fine posters. They did great business for us last year. . . .
Cover the town with them.

See the " Vote Dry " button on this letter.. Put one on every man,
woman and youngster who will wear it. . . .

Get the folks to singing local option songs in your campaign meetings, Sunday School and young people's societies. We've a fine anti-
saloon song book with 58 numbers. . . .

There follows a list of available speakers.

The foregoing does not pretend to be an exhaustive treatment of League propaganda. The Speakers' Bureau, the Press
Bureau and the World League Against Alcoholism have not
been discussed. It is felt that these are rather outside the
scope of the present chapter. It should be mentioned here that
not all of the publishing of the Anti-Saloon League was done at
Westerville. In 1917, there were no less than six state periodicals published independently in the respective states. These
publications had suggestive names, *The Alabama Citizen, The
California Issue,* now *The California Liberator, The Connecticut Citizen,* [89] *The New Hampshire Issue, Home and State*
(Texas), *Civic League Record* (Waterville, Maine).

" If you turn the light into a rat hole," said Abraham Lincoln, " it will soon cease to be suitable as a rat hole." The
Anti-Saloon League turned the light of publicity into the rat
hole of the American saloon.

[89] *The Connecticut Citizen* is not strictly a League publication. It is the
organ of the Connecticut Temperance Society which, though nominally independent, is closely affiliated with the Anti-Saloon League.

# CHAPTER III

## METHODOLOGY OF REFORM

Prohibition laws in the United States did not spring full-blown from the Jovian brow of Wayne Wheeler and the Anti-Saloon League. A careful reading of the record demonstrates, if it demonstrates anything, that the Eighteenth Amendment was not " put over " on the American people. The Anti-Saloon League did not, as many good people believe, come like a thief in the night to steal away our liberties. Nor was prohibition adopted in a fit of civic absent-mindedness. The step from school and church district remonstrances to a constitutional amendment outlawing the liquor traffic throughout the nation is too great to admit of so facile an explanation.

In a very real sense national prohibition represents a growth, and a rather slow, deliberate growth at that. It is true that the political activities of the myrmidons of morality must account for a large measure of the success which has attended the temperance people. But it is not the sole explanation. Moral and economic beliefs are not crystallized into law without the backing of a considerable constituency and the existence of a pretty well-defined opinion. The most that can be said of the Anti-Saloon League is that it provided an organization through which this constituency made itself effective. In final analysis, its success depended not only upon its ability to make prohibition sentiment, but also upon its ability to build an effective political machine upon the basis of an already existing body of opinion.

In the following discussion of the political methods of the Anti-Saloon League it should be borne in mind that a political contest implies an issue. If the issue is real and persistent, it implies that the question involved has already become momentous. This description of the tactics of the prohibition agitation is not an attempt to give a complete picture of that movement. An effort will be made to set forth only the main tactics employed in crystallizing prohibition sentiment into law.

The outstanding features of the methods used by the Anti-Saloon League are: (1) centralization of authority; (2) singleness of purpose; (3) political utilization of the power of the Protestant churches; (4) avoidance of entry into politics as a separate political party.

The concentration of authority within the organization has been described. Singleness of purpose means, simply, that the League devoted all of its energies to outlawing the saloon and the organized liquor traffic. No other issue was permitted to becloud its political horizon.

The banishing of booze was the League's sole concern, and until that was accomplished it held all else at naught. This policy has enabled the League to keep its identity and has prevented internal dissension; any other would have seriously limited its effectiveness. The Prohibition Party failed to make itself politically effective largely for this reason. The leaders found themselves in a constant dilemma:

If they refused to commit themselves on any issue other than prohibition, they found it impossible to persuade any considerable number of voters to disregard their opinions on all other political issues for the sake of united action against the liquor traffic. But if they took a clean stand on contentious party issues, as they did in 1884 and 1888 on the tariff, they repelled possible converts from the ranks of the Democrats and low-tariff Republicans without securing the support of the high-tariff temperance men who believed the tariff to be a matter of great importance. Or they split their party as they did in 1896, when both silver and gold Prohibitionists put independent presidential candidates in the field.[1]

[1] A. N. Holcombe, *The Political Parties of Today*, New York, 1924, pp. 322 ff. The tactics of the Anti-Saloon League in this respect may be compared

The Anti-Saloon League has avoided the danger of this political Scylla and Charybdis. Working through the existing party organizations, it was able to avoid the disastrous consequences of meeting a dilemma like that above described. Of course this procedure is not peculiar to the League. It is essentially the same as that employed by all pressure groups, with whom much of our legislation originates. Associations of business men and corporations interested in legislation have frequently supported candidates friendly to their interests, regardless of their other political views.[2]

## The League and the Prohibition Party

The relation between the Anti-Saloon League and the Prohibition Party has been grossly misrepresented. Many otherwise well-informed people suppose that the League is simply an adjunct to the Prohibition Party or the residuary legatee of that party. Such a view is misleading. Within the Prohibition Party itself the Anti-Saloon League has been severely censured for its tactics, and many ardent Prohibitionists regarded it as a greater enemy than the liquor traffic itself. Eugene Chafin, the Prohibition Party candidate for President in 1908, declared:

There is nothing so damnable and wrong in the United States as the proposition of local option. We have got to kill the Anti-Saloon League and then lick the Republican and Democratic Parties. [The Anti-Saloon League] is nothing but an annex to the Republican Party and is only kept alive by them that Republican candidates

---

to those employed by the Anti-Corn Law League in England (1838–46) which succeeded so notably by concentrating on a single issue. In contrast may be cited the Chartists, with their six points, who accomplished so little. See H. D. Jordan, " Political Methods of the Anti-Corn Law League," *Political Science Quarterly*, March, 1927, Vol. 42, pp. 58–76.

[2] It is not unusual for business men of " large interests " to contribute to the campaign funds of candidates of opposing parties whom they regard as " sound." See James K. Pollock, Jr., *Party Campaign Funds*, New York, 1926, p. 112.

may avoid the real issue and poll both the Sunday School and the whisky vote.[3]

This charge has been frequently repeated. Much has been made of the fact that the original founders of the organization were Republicans.[4] At the League convention in 1925, the Rev. Sam Small, a former League worker, asserted that Wayne Wheeler was making it a part of the Republican machine.[5] To one familiar with the history of the Anti-Saloon League, such charges are amusing. Oberlin, its birthplace, was a Republican stronghold, and it was natural and practical to take on the political complexion of this environment. But, even in Ohio, the League did not become a tail to the Republican kite. In 1904 it was largely instrumental in defeating Herrick, Republican candidate for governor, and electing Pattison, a Democrat.[6] William Jennings Bryan could scarcely have been seduced by an organization that was but a shadow of the Republican Party. The success of the League in the Democratic South certainly cannot be attributed to Republican leanings.[7]

[3] Quoted in the *American Issue,* Maryland Edition, Feb. 26, 1910.
[4] Leigh Colvin, *Prohibition in the United States,* New York, 1926, p. 384.
[5] *New York World,* Nov. 10, 1925.
[6] William M. Burke, Superintendent of the Oakland district league, " The Anti-Saloon League as a Political Force," *Annals of the American Academy,* 1908, Vol. 32, pp. 497–507.
[7] The League's analysis of the affirmative votes in various legislatures for Anti-Saloon League legislation may be cited as showing the non-partisan or rather omni-partisan nature of the organization.

| STATE | REPUBLICAN VOTE | DEMOCRATIC VOTE | OTHERS |
|---|---|---|---|
| Alabama | 2 | 139 | |
| Michigan | 127 | 5 | |
| Georgia | 0 | 219 | |
| Wisconsin | 102 | 25 | 6 |
| Mississippi | 0 | 178 | |
| Tennessee | 33 | 99 | |
| Illinois | 133 | 68 | 3 |
| Kentucky | 65 | 73 | |

*American Issue,* Maryland Edition, June 13, 1908.

The vote in the Ohio legislature of 1908 on the Rose County Option Law (an Anti-Saloon League bill) showed 80 Republicans, 75 Democrats and 3 Independents for the measure.[8] In 1912 the committee chosen by the League to draft a suitable Interstate Commerce Liquor Shipment bill included both Democrats and Republicans.[9]

The fact is, the tactics of the League require it to work through the dominant party in one-party states. In Pennsylvania, Kansas, Wisconsin, Michigan and Maine the League is Republican; in Texas, the Carolinas, Georgia and Alabama it is Democratic; in Ohio it tends to be Republican. In New York, where the Democrats are wet, the League works through the Republican Party, without being married to it. In the New York senatorial election of 1926, for example, the League, finding both parties unsatisfactory, worked independently.[10] In the national arena the Anti-Saloon League was Republican when the Republicans were in office and Democratic when the Democrats were in. A Democratic Congress passed the Webb-Kenyon Law and submitted the Eighteenth Amendment; a Republican Congress gave us the Volstead Act.[11]

This policy of working through the Democratic and Repub-

---

[8] *American Issue,* Ohio Edition, June, 1908.

[9] The membership of this committee was: Dr. A. J. Barton of Texas, D.; Hon. F. S. Caldwell of Oklahoma, D.; Dr. James Cannon, Jr., of Virginia, D.; Hon. J. F. Hanly of Indiana, R.; the Rev. S. E. Nicholson of Washington, D. C., R.; Senator Curtis of Kansas, R.; Senator P. J. McCumber of North Dakota, R.; Hon. E. Y. Webb of North Carolina, D.; Hon. Morris Sheppard of Texas, D.; Hon. Fred S. Jackson of Kansas, R.— *American Issue,* Maryland Edition, Feb. 3, 1912.

[10] Superintendent Anderson of New York in 1920 declared, " The Republican state platform declaration on prohibition is a cowardly falsehood." — *New York Times,* July 29, 1920.

[11] At a conference held in Westerville in June, 1923, it was decided by the League superintendents of eleven Southern states to make a concerted drive to eliminate Alfred E. Smith as a candidate for the Democratic presidential nomination. At this conference Senator McKellar of Tennessee declared that the " wet-dry " issue would be fought to the death in the Democratic convention. The League superintendents asserted that in the eleven Southern states which they represented, only a " dry " Democrat could hope for success. " The Solid South will not remain solid if a wet is nominated." — *New York Times,* June 18, 1923: *Christian Science Monitor,* June 22, 1923.

**HOLDING THE DOOR OPEN FOR HIM**

This cartoon from the *American Issue*, Illinois Edition, September 10, 1915, illustrates the Anti-Saloon League's attitude toward the Prohibition Party's policy of nominating independent dry candidates.

lican Parties was denounced by Prohibition Party leaders as actually impeding the cause of prohibition.[12] Such a view, however, would be difficult to sustain. The political arena has been literally strewn with the cadavers of one-issue political parties. The voters are rarely willing to turn the reins of government over to men so politically myopic as to see but one issue. To compete with the regular parties on other issues was impossible, for the Prohibitionists themselves were not agreed on them. The Anti-Saloon League in its campaign for temperance legislation chose rather to follow the tactics of other pressure groups within the old parties. The Prohibitionists might as fairly be accused of playing into the hands of the liquor interests. On occasion, when the League endorsed dry candidates of a major party, the Prohibitionists confused the issue by entering their own candidates, thus opening the way for the election of avowed wets.

Certainly the liquor dealers did not regard the League as friendly.[13] " It is the Anti-Saloon League which is chiefly responsible for the big conquests which liquor exclusion has been making in recent times. The League has no politics. It works as effectively in Democratic as in Republican communities. All parties look alike to the Anti-Saloon League." [14] The September number of *Bar and Buffet*, 1908, discussing the progress of the Anti-Saloon League campaign, asked in a headline, " What Shall We Do to Be Saved? "

Many wet papers were quite willing to fall in with the Prohibition Party's criticism of the Anti-Saloon League. It is not unusual to find in the files of wet newspapers articles and edi-

---

[12] " By giving its influence to the perpetuation of the old parties . . . the League helped to keep alive the old alignments and helped to make other issues paramount. . . . The League thus minimized its own issue and encouraged its subordination." — Colvin, *op. cit.*, p. 397.

[13] See *Bar and Buffet*, Feb., 1908; *American Brewers' Review*, March 1, 1908; also *Toledo Blade*, Jan. 15, 1908.

[14] *Pittsburgh Liquor Dealers' Journal*, Feb. 26, 1908. See also, *Year Book of American Brewers' Association*, 1919, and *Cleveland Plain Dealer*, Feb. 6, 1908.

torials praising the Prohibition Party and denouncing the Anti-Saloon League. An editorial in the *Baltimore Sun* of July 20, 1908, illustrates this. This thoroughly wet journal said:

> The Prohibition Party appeals to the moral sense. . . . The Anti-Saloon League uses threats and violence. It offers its support on election day to the candidates of the political parties, it does not care which, in return for a pledge to vote for its measures. . . . The offer to deal is accomplished by threats. . . . Such methods constitute an ever present danger to good government. The clear, courageous and straightforward methods of the Prohibition Party command respect. The methods of the Anti-Saloon League tend to provoke bitterness and opposition.[15]

It would, of course, be erroneous to minimize the importance of the Prohibition Party in creating dry sentiment. The long and persistent battle which it waged certainly made the League's fight less difficult. Not all Prohibitionists were unfriendly to the Anti-Saloon League. J. G. Wooley and ex-Governor Hanly, Prohibition candidates for the presidency in 1900 and 1916, respectively, became two of the League's most effective speakers. Wooley explained his abandonment of the party thus:

> The Prohibition Party was like a fire bell. It awoke the people. They are up and doing. In such a case there are two things to do, ring the bell more, or put out the fire. I am for putting out the fire, whatever becomes of the bell . . . no political party is my landlord . . . I am no political squirrel bound to make my progress, if at all, within a party whirligig. I pay no vows to Saint Fixity, Saint Party, or Saint Consistency. I grow; or try to. And whither the sealed orders of my conscience read when once I open them, I go, in company or alone. I owe nobody an apology for what I am or what I do as an elector within the triangle of my own conscience, my own judgment and the law of the land.[16]

[15] See, for an opposite interpretation, *New York Evening Mail*, Nov. 22, 1907.

[16] *American Issue*, Maryland Edition, July 10, 1909.

*The League's Singleness of Purpose*

The League was subject to constant temptation and no little pressure from interested persons to declare itself and to use its influence on behalf of other reforms. This it has generally refused to do. Child labor, free silver, taxation, the League of Nations, imperialism and a host of other issues, found no place in the League's platform.

There were certain exceptions to this which deserve mention. In Connecticut, as the successor of the old Connecticut Temperance Union, it handled practically all the agitation about probation, juvenile courts, reformatories, gambling and prize fighting.[17] Other instances might easily be cited where the League has favored social legislation.[18] But where such questions were allowed to enter at all, it was only because the League believed them to be closely allied to its war on drink.

One of the reforms most actively supported was the extension of the suffrage to women. Purley A. Baker, general superintendent of the Anti-Saloon League, declared to its 1911 convention: " The antidote that is to meet the saloon opposition to American citizenship is to be found in the enfranchising of American womanhood." Every mention of woman suffrage during this convention was greeted with applause. Had the League been convinced that the enfranchised women would vote wet, it would have been just as strenuous in its opposition as it was in its support.[19] The opposition of the brewers to woman suffrage confirmed the League in its opinion that the woman vote would be dry.[20] It was the belief of those

[17] J. C. Jackson, editor of *American Issue*, " Work of the Anti-Saloon League," *Annals of the American Academy*, Vol. 32, pp. 482–97.

[18] *American Issue*, New Jersey Edition, May 17, 1912.

[19] The Rev. William O'Ryan of Denver, Colorado, voiced the League attitude when he said, " I will utterly despise woman suffrage and curse the day I voted for it if the women of Denver are not alive to the necessity of voting as one, for local option at the coming election." — *American Issue*, Maryland Edition, Feb. 1, 1908.

[20] " We will gladly give space in the *American Issue* if some brewer or liquor dealer will tell why his crowd is against the equal suffrage proposal." (*American*

responsible for the League policy that the sentiment opposed to woman suffrage was wet.[21]　Consequently, it was considered good tactics to favor the reform.　It now seems clear that the League was not mistaken in its belief.[22]

*Issue*, Ohio Edition, June 8, 1912.)　Some of the brewers at least believed opposition to woman suffrage to be a serious political blunder and advised against it. (Correspondence between officers of the United States Brewers' Association in *Senate Document No. 62*, 66th Congress, 1st Session, pp. 1016, 793, 779.)

[21] C. E. Gehlke has attempted to work out the relation between the votes on suffrage and temperance, and his findings lend some support to the League assumption.

In 1912, Ohio voted on several constitutional amendments, among which were the extension of the vote to women and the licensing of the sale of liquor, which had previously been unlicensed and subject only to the liquor tax law.　Though the issue was not clearly drawn, those who favored prohibition tended to vote " no " on the licensing amendment, and in general "the trade " supported the license proposal.　Dr. Gehlke's sampling seems regrettably limited, but he gives the following from certain Cleveland precincts:

| | | | | | |
|---|---|---|---|---|---|
| For Suffrage | 78 votes | Against Suffrage | 42 votes | For Suffrage | 65% |
| Against License | 94 votes | For License | | Against License | 78% |

Again in 1914 the woman suffrage and state-wide prohibition amendments were submitted together.　This time the issue was quite clear:

| | | | | | |
|---|---|---|---|---|---|
| For Suffrage | 77 votes | Against Suffrage | 33 votes | For Suffrage | 70% |
| For Prohibition | 92 votes | Against Prohibition | 41 votes | For Prohibition | 69% |

*Proceedings of the American Statistical Association*, 1917, p. 524.

[22] The actual determination of how women did vote after they were enfranchised is difficult.　The following table shows little immediate influence on the part of the enfranchised women:

| STATE | WOMAN SUFFRAGE ADOPTED | PROHIBITION ADOPTED | TIME ELAPSED BETWEEN SUFFRAGE AND PROHIBITION |
|---|---|---|---|
| Wyoming............ | 1890 | 1918 | 28 years |
| Colorado............ | 1893 | 1914 | 21 " |
| Utah................ | 1896 | 1917 | 21 " |
| Idaho............... | 1896 | 1915 | 19 " |
| Washington.......... | 1910 | 1914 | 4 " |
| California........... | 1911 | 1919 | 8 " |
| Arizona............. | 1912 | 1914 | 2 " |
| Kansas.............. | 1912 | 1880 | − 32 " |
| Oregon............. | 1912 | 1914 | 2 " |
| Montana............ | 1914 | 1916 | 2 " |
| Nevada............. | 1914 | 1918 | 4 " |
| New York........... | 1917 | 1919 | 2 " |
| Michigan............ | 1918 | 1916 | − 2 " |
| Oklahoma........... | 1918 | 1907 | − 11 " |
| South Dakota........ | 1918 | 1907 | − 11 " |

*The League's " Nihil Obstat "*

The Anti-Saloon League was, as we have seen, non-partisan, bi-partisan, omni-partisan.  With no nominees of its own, it held itself free to support any candidate it approved.  It frequently supported both Republicans and Democrats in the same election.  The only question put to candidates was, " How do you stand on temperance? "  " He who is not with me is against me," and no man could hope for Anti-Saloon League support if he failed to commit himself definitely to its program.  A candidate's unimpeachable merit in other respects mattered nothing.  If he failed to reply satisfactorily to the League's questionnaire, he could not look for League support.  " In season and out of season the League workers have fought in defense of worthy public officials and have persistently demanded the scalps of those who have not been in sympathy with its aims." [23]  Of course it could see no worth in public officials who did not sympathize with its own aims.

The Anti-Saloon League did not insist that a candidate be a personal abstainer.  If his vote was dry, he himself might be wet.  The League's theory was that it is better to have a drunkard who will " vote right, than to have a saint who will vote wrong." [24]  This was consistent with the early declaration that

---

In Washington and Montana, where the author lived during the prohibition and suffrage contests, it was felt that the votes of the women made these states dry; but, without a careful statistical analysis, such affirmations are little better than guesses.

Ogburn and Goltra, in their study of " How Women Vote " (*Political Science Quarterly*, Sept., 1919) analyzed the votes of men and women on prohibition in Multnomah County, Oregon, in 1914 and found that 49% more of the women voted for prohibition than men.  (*Political Science Quarterly*, Vol. 54, pp. 413 ff.)

The belief that the triumph of prohibition was due to women has been frequently expressed since the adoption of prohibition.  (*California Liberator*, April, 1926, editorial, " The Nineteenth Amendment Rivets the Eighteenth Amendment.")

[23] H. M. Chalfant, editor of the Pennsylvania Edition, *American Issue*, " The Anti-Saloon League," *Annals of the American Academy*, 1923, Vol. 47, p. 279.

[24] Burke, *op. cit.*

it was an anti-saloon organization interested in ridding society of the saloon, and not a prohibition league. It did not concern itself with the personal habits of individuals, nor has this policy been altered since the adoption of prohibition, although in many states only total abstainers are supported.

The League did not wait for the candidates to be selected. Every effort was made in primaries and conventions to secure the nomination of drys. In some instances, informal conferences or direct questionnaires were employed to determine the attitude of the various candidates toward the League measures. Failing to get a satisfactory answer, the League abandoned the contest altogether or put up a candidate of its own. The latter alternative had two advantages. In the first place it might, especially where the influence of the League was considerable, force one or both of the regular parties to reconsider, in which case the League candidate readily withdrew.[25]

[25] An illustration of the manner in which the announcement of an independent Anti-Saloon League candidacy served to force concessions from the regular parties is to be seen in the New Jersey senatorial election of 1924. State Senator Shields, superintendent of the League in New Jersey, announced during the primary contest that if Senator Edge, Republican and wet, were renominated, he would enter the final contest as an independent Republican. During the primary campaign the League vigorously supported H. F. Kean against Edge, but Edge was nominated. Shields thereupon proceeded to carry out his threat and resigned. The Republicans became alarmed, and with reason. With less than 40% of the Republicans of the state participating in the primary, Kean had received 180,000 votes to 225,000 for Edge. There was evidence that many of the non-voters were dry. With Shields in the race, Donnelly, the Democrat, seemed likely to win. Hurried conferences were held in Washington between Senator William M. Butler, Wayne Wheeler, Munro and Hobart of the League Headquarters committee, and Marna S. Poulson, the new League superintendent. Butler requested as a " personal favor " to President Coolidge that Shields be prevailed upon to withdraw. In return for this courtesy the League was assured that there would be " a radical change in the administration of the [prohibition] law " in New Jersey if the Coolidge administration continued in power. Coupled with this was a pledge from Senator Edge that he would support the bill providing for the reorganization of the prohibition unit. On October 6 Shields withdrew, and instructions were issued forthwith to Anti-Saloon League supporters to disregard his name if it appeared on the ballot. Edge was reëlected, though he ran 86,000 votes behind the national ticket. Immediately things began to happen in New Jersey. Six Federal prohibition agents were dismissed by Attorney General Stone; over fifty raids on New Jersey saloons took place; District Attorney Walter Van Riper was asked to resign, and wholesale investigations into local police and enforcement activities

Secondly, the presentation of a temperance candidate kept the issue before the people and enabled the League to gauge its own strength. Where all candidates were dry, the League took no active part in the contest. Usually it was not necessary to put forward an independent, and such procedure was the exception.

### The Balance of Power

The League's objective was to hold the balance of power. Actively to enter the contest as a political party would have destroyed this possibility. With the virtual control of a large block of votes, through the political organization of the churches, the League could frequently force the major parties to nominate candidates friendly to its interests. For a party to ignore the League's demands might easily prove fatal, as it did in Ohio in 1904.

Governor M. T. Herrick of Ohio had incurred the enmity of the drys by his veto of a local option measure. Herrick claimed that his veto was required by certain preëlection promises to Mark Hanna. Wayne Wheeler received a letter from Hanna denying any such pledge. When the question of Herrick's renomination came up in 1904, the Anti-Saloon League and the temperance people bombarded the Republican leaders with protests. The Cox machine, representing the wet element, renominated him. The Democratic Party had the good sense to choose J. M. Pattison of Cincinnati, president of the Union Central Life Insurance Company and a substantial supporter of the Anti-Saloon League. Local option became the outstanding issue. The League began its campaign by sending

---

of officials produced indictments involving prominent political personages and indirectly implicating a U. S. Senator. This commotion lasted four months. — As related to the author by Messrs. Poulson and Munro. See *American Issue*, New Jersey Edition, Oct. 11, 18, and Nov. 15, 1924; *New York World*, Oct. 7, Dec. 7, 18, 19, 20, 21, 22, 1924; Jan. 3, 7, 8, 9, 10, 14, 24 and March 3, 1925; *New York Times*, Dec. 21, 28, 1924; Jan. 1, 4 and Feb. 22, 1925.

100,000 letters to the voters urging Pattison's election and intimating that Herrick was a tool of the liquor interests. This, Herrick vigorously denied. Nevertheless, " to help him out," the Fleischmann Distilling Company sent out 75,000 copies of a pamphlet lauding him. As the campaign neared its end, the Brewers' Association by letter urged its members throughout the state to turn over part of their employees to the Herrick committee but to do it secretly. " We got this on Thursday before election," said Wheeler, " photographed it and sent out thousands of them to churches on Sunday." [26]  Over three hundred meetings under League auspices were held during the last few weeks of the campaign. The result was a victory for the League. Pattison was elected and Herrick, who in 1900 had won by a majority of over 100,000, ran almost 300,000 votes behind the National Republican ticket, losing to Pattison by 42,000 votes.[27]

Politicians early recognized the power of the League, just as they recognized the power and influence of the saloon, and they were prepared to deal with it. A League superintendent quoted a member of the assembly of an Eastern state: " While I am no more of a Christian than I was last year, while I drink as much as I did before, you have demonstrated to me that the boasted power of the saloon in politics is a myth, and you have also demonstrated that there are more Anti-Saloon votes in my district than there are saloon votes; therefore I will stand with you both with my influence and my vote if you will give me your support." [28]

The League, unlike the average American voter, was not satisfied with glittering promises during the campaign and com-

[26] *Proceedings of the Tenth Convention of the Anti-Saloon League,* 1905.

[27] *Proceedings of the Tenth Convention of the Anti-Saloon League,* 1905; Burke, *Ibid.; World Today,* Nov., 1910.

[28] Burke, *op. cit.* " The politician is not tied up with the saloon keeper for the love of him, but only for the votes that are in it. Once make him see that he can get more votes, more power and more advancement by opposing the saloon than he can by promoting it and he will break the alliance." — *Collier's Weekly,* Feb. 8, 1908.

plete apostasy once victory had been gained. In selecting the candidates which it recommended to its constituency, the League inquired first into legislative records, and if the record of a candidate showed a false move on a temperance question, he became tabu so far as future support was concerned. Elaborate indexes of politicians and their records were kept at Washington and in most of the states, and professions of sympathy were matched with deeds. The voters were constantly apprised of the doings of their representatives. When a man had kept faith with the League, it did not desert him.

Where no legislative record was available, a strong written pledge was required for League support. The nature of these pledges varied greatly, but this from the state of Washington is typical of those used by the state organizations:

### ANTI-SALOON LEAGUE OF AMERICA

WASHINGTON-IDAHO STATE DEPARTMENT
604–608 Thompson Building, Seattle
Main 3643

JOSEPH POPE
*Superintendent*

E. E. COLLINS
*Attorney and Asst. Supt.*

August 12, 1924

DEAR SIR:

We receive many inquiries requesting information in relation to the attitude of candidates for public office on the question of prohibition, its modification and its enforcement.

That we may the more intelligently answer these inquiries, and to give the same such publicity as may be deemed advisable, we respectfully submit the following questions:

1.  Do you believe in prohibition as a public policy?
2.  Do you favor a repeal of the state prohibition statutes, similar to the action taken by the Legislative Assembly of New York?
3.  Do you favor an amendment to the Volstead Act, or to the state prohibition law, to legalize the manufacture of beverages with an alcoholic content in excess of that provided in Initiate Measure No. 3, adopted by the people of the state of Washington, Nov. 3, 1914?

4. Do you believe the prohibition law should be observed as conscientiously and enforced as rigidly as any other laws on the statute books?

5. If nominated and elected, will you pledge your personal and official efforts in support of the observance and enforcement of the prohibition law, and to support such additional measures as in the light of experience may be deemed advisable to suppress the beverage use of intoxicating liquors?

> Signed  ..............................
>
> Candidate for  ........................
>
> Affiliated with  ................... party
>
> Address  .............................
>
> Date  ................................

Yours very respectfully,
THE ANTI-SALOON LEAGUE OF WASHINGTON
By ...................................
*State Superintendent*

Such a questionnaire left little room for misunderstanding or ambiguity. Politicians who like to carry water on both shoulders are loath to make definite declarations on public questions. To such, the Anti-Saloon League questionnaire was a source of embarrassment. To prevent the Maryland League from exacting pledges from candidates, a bill was introduced in the 1910 legislature making the sending of such questionnaires a violation of the Corrupt Practices Act.[29] In discussing this bill, the Anti-Saloon League said that its sponsor had been elected to the legislature by claiming to be for local option and had then voted against it and in favor of repealing Washington County's local option law. The bill was passed, but the governor refused to sign it.[30]

[29] *Baltimore Sun*, March 23 and April 8, and *Baltimore News*, April 7, 1910.
[30] *American Issue*, Maryland Edition, April 2, 1910.

When the attitude of the candidate had been determined, the headquarters committee placed this information, together with his legislative and personal record, in the hands of all the voters it could reach. Tens of thousands of letters were sent out. Literature was distributed through the local churches and auxiliary organizations as well as through League agents. No attempt was made to dictate how a person should vote, but the record of the candidate left little room for doubt as to how a true Christian should cast his ballot. An example of the type of information given to the voters is the following:

## DRY CONGRESSIONAL AND LEGISLATIVE CANDIDATES

### *U. S. Senator*

Irving L. Lenroot, rep: must be reëlected. Next to Volstead, perhaps the most important man in Congress for the Drys. Defeat might mean repeal of the Volstead Act.

### *Governor*

Robert Bruce McCoy, dem: member Congregational Club which took active part in voting Sparta dry. Opposes legalizing beer. For law enforcement and removal of sheriffs and district attorneys who are lax.

John J. Blaine, rep: voted for county option. Now receiving support of beer advocates, refuses to state position on legalizing beer.

### *Attorney General*

William J. Morgan, rep: openly opposed to legalizing beer. Lifelong Dry fighter, pledges law enforcement.

### *Congressmen*

First District: H. A. Cooper, rep: voted for the Eighteenth Amendment, no statement on beer and wine.

Third District: James W. Murphy, dem: openly opposed to legalizing beer and wine. John M. Nelson, rep: voted for the Eighteenth Amendment. Refuses to state position on beer and wine: receiving support of beer and wine advocates.

Fourth District: Gerald P. Hayes, dem: bone-dry, declares against legalizing beer and wine.

Seventh District: Joseph B. Beck, rep: opposed beer and wine.

Eighth District: David G. Classon, rep: voted against Eighteenth Amendment, voted for Volstead Act. Andrew R. McDonald, dem: endorsed by Farmer-Labor; bone-dry, union labor leader.

Tenth District: James Frear, rep: has dry record.

Eleventh District: Adolphus P. Nelson, rep: dry floor leader.[31]

Having determined upon a satisfactory candidate, no stone which the League could remove was left to block the smooth highway that led to public office. The message was sent down the line through the organizations associated with the League and through the churches. Seldom has a political machine worked with such efficiency and despatch. Pulpits were thrown open to League speakers. The local minister became for the time being, and with reference to the temperance question, a veritable local boss,[32] taking his instructions from a superior who was paid by the churches for leading them on the straight path through the political wilderness. The W. C. T. U., the Good Templars, the Sons of Temperance, the Intercollegiate Prohibition Association and upwards of twenty temperance organizations, in addition to the churches, were pressed into service.

Thousands of clergymen and laymen only wait definite instructions to exert their energy and influence in favor of given policies. . . .

[31] The League's endorsements by party in this instance were:

    For U. S. Senator — a Republican
    For Governor — a Democrat
    For Attorney General — a Republican
    For Congress — five Republicans, three Democrats
    For Assembly — sixty-three Republicans, five Democrats and three Independents

— *Report of the Anti-Saloon League of Wisconsin*, Nov. 4, 1920, under Federal Corrupt Practices Act, in files of the Clerk of the House of Representatives.

[32] The extent of the Anti-Saloon League machine is evident when it is recalled that in Pennsylvania in 1923 there were more than five thousand churches affiliated with the League. (H. M. Chalfant, *op. cit.*) Joseph Pope, superintendent of the Anti-Saloon League in the State of Washington claimed, in a conversation with the author, to be able to deliver over 30,000 votes in a primary or general election.

The official agents are sentinels . . . and captains. Those who constitute the great army of workers simply await the warning, the proclamation or command that will cause it [the machine] to move simultaneously. to the point of defense or attack.[33]

Women and children were urged to go to the polls, women to see that their husbands voted right or not at all. A description of the manner in which the women and children were used on an election day in North Carolina gives a striking picture of this type of political persuasion:

Stirred by the representations made by the prohibition forces and headed by the ministers of their respective churches, the hundreds of women and children of the town were stationed along the sidewalks of the streets upon which the polling places were located. These workers had been thoroughly coached in their parts; they worked openly and appealed directly to the voters with pretty much the same effrontery as would invite indictment and result in a prison sentence in New York City. . . . When a voter came within range he was immediately surrounded by the ministers and the women and children. The clergymen employed words of advice and confined their activities to the proprieties. But the women and children were less tactful. They clutched at the coats of the voter. They importuned him to vote the dry ticket. A phrase constantly employed was " Mister, for God's sake don't vote for whisky," repeated with parrot-like accuracy that results from thorough coaching. . . . A few of the wets ran the gauntlet of the women and children to whom they were personally known, who pleaded the cause of the Anti-Saloon League, but the greater majority of the voters viewed the conflict from afar and returned to their offices and homes. The drys won the day.[34]

Such tactics were not confined to the South. They were used in New York and Maryland also. The women and children were paraded before the polling places wearing badges with these words: " Vote Against Whisky and For Me," and " Vote Against the Saloon — I can't Vote."

[33] H. G. Furbay, " The Anti-Saloon League," *North America Review,* 1903, Vol. 177, pp. 434 ff.
[34] Louis Seibold in *New York World,* May 13, 1919.

*Frame-up*

If a candidate could be shown to have the backing of the saloon people and the liquor interests, it was frequently possible to blast his reputation with his constituents. An illustration of the manner in which this was attempted shows the extremes to which the League would sometimes go to gain its end. Speaker Sweet of the New York assembly, although politically dry, had found it impossible to coöperate with the new League superintendent, Anderson. In an effort to defeat Sweet, Anderson hired a detective, one Campbell of the Central Detective Agency of Grand Rapids. He was sent into Oswego County (Sweet's bailiwick), where he represented himself as coming from the brewers and liquor dealers to help Speaker Sweet because the Anti-Saloon League was out to beat him. Presenting himself to the liquor dealers as an agent of the New York liquor interests, he procured their business letterheads. On these he dictated a letter attacking the Anti-Saloon League and lauding Speaker Sweet. This letter [35] he then took to the

---

[35] M. SALZMAN AND CO., WINE AND LIQUOR MERCHANTS
196 First Street, Oswego, New York

October 3, 1914.

To whom it may concern:

I want to write you as one who is interested in the liquor business, and who ought to stand by all those who are looking after our interests. The Anti-Saloon League men are working here in Oswego County against Thaddeus C. Sweet of Phoenix, as a member of the assembly. This man Burke, who has been speaking in the county and talking to our people has been run out of Illinois just as his boss was, Anderson, who is the state superintendent. They got a bill through in Illinois that has put a lot of towns in the hypocritical Prohibition column, but it has put a lot of our fellows out of business. They would never have been able to do it if our fellows had done their duty in the beginning, and worked together. They are fighting Assemblyman Sweet because he is with us, and appointed a committee who held their local option prohibition bill and other temperance bills so they could not get them out for a vote.* Speaker Sweet should have the support of every one of us fellows who are engaged in the liquor business, and everyone who believes in personal liberty. He stood by us there, we should stand by him here. You can count on him giving the boots to Anderson, Burke and the whole Anti-Saloon League lot. Sweet's opponent, Rounds, used to be a party Prohibitionist. Yours for a square deal.

Your friend,
(by) F. Knodel, Mgr.

* A charge which Anderson had made against Sweet but which he vigorously denied.

dealer for his signature, suggesting that it would be more effective if signed by a local man. The letter was now turned over to Anderson and his assistants who used it in their addresses, charging that Sweet was supported by the liquor dealers. Hearing of the charge through his own minister, Sweet investigated Campbell's alleged connection with the liquor dealers. At a public meeting, he confronted Anderson with the evidence of his frame-up. Anderson was forced to admit the truth of the facts as here related and was publicly rebuked. This bit of political chicanery having been exposed, Sweet was reëlected by an increased plurality of two thousand.[36]

### Signs of Strength

Such tactics were of course exceptional. For the most part the League fought fairly and in the open, and usually with more success. In Ohio, between 1895 and 1903, over seventy members of the legislature, who were entitled by the custom of their parties to renomination but who had been antagonistic to the League's legislative program, were opposed and every one of them was defeated. In Cuyahoga County, in 1902, a candidate for county prosecutor had, while in the legislature, incurred the League's displeasure; his record was placed in the hands of every voter, and he suffered an overwhelming defeat although the rest of the ticket was elected.[37]

The League stands by politicians who support its measures. In New York in 1906 it promised that any member of the assembly who voted for its local option bill could call upon it for

[36] The story in the text is substantially as it was related to the author by Mr. Sweet. At the meeting referred to, Sweet said with regard to Anderson, "I tore his shirt off, lashed him and rubbed salt into it." *The Lyons Republican* (Nov. 6, 1914, and Jan. 15, 1915) published affidavits of six persons who affirm the facts as here set forth. Anderson, of course, denies that he tried to frame Sweet, but, in a recent letter to the author, Sweet affirms the facts and adds with rigor that "It would make your blood run cold and hair stand up to know all the antics and tactics entering into the case."
[37] Furbay, *op. cit.*

aid in his campaign, should he be opposed because of his dry vote. Thirty-six dry members requested such assistance and all were reëlected.[38]

The League is familiar with most of the tricks of politics and skilled in their use. In the campaign for Attorney General in Delaware, in 1908, the leading candidate was the Republican nominee, Davis, who did not satisfy the League. Sample ballots were therefore printed with Davis' name crossed out and that of Gray, a dry, substituted. Gray was elected by a plurality of 1500.[39]

When Nicholson was superintendent of the Pennsylvania League he kept a file of 50,000 to 75,000 voters giving their addresses, political affiliations, even in some cases their telephone numbers. These were obtained through the churches and were used with considerable effect. For example, Perry County had not sent a Democrat to the legislature in forty years. In 1908 the Republican candidate was unacceptable. The Democratic candidate's questionnaire was satisfactory and it was decided to support him. Nicholson consulted his file of voters in the county, and wrote letters to some twelve hundred Republicans, explaining the League's stand. Enough of these followed the League's advice to elect the Democrat.[40]

When in December, 1914, all of Indiana's Congressmen voted against the submission of the Hobson Federal Prohibition Amendment, the League promptly declared war on them and all but three were retired at the next election. These three joined with the new ten in 1917 and voted solidly for the submission of the prohibition amendment.[41]

The following tactics employed in New Jersey further illustrate the effectiveness of the League's methods. For fifteen years

[38] New York Report, *Proceedings of the Twelfth Convention of the Anti-Saloon League,* 1907.
[39] *American Issue,* Maryland Edition, Nov. 28, 1908.
[40] Related to the author by Mr. Nicholson.
[41] Indiana Report, *Proceedings of the Nineteenth Convention of the Anti-Saloon League,* 1919, p. 264.

the New Jersey League had agitated for a municipal local option law. In 1916 a majority of the members in the senate were pledged to its support. In New Jersey each of the twenty-one counties has one senator. Representatives in the assembly are apportioned among the counties according to population and elected by the county at large. Hudson and Essex Counties, having approximately forty percent of the state's population, occupy a key position in the lower house. In 1917 the League was particularly determined to have a legislature pledged to its local option policy. It was recognized that if it could elect the senator in Essex County, a strict party vote would probably enable it to sweep in the entire slate. To insure this a careful plan of organization was carried out.

For one year prior to the primary election of 1917, the Anti-Saloon League employed organizers who worked chiefly in the suburban towns and cities securing signatures of voters who promised to attend the next primary election and to vote for candidates on the Republican ticket pledged to local option. We thus enrolled several thousand voters. A few weeks before the 1917 primary we employed some forty men, chiefly young clergymen, to canvass the districts, assigning to each a separate territory, giving to the canvasser a section of the map of Essex County that he was to cover, also a list of the voters whom we had enrolled, with their addresses and voting district, and, whenever possible, their telephone numbers. It was their duty to call upon each of the card signers and in turn get them to promise to see their neighbors or at least ten voters in the district and urge them to attend the primary election to vote for local option candidates whose names were given to them. This work was entirely unknown to the Republican wet machine officers who boasted that our local option candidates wouldn't have " a look in." The result . . . was an overwhelming victory for the Republican candidates . . . who were pledged to local option, and in turn the twelve assembly candidates were elected, and the legislature that met that winter enacted the municipal local option law for New Jersey.[42]

[42] Letter to the author, from M. S. Poulson, superintendent of the New Jersey League, dated April 13, 1926.

The results of the 1924 election in the national field were summed up by Wheeler thus:

The drys endorsed 532 candidates for seats in the House, of whom 320 were elected. The number of endorsements is explained by the fact that in many states all the candidates were dry. The Association Against the Prohibition Amendment made 174 endorsements of candidates for Congress, of whom 82 were elected. They openly opposed 262 candidates, of whom 219 were elected. Eight of the candidates endorsed by the wet organization either repudiated the endorsement or had dry voting records.

In the Senate, of the thirty-three Senators elected, twenty-eight had League support, only three were outspokenly wet, while two were moderates who generally supported enforcement legislation.[43]

The Anti-Saloon League does not hesitate to wreak political vengeance on a legislator who has become unresponsive to its dictates. Senator Wadsworth of New York had voted against the Eighteenth Amendment, joined the Association Against the Prohibition Amendment and advocated its repeal. Any one of these acts was sufficient to bring down upon him the wrath of the League. It charged that Wadsworth was determined to carry the entire Republican state organization into the camp of the wets. Now, the Republicans in New York have been the last hope of the drys. It was they who passed the Mullan-Gage law, and, after its repeal, perennially pledged its reënactment. Lieutenant Governor Seymour Lowman, a dry Republican, suffered from the unfortunate handicap of believing that the Republican prohibition plank was something to stand on rather than something to get in on, and had coöperated with the League in an effort to put an enforcement law through the legislature. The measure failed, due, according to the League, to Wadsworth's influence.[44]

[43] *New York Times*, Nov. 23, 1924.
[44] *New York World*, Jan. 15 and 17, 1925. In explaining Wadsworth's wet attitude, the League asserted that he was " more concerned with his own politi-

Wadsworth had assumed the responsibility of bossing the party. The League therefore held him responsible for the defeat of enforcement legislation in 1925 and again in 1926. When on March 22, 1926, the state senate defeated the Wales-Jenks enforcement bill, the superintendent of the League declared:

The vote in the Senate is part of the Wadsworth agreement to save Al Smith the embarrassment of considering a state enforcement law.

The League will be definite and show how his [Senator Wadsworth's] job has been and is being done, citing, for example, the fact that Wadsworth's campaign manager, Fred Hammond, is clerk of the assembly. He walks in without knocking. He attends the conferences. He delivers the ultimata. He represents Wadsworth's view. He can mould party judgments and form party policies so as to benefit Wadsworth, no matter what happens to the rest of the party and no matter what violence is done to the promises made to the people.[45]

As early as February, 1926, the League board of trustees met at Utica, New York, and announced its intention to encompass Wadsworth's defeat. There was scant hope that the state convention would desert Wadsworth for a dry candidate, and only an act of God could induce the Democrats to name a dry. The League demanded a Republican who would stand four-square for prohibition. Although it had no illusions about electing an independent dry, it was thought that the selection of such a candidate would be justified if by such tactics Wadsworth could be defeated. In addition to its disciplinary value, it was felt that Wadsworth's defeat would head off a serious rift in the Republican party throughout the nation. Should Wadsworth

---

cal future than with that of the party in the state, and has entered into an agreement with Smith which leaves the way clear for Wadsworth to be returned to the Senate in 1926." (From a speech by Orville S. Poland at Watertown, Sept. 28, 1924.) In the opinion of League officials, it was for this reason that Wadsworth dictated the nomination of Col. Theodore Roosevelt in 1924, knowing that he could not be elected.

[45] *American Issue*, New York Edition, April 3, 1926.

be reëlected, his control of a large block of delegates to the Republican convention in 1928 would be a serious blow to prohibition within the party.[46]

In May, 1926, after a joint meeting of the responsible officials of the W. C. T. U., the Prohibition Party, the New York Conference of the Methodist Church, the Anti-Saloon League of New York, the Civic League and the New York Women's Committee for Law Enforcement, the following statement was issued:

> The dry organizations intend to select a candidate for the United States Senate, in opposition to Senator Wadsworth, who will draw the votes of Independent Republicans and secure the collective and individual support of those who are opposed to the continuance of the leadership of Senator Wadsworth.

The Independent Republican Committee in June tendered the nomination to F. W. Cristman, a former state senator and an ardent dry. The details of the campaign cannot be discussed in this place. It is sufficient to record the result. Wadsworth was duly nominated by the Republican convention in September. In the election bulletin sent out by the League the object which the drys had in mind is evident. Of Wadsworth it is said: " A wet leader and a leader of the wets, his defeat would be the greatest loss the wets could suffer. . . . He has asked for the defeat or coercion of three-fourths of the Republican Congressmen from New York [i. e., through his membership in the Association Against the Prohibition Amendment], and now seeks support on the grounds of party regularity." Robert F. Wagner, the Democratic candidate, is described as: " A man of ability and a wet. His vote on prohibition in the Senate would be the same as Wadsworth's except that he would only cast a vote and would have no influence." In describing Ogden L. Mills, the Republican candidate for governor, the bulletin says:

[46] *American Issue,* New York Edition, Sept. 25, 1926.

" His position and Smith's are apparently identical except that Smith may claim prior rights." [47]  Much space, of course, is devoted to praise of Cristman, but it is significant that the regular Democratic candidates are in each case treated with a cordiality denied to the regular wet Republicans.

The drys participated vigorously in the campaign, the Rev. S. E. Nicholson, associate superintendent, acting as manager. Wagner defeated Wadsworth by about 116,000 votes.  That the League tactics were responsible for this, there is little doubt. Cristman polled over 230,000.  It is hard to imagine that many of these came from the Democratic ranks.  Had Cristman not been nominated, Wadsworth would almost certainly have been reëlected.  Commenting on the result, Arthur J. Davis, superintendent of the New York League, said: " The Republican party in the nation is dry.  The Republican party in New York state can no longer bore from within, in order to filch liquor votes from Tammany Hall."

[47] *American Issue*, New York Edition, Oct. 30, 1926.

# CHAPTER IV

## " PRESSURE "

Difficult as it is to determine the precise extent of League influence in the selection and election of public officials, it is even more difficult to bring to light the full extent of its influence upon the conduct of legislative bodies. Lobbying is as old as legislation. Those interests which are able to make themselves politically articulate are the interests which find protection and privilege in law. The final form of a tariff bill is more frequently determined by the pressure organizations that influence the politician than by the economic or political beliefs of the politician himself. Burke and Macaulay might with a fine, almost contemptuous, independence refuse to become mere recording machines for the wishes of their constituents. We may argue until Gabriel's trumpet sounds concerning the relative merits of delegation versus representation, but the fact will remain that legislation frequently finds its source, not in the brain of an independent, courageous statesman, but in the devious channels of pressure politics. The history of any law carries with it, in large part, the history of the organized groups whose wishes and wills it embodies. The majority will — the delight of political theorists — is really little more than the unquestioning, too frequently unknowing, acquiescence of men and women in the declared will of the state.

The Damoclean sword which the Anti-Saloon League dangled over the heads of practical statesmen was the threat of political defeat. The man or the organization which seeks to make itself effective in lawmaking under the system of representative government must, directly or indirectly, command votes. The politician who is satisfied with one term of office and subsequent obscurity is rare.  A politician who has no interest in reëlection or no fear of defeat can tell the organized minorities which seek to control his vote, to " go to."  Had the Anti-Saloon League not demonstrated its ability to elect and defeat candidates for public office, it is probable that the Eighteenth Amendment would still be a chafing word-symbol in the mind of some political ideologist.  Had the League been confined to moral appeals, it would have accomplished no more in the realm of practical legislation than Christian missionaries could accomplish in a well-fed heathen land.  But with the strong appeal of bread to starving heathens, and with the appeal of reëlection to aspiring politicians, converts are readily made.  It should be kept in mind that whatever power or influence the League developed in legislative lobbies is attributable to the votes of the people back home who take their political advice from the League.  It has little money for bribes, even if it admitted such a method of influence.  Its single weapon was its actual or assumed control of votes.  So much has been written about the League's browbeating tactics that it is easy to forget that whatever browbeating and intimidation was done was made possible by the consent of those voters who are called out with astronomical regularity to render their solemn judgment.  True, the League boasted of its power, but it is even truer that without a substantial foundation in the hearts of the electorate, its influence in the lobby and committee room would have been negligible.

The League began as a lobbying organization.[1]  The superintendent of the New York League declared, in 1912:

[1] Because of its avowedly altruistic purpose, the League frequently secured exemption from laws governing lobbyists.  This is reflected in the ruling of the Attorney General of Wisconsin, in 1909, holding that the Anti-Saloon League lobbyists, since they were not interested in securing the enactment of legislation financially beneficial to their employer, were not required to register as lobbyists.— *Fifth Biennial Report of the Attorney General of the State of Wisconsin,* 1910, p. 772.

The Anti-Saloon League is the only reform organization in New York state which has a personal representative or representatives at the capitol each day of the legislative session. During the last legislative session eight bills were drawn by the League and introduced in the legislature by the League friends.[2]

In Kentucky, in 1912, legislation favoring the liquor interests was defeated and anti-liquor legislation was passed, " as the result of vigorous lobbying and agitation by the temperance people under the leadership of the Rev. N. A. Palmer, state superintendent of the Anti-Saloon League." [3]

In addition to fighting for affirmative temperance legislation, the League also had the task of defeating legislation favorable to the liquor business. Superintendent Nicholson had directed the activities of the Anti-Saloon League in Indiana for a number of years with considerable success, and in 1902 had secured the enactment of twenty-three local laws, drafted by the League and introduced by its friends. When he took charge in Pennsylvania he found his task primarily one of preventing unfavorable legislation. In 1908 the League had opposed the candidates of the regular Republican organization and had in a number of instances succeeded in electing Democrats. John Cox, whom the Republicans were proposing for speaker, was unsatisfactory to the League and Nicholson protested to Penrose against his selection. Penrose assured Nicholson that the organization would deal fairly with local option legislation, but asked him to " lay off " Cox on the promise that no pro-liquor legislation would be passed. Under the

---

[2] Report of Superintendent, *American Issue*, New York Edition, Sept., 1912.

[3] House Bill 278 sought to repeal the law which forbade the shipment of liquor from any part of Kentucky into local option territory. "The liquor people made a thorough canvass and resorted to the most clandestine methods . . . but our people rallied and met them and drove them to the same fate they suffered in every other attempt they made to secure adverse, or prevent the enactment of favorable, temperance legislation." Other laws which were passed related to the sale of liquor to minors and the shipment into dry territory of beverages containing *any* alcohol. — *American Issue*, Kentucky Edition, April, 1912.

constitution of Pennsylvania at the time there was no prohibition against special legislation. Numerous laws had been passed extending the principle of local option to certain localities and prohibiting saloons in other districts. There were constant efforts on the part of the liquor people to bring about the repeal of such legislation. Nicholson discovered on the house calendar two bills to repeal certain of these old temperance laws and immediately wired Penrose reminding him of his promise and protesting against their passage. He was assured that the bills would be killed in the senate. Nicholson showed Penrose's telegram to Speaker Cox. Cox confirmed the wire in a telephone conversation with Penrose, and then asked the authors of these bills to consent to their recommital and they died in committee.[4] Such brusque dealings with an almost invincible political machine would not have been possible had the League not demonstrated in 1908 that it was a power to be reckoned with.

### Anderson at Annapolis

A good example of League lobbying methods is to be found in the fight made for a local option bill in Maryland in 1908. Anderson, who had served in Illinois and New York, was transferred to Maryland as superintendent early in 1907 and immediately began to work for a state-wide local option law. It was a bill patterned after an Illinois law that Anderson wished to have adopted in Maryland. To guard against subsequent attacks upon its constitutionality, he employed a former Maryland attorney general to put the bill into proper form.

Anderson registered as legislative counsel for the League, pursuant to the state law, and at the same time was admitted to practice at the bar of the state. A room in the Carroll Hall Hotel in Annapolis was fitted up as League headquarters dur-

---

[4] As related to the author by Mr. Nicholson.

ing the session. The *American Issue* published a complete list
of members of the legislature, urging citizens to write favoring
temperance legislation.[5]  So great was the response, Senator
Beasman declared, that the temperance committee, of which
he was chairman, was overwhelmed with letters and petitions on
local option.  Every member received, at the opening of the session, a personal letter from Anderson and a pamphlet explaining the bill.  The following Sunday was " Concerted Discussion " day in the churches.  Two thousand ministers throughout
the state spoke in favor of the bill.  In Baltimore, following the
services in the churches, a mass meeting in the Lyric auditorium
was attended by more than thirty-five hundred people and over
two thousand dollars was pledged.  The audience was almost exclusively male, since it was to the voters that the League wished
to appeal.  Cardinal Gibbons, later a powerful opponent of the
League, sent a personal representative.  The president of the
Merchants and Manufacturers Association of Baltimore pre-
sided, adding a tone of economic respectability.  " With the
precision of a military maneuver the church militant moved
against the saloon," said the *Baltimore News*.[6]  A special
steamer was chartered to carry to Annapolis enough " petitions
in boots " to overflow the state capitol.[7]

### The Bill Is Launched

The bill was introduced by a Democrat in the house and a
Republican in the senate.  Describing Jones, the introducer in
the house, the *American Issue* said, " The League had been
looking for a man who would stand without hitching, who had
no political alliances that would prevent his standing and fighting for the bill regardless of pressure that might be brought to
bear.  We believe we have found such a man in Mr. Jones."
After much stalling, a date was set for the dry hearing.  An-

[5] *American Issue,* Maryland Edition, Jan. 18 and Feb. 1, 1908.
[6] Jan. 27, 1908.
[7] *American Issue,* Maryland Edition, Jan. 11 and Feb. 15, 1908.

derson sent out thousands of letters urging all friends of the bill to hurry to Annapolis. The trip by boat was abandoned because of ice and they went by train. It required two trains aggregating twenty-two cars to carry them to the capital city. The temperance committees were so smothered by local optionists that some of the committee members were unable to get into the room.

The drys began the hearing with " Onward, Christian Soldiers " to relieve some of their pent-up enthusiasm. Anderson marshaled his forces. Business men, educators and churchmen were called upon. All appealed for local option to enable communities desiring to do so to drive out the serpent saloon from the " Eden of their homes and firesides." Most of the speakers insisted that the passage of the local option bill in itself would accomplish nothing. It was, they said, merely an extension of the right of local self-government to the various communities in the state. Baltimore, it was pointed out, had twenty-four wards (this bill would have extended local option to wards) averaging twenty-five thousand people. Certainly, it was declared, twenty-five thousand people ought to have the right to decide whether they want saloons. To constitutional objections they replied that a former attorney general had pronounced the bill valid, that a similar law had been sustained by the supreme court of Illinois, and that " no law drafted by the Anti-Saloon League has ever been declared invalid."

To speed things up, Anderson wrote the chairmen of the committees suggesting that a date be immediately set for the hearing of the opponents of the bill. Dawkins, chairman of the house committee, replied hotly that Anderson had insinuated that the committee was being willfully dilatory. Anderson, in answer, assured him that he meant nothing of the sort but that, in view of the customary tactics of the liquor people, he had written solely to warn him lest the wets delay their hearing so long as to kill the bill in the last-minute rush of legislative business, known as " the slaughter of the innocents." [8]

At the wet hearing a few days later, over two thousand persons appeared, representing the retail liquor dealers and the German-American Alliance.  They protested that the bill was confiscatory, that it would be unconstitutional and that it was a violation of liberty.  Everything which the drys claimed the bill would do, the wets denied.  In describing this delegation, the *American Issue* [9] said, " They were a quiet, orderly crowd, many of them excellent citizens who have been misinformed as to the real issue, though there was a considerable sprinkling of typical saloonists."

## Defeat

On March 11 the bill was reported unfavorably.  It was thoroughly debated and, when the vote was finally taken, was defeated 56 to 43.  One of the absentees and seven who voted against the bill were pledged to support it but failed to deliver the goods, because, as Anderson claimed, " of the pressure of the Baltimore machine." [10]  The apostasy of these men moved the drys deeply:

We have seen many dramatic situations in legislative halls and experienced tense moments when it seemed that human hearts could actually be heard beating, but we have never been in a room where the gravity of the situation seemed to weigh down upon the members with more terrific pressure.  The tension was extreme.  Some men blanched and went white as they voted.  Political futures were blighted, and the tragedy of it was that some men went home to constituents whose wishes they had misrepresented, to live among neighbors who will always wonder why they voted against so fair and righteous a measure.[11]

[8] On this exchange of notes the *Baltimore News*, Feb. 15, 1908, commented: " Some people at Annapolis act as if there is nothing they would like better than a good excuse to pick a quarrel with Mr. Anderson."

[9] Maryland Edition, March 7, 1908.

[10] *American Issue*, Maryland Edition, March 21, 1908.

[11] *Ibid.*

### Anderson Rallies

Anderson, not to be outdone, called a hurried session of the headquarters committee and announced that an amended bill would be brought up in the senate and thence sent to the house. An indignation meeting was held at the Lyric where those who should dare to oppose the new bill were threatened with political disaster.[12]

Senator Beasman, chairman of the senate committee, however, announced that his committee had unanimously decided not to report the bill in any form, because it had failed in the house. An attempt to direct the committee to report was defeated by a vote of 15 to 12, and dry hopes faded. Here again the League charged that seven men deserted " at the crack of the whip," including five from dry eastern shore counties. " A number of senators said they would vote for the bill ' if the senate decided to consider it.' And then they voted against bringing it up so that they could not vote for it." [13]

### War on the Faithless

The wets were happy. One paper, after describing Anderson as a political pariah, said: " The legislature . . . yesterday smashed Anderson like a cockroach. . . . To the eternal reproach of Washington County, four men voted for Anderson, the political outcast from Illinois." For the drys, the defeat only added zest in their compaign for local option. The League began at once to secure signed pledges from church voters to vote only for local option candidates. It sought particularly to vent its wrath upon Dawkins and Beasman. The former had been appointed a justice of the peace as a preliminary to becoming a police magistrate, a post involving the enforcement of liquor laws. The League vigorously protested to the Governor, and Dawkins was not appointed.[14] Beasman did not come up

---

[12] *Ibid.*    [13] *American Issue,* Maryland Edition, March 28, 1908.
[14] *American Issue,* Maryland Edition, May 30, 1908. The *Liquor Trade*

for reëlection that year, but the League set out to elect a senate
that would oust him from the chairmanship of the temperance
committee, and in this they were successful.  During the campaign Anderson entered Beasman's bailiwick challenging him
to debate and accusing him of having violated a preëlection
pledge.  Beasman denied having made such a pledge, but declared that in spite of his failure to respond to the League questionnaire his name had been included among those favoring
local option.  He contemptuously refused to debate, charging
that Anderson's consuming political ambition and offensive
tactics were a chief obstacle to temperance reform.  In reply
to Anderson's challenge he wrote:

I was not aware that the people of my county or the state had
constituted you the judge and arbiter of its servants. . . .  It is
common knowledge that the defeat of local option in the lower house
of the last legislature was due very largely to your own dictatorial
and demagogic methods. . . .  Your clumsy attempts to make it
appear that you were the spokesman of the churches and that all
who were opposed to you were the friends of iniquity . . . all
helped to weaken the cause of temperance day by day at Annapolis.
. . .  You are trying to get your hands into the local politics of
every county in the state. . . .  You are trying to say who shall be
Congressmen and dictate nominations . . . you are after political
power.  It pays you well.  But I, for one, am not willing to recognize you as a political dictator.[15]

---

Journal of Baltimore, May, 1908, bitterly criticized Governor Crothers for
obeying the orders of the Anti-Saloon League.
  [15] Baltimore Sun, July 23, 1908.  The Cecil Whig, a Republican journal,
commented on Beasman's duplicity and added, " When Anderson asked the
senator how he reconciled these conflicting currents . . . the Hon. Senator did
just what every man does when he gets rearin-tearin-cussin-mad . . . fell down
and broke his molasses jug.  Evidently the Hon. Johnzie needs a lot of training.
. . . [When someone calls attention] to the fact that your promises and performance do not look alike. . . .  Then is the time to walk most complacently
down the middle of the road with the High Priest on one arm and Pontius
Pilate on the other. . . .  But this crying out!  Oh, Johnzie! Johnzie! you were
never meant to be a politician. . . .  The idea of arguing with the people!
What you want to do is fool 'em." — Quoted in American Issue, Maryland
Edition, Oct. 10, 1908

*Defeat Assuaged*

The League never did succeed in getting state-wide local option for Maryland. In 1910 and 1912 a majority of the legislature had answered the League's questionnaire favorably, but in both instances the Baltimore wet machine proved too powerful.[16] In the latter year things looked particularly auspicious; even the wet *Baltimore News* demanded a square deal for the local option bill and predicted its passage.[17] The house committee, however, had been packed with wets. A demand for a special rule to permit immediate consideration without reference to this committee was rejected.[18] " If the committee does what it was apparently appointed to do," said Anderson, " and represents the gang in another effort to kill the local option bill, the speaker will be added to the list of respectable gentlemen who have permitted the gang to use them in doing its dirty work." [19] The bill was defeated in the house amid the great joy and tumult of the wets.[20]

After 1912, the League wavered between constitutional and statutory state-wide prohibition, but secured neither. In 1919, however, it succeeded in placing Maryland sixth among the states to ratify the Eighteenth Amendment.[21] The League's main victories were in connection with local option elections held under special acts dealing with various units within the state. In the absence of a constitutional restraint on special legislation, the legislature was able to "buy off " counties where the dry sentiment was strong. Under such laws much of the state was dry when the Volstead act arrived. The only wet territory was Baltimore City, most of Baltimore County, Ellicott City and most of Anne Arundel and Allegany Counties.[22]

[16] *American Issue,* Maryland Edition, Jan. 15, 1910.
[17] *Baltimore News,* Feb. 3 and 17, 1912; also, *Baltimore Sun,* Feb. 17, 1912.
[18] *Baltimore Sun,* Jan. 5, 1912.
[19] *American Issue,* Maryland Edition, Jan. 27, 1912; *Baltimore News* and *Sun,* Jan. 18, 1912.     [20] *Baltimore News,* March 31, 1912.
[21] Wheeler, *Federal and State Laws Relating to Intoxicating Liquor,* Third Edition, Westerville, 1921, p. 382; *Anti-Saloon League Year Book,* 1925, p. 102.
[22] *Anti-Saloon League Year Book,* 1925, p. 102.

### A Lobby of Love

Professional lobbyists though they were, dealing with hard-
boiled politicians, League men never lost an opportunity to appeal to simple sentiments in softening steely legislative hearts.
When League leaders gathered to take counsel together, they
inspired each other with stories of the wonder-working power
of love.  At one such gathering the Rev. Louis Banks touched
his hearers' hearts with such a tale:

When the prohibition amendment was in the balance in the Kansas house of representatives the vote was taken at midnight.  The roll
of ayes and nays was called. . . .  Busy pencils kept the tally and
when the voting ceased a sigh from many a temperance man's heart
accompanied the words, " We've lost our cause by just one vote."
But look!  A woman, gentle, modest, sweet, advances from the
crowd.  What! is she going down that aisle where never woman trod
before, and in among that group of party leaders?  Yea, verily, and
every eye follows with intense interest, and the throng is strangely
still as she goes straight to her husband, takes his big hand in her
little one, lifts her dark eyes to his face and speaks these thrilling
words: " My darling, for my sake, for the sake of our sweet home,
for Kansas' sake, and God's, I beseech you change your vote."  When
lo, upon the silence broken, a man's deep voice: " Mr. Speaker, before
the clerk reads the result I wish to change my vote from no to aye."
How loud rang out the cheers of the men.  How fell the rain of
women's tears, for love had conquered as it always will at last.[23]

---

[23] *Proceedings of the Seventeenth Convention of the Anti-Saloon League,*
1916, p. 163.  Such testimonials occur in all the League's convention reports,
although few reach the heights, or depths, of Dr. Banks.  During the fight for
local option in Indiana an aged mother was used as a lobbyist and a daughter
sat with her father to see that he voted " right."  (*American Issue,* Indiana
Edition, Oct. 24, 1908.)  In Florida when the submission of the state prohibition amendment was in the balance, in 1908, " On the night before the fight in
the senate the wires told our floor leader in that house, Hon. Don C. McMullen,
that his old mother had just died four hundred miles away.  Next morning C. L.
Collins, the League superintendent at the capitol, asked, ' When must you go
home, Senator? '  Quick as a flash he replied, ' I shall not go at all.  I shall stay
here and do my part as my mother would want me to do.'  And through five
long hours of debate . . . he stood at his post of duty."— Florida Report,
*Proceedings of the Thirteenth Convention of the Anti-Saloon League,* Dec.,
1909, p. 92.

*Advice from the Chief*

No party boss or professional politician studied more diligently or with more insight the workings of the legislative machine than did the leaders of " the Church in Action Against the Saloon." What Platt, Quay, Penrose, Cox and Taggart were to their organizations, Russell, Wheeler, Dinwiddie, Nicholson, and Anderson were to the Anti-Saloon League.

Summing up the lessons learned in about fifteen years of legislative lobbying, Wayne B. Wheeler described the methods he regarded as most effective.

1.   The League should make every effort to see that the committees to which temperance legislation is referred are friendly. It is best to have a regular committee, since a special committee may be packed hostilely.

2.   The bill should be introduced early in the session. During the closing days each member has some pet measures and it is harder to get a fair consideration. The bill should be introduced first in the house . . . the senate being more conservative.

3.   The introducer should be an able representative, with few enemies, one skilled in the procedural mysteries, who knows the bill from A to Z.

4.   The bill should not be extreme. Do not be " whole hog or none."

5.   Hearings should be promptly held and well attended by representative people from the entire state, and from different walks of life.

6.   Temperance bills should, if possible, be made a special order at least ten days after they are reported.

7.   As for the liquor lobby " all that is needed is to throw the light in upon them and let the legislature and the people know what they are doing."

8.   The League should take no official stand on other measures.

9.   " Petition in boots " and letters and telegrams from constituents are often a determining factor.

10.   The day of the third reading is the day of crisis. Advocates from all parties should speak for the bill to shut off the cry that it is a partisan measure. The galleries should be crowded with spec-

tators, but demonstrations against the opponents of the bill should be discouraged. A yea and nay vote should be demanded on each important question. Effort should be made to prevent amendments. An amended bill means a conference committee and conference committees are dangerous, unless the leaders of the houses are temperance men.

Generally speaking, the foregoing describes the methods employed by the League, but as Wheeler emphasizes, while lobbying is very important, the most substantial and effective work must be done before the legislature convenes, in the nomination and election of friendly officials. " The foundation of victory is the average public sentiment which the League helps to educate in years of faithful and often unnoticed service." [24]

## LOCAL OPTION

The Anti-Saloon League was early dubbed the " Local Option League " ; indeed its first step toward prohibition was the enactment of laws under which political units within the states could banish the saloon. There were several varieties of option. The simplest and most easily secured was that which prohibited saloons within a certain distance of churches and educational institutions. Frequently zones were established directly by the legislature without local vote. By making the areas large enough it was sometimes possible to dry up practically a whole state, as was done in Tennessee. Other forms of local option had the city, town, village, ward or election district as the unit. As a rule, the League demanded the county as the unit, with provision for taking a vote in smaller units if desired.

The Maryland bill of 1908 may serve to illustrate the type of legislation generally favored by the League. It provided that " one-fourth of the voters of any county, election district, city, town, village or ward " could, by filing a petition sixty days before a November election, secure the right to vote on

[24] *American Issue*, May, 1909, Anniversary Number.

the question, " Shall this district . . . become anti-saloon territory? " A majority of those voting on the question was sufficient to decide the issue. Territory could be changed back
only by a similar process, in which event the laws existing prior
to the first election were restored to effect.[25]

### Heads I Win — Tails You Lose

The wets complained that this scheme was one-sided. The
only question submitted was: " Shall this become anti-saloon
territory? " The saloon could be voted out of license areas,
but it could not be voted into no-license areas.[26] The League
intended that local option should mean but one thing, the option
to prohibit.[27] Its official attitude was summarized thus:

> The League believes in self-government. It has faith enough in
> its cause to be willing to submit it to the arbitrament of the majority.
> The League works for local option laws which will give effective
> expression to anti-saloon sentiment wherever it is strong enough to
> sustain itself. . . . The League stands for prohibition in those
> states which have or are ready for such laws. Elsewhere it favors
> local option. . . . Such legislation does not in itself close a single
> saloon, but hands the question back for determination to a majority
> of the voters of the locality immediately concerned. . . . The type
> of legislation favored by the League is always restrictive. It pro-
> vides for a vote in the Largest Possible Unit and facilitates the
> removal of existing saloons as fast as possible, in counties, townships,
> cities, and villages, wards, precincts and residence sections. . . .
> The League proposes that the legislature hand back to the people
> the privilege of exercising their inherent right to control the liquor
> traffic.[28]

The Anti-Saloon League eschewed the Prohibition Party's
all-or-none policy. It would take what it could get and wanted
local option " for the largest possible unit." In the absence of

[25] *American Issue,* Maryland Edition, Jan. 15, 1910.
[26] *Baltimore Sun,* Feb. 16, 1912.
[27] *American Issue,* Ohio Edition, Oct. 24, 1908; Maryland Edition, Aug. 15,
1908.
[28] Anderson, *Church in Action,* pp. 30 ff.

state-wide prohibition, this meant the county, although it was careful to permit a vote in units within the county as well as in the county as a whole.[29]

The manner in which such a law worked is further illustrated in the following colloquy:

Q. If under the new county unit law a county which is partly dry should vote wet, will the dry territory thereby be made wet?
A. Unquestionably not.
Q. If any part of the county is wet and the county as a unit votes dry, will the wet portion thereby be made dry?
A. Yes. The larger unit can vote the smaller unit dry, but the larger unit cannot vote the smaller unit wet.

This was based on the proposition that the saloon was presumptively an outlaw and on the practical fact that though a dry town in a wet county did not make the whole county dry, a wet town in a dry county made the entire county wet.[30] The difficulty of actually enforcing prohibition legislation in one community with a wet area near-by was almost insuperable. The logic of this argument led of course to state-wide prohibition, the Webb-Kenyon act and ultimately the national amendment. The wets, however, explained it thus:

Since the Anti-Saloon League cannot effect this [prohibition] by the direct will of the residents in a chartered town or city . . . they bring pressure on the legislature to pass bills making the county a unit for a wet-dry vote. Then by means of the rural vote outside the chartered municipalities they impose " no-license " upon them.[31]

This seemed to the wets violative of the spirit of local self-government. " Talk about local self-government! " said a prominent League speaker in reply. " What are your large cities doing to the smaller counties today? The people of these

[29] *American Issue*, Illinois Edition, May 31, 1912.
[30] *American Issue*, Kentucky Edition, April, 1912.
[31] *Mida's Criterion*, Jan., 1909; see also *Champion of Fair Play*, Dec. 7, 1907; *Baltimore Sun*, Aug. 10, 1909.

counties rose up in their power and drove the saloons from their borders, yet the whisky dealers of Nashville, Memphis and Chattanooga ship into these counties their poison every day. . . . They are nullifying the local option in those counties and at the same time demanding that their own local option in these cities be respected." [32]

### Home Rule

The argument that local option was but the extension of self-government and home rule appealed to many people who personally disliked prohibition, because it seemed consonant with the idea of democracy. Thus Governor Woodrow Wilson of New Jersey, who had no sympathy with prohibition, wrote, " I am in favor of local option. I am a thorough believer in local self-government and believe that every self-governing community which constitutes a social unit should have the right to control the matter of the regulation or the withholding of licenses." [33] Similarly, Cardinal Gibbons supported local option in Maryland.[34]

The interest of the League in home rule, however, extended only so far as it meant the banishing of the saloon. Oregon in 1910 had a county option law under which twenty-three counties had voted out the saloons, leaving eleven wet. At the election in that year a state-wide prohibition amendment submitted at the behest of the drys was defeated by a large majority. At the same time an amendment giving municipalities home rule on the liquor question was adopted, and within three years the saloons reappeared in municipalities in twenty of the twenty-three counties that had previously voted dry.[35]

---

[32] *American Issue,* Maryland Edition, July 25, 1908.
[33] *American Issue,* Vermont Edition, March, 1912.
[34] *Baltimore Sun,* Aug. 25, 1909; *News,* Jan. 26, 1908; *American Issue,* Maryland Edition, Feb. 15, 1908; *Proceedings of the Seventeenth Convention of the Anti-Saloon League,* 1916, p. 468.
[35] Oregon Report, *Proceedings of the Fifteenth Convention of the Anti-Saloon League,* 1913, p. 320. Constitution of Oregon, Art. XI, Sec. 2: " . . . exclusive power to license, regulate, control, or to suppress or prohibit the sale of

In 1914, Ohio likewise adopted an amendment to the state constitution giving cities and towns home rule on the liquor question. The League opposed the amendment because it repealed the county option law which had been adopted in 1908 and forbade laws prohibiting the liquor traffic in units larger than townships and incorporated municipalities.[36] Before the adoption of this amendment there were forty-five dry counties in the state.[37] The new law enabled the towns and cities to license saloons regardless of how the county as a unit voted, with the result that by 1917 there were only thirteen wholly dry counties in the state.[38] Towns and cities like Marion in Marion County, Mansfield in Richland County and Xenia in Greene County, which had been forced into the dry column, were now able to restore the saloons. It was natural that under these circumstances the League should oppose such home rule.

In those counties where the urban population outnumbered the small-town and rural population, prohibition had never been adopted. Such counties as Cuyahoga (including Cleveland), Summit (including Akron), Franklin (including Columbus), Lucas (including Toledo), Montgomery (including

---

intoxicating liquors therein is vested in such municipality; but such municipality shall within its limits be subject to the provisions of the local option law of the State of Oregon." State v. Schluer, 59 Or. 18, 1911, 115 Pac. 1057; State v. Hearn, 59 Or. 227, 1911, 115 Pac. 1066; State v. Boysen, 76 Or. 49, 1915, 147 Pac. 927; State v. O'Donnell, 77 Or. 116, 1915, 149 Pac. 536. See also H. L. McBain, *The Law and the Practice of Municipal Home Rule,* New York, 1916, p. 592.

[36] " No law shall be passed or be in effect prohibiting the sale, furnishing or giving away of intoxicating liquors operative in a subdivision of the state upon the option of the electors thereof or upon any other contingency, which has force within a territory larger than a municipal corporation or a township outside of municipal corporations therein. All laws in contravention of the foregoing are hereby repealed. Nor shall any law hereafter be passed prohibiting the sale, furnishing or giving away of intoxicating liquors throughout the state at large." — *Constitution of Ohio,* Art. XV, Sec. 9a; Page's Ohio General Code, Vol. 3, pp. 6580–82; sustained in Hockett v. Liquor Licensing Board, 91 Oh. St. 176, 1915.

[37] *Anti-Saloon League Year Book,* 1917, p. 198; *Proceedings of the Sixteenth Convention of the Anti-Saloon League,* 1915, p. 316.

[38] *Ibid.,* p. 197.

Dayton), were dripping wet. Of course the dry area was much greater than the wet area and the League made much of this in its propaganda. In 1917, 85 percent of the territory of Ohio was dry, but in this area lived only 42 percent of the state's population.[39] Only 20 percent of the dry population lived in communities of 1000 or more. The thirteen wholly dry counties had a total population of but 311,000. Not one big city in the state was dry. The seven largest cities, with an aggregate population of 2,500,000, included approximately 90 percent of the population living under license.

## The League and Direct Legislation

In the United States our city population is grossly underrepresented and our state legislatures are for the most part under the control of rural and small-town representatives. The League, recognizing this, preferred legislative action to direct popular vote. In the Ohio general assembly each county, no matter how small its population, had at least one member. Thirteen rural counties could offset the vote of Hamilton County, which includes Cincinnati.[40] Under the initiative and referendum, when the state-wide prohibition amendment was voted on in 1914, Cincinnati alone returned a wet majority of 75,000. Forty dry counties could not offset this. Although seventy counties, of the state's eighty-eight, voted dry, the amendment was defeated by an 83,000 popular majority. Apart from Hamilton County, however, the drys had a majority of 13,000.[41]

In 1912, the League issued a pamphlet vigorously denouncing the initiative and referendum for Illinois on the ground that it would enable the wets in Chicago to dominate.[42] Much

---

[39] *Anti-Saloon League Year Book,* 1917, pp. 197 ff.
[40] *Ibid.,* p. 201.
[41] Ohio Report, *Proceedings of the Sixteenth Convention of the Anti-Saloon League,* 1915, pp. 488–89.
[42] *Christian Science Monitor,* June 6, 1918.

of the League's opposition to some of the popular referenda since the adoption of prohibition is to be explained in light of the above facts.

It must not be assumed, however, that the Anti-Saloon League always opposed direct legislation.  On several occasions it demanded submission of the liquor question directly to the people.  The California League in 1909 fought for a state initiative and referendum law, declaring that opposition to such a law came chiefly from the liquor dealers.  Generally speaking, however, the Anti-Saloon League cared little for popular referenda except where it gave promise of aiding in the fight against liquor.

### Blocks of Ten

One important reason for the League's hesitancy in adopting a policy of state-wide submission lay in its insistence that rural dry voters are more difficult to organize than are the wet voters in the cities.  Time after time the League attributed the defeat of state-wide prohibition laws to the difficulty of getting rural voters to the polls.[43]  Oregon voted on such an amendment in 1910 and again in 1914.  In the first election, organization was poor and the wets won.  Immediately, the League set about perfecting an organization which would get out the dry rural vote.  The state was carefully divided into precincts averaging one hundred and twenty families.  The churches were given

[43] In the New Jersey gubernatorial election of 1925, Arthur Whitney, the dry Republican candidate, was defeated by A. Harry Moore, the wet Democrat. Out of a total of twenty-one counties Moore carried only three, Hudson by 103,000, Passaic by 1,903, and Middlesex by 2,807. Outside of Hudson County, Whitney's plurality was 68,000. The League claimed that it was the unorganized rural and suburban non-voters who defeated Whitney. The percentage of the registered vote, according to the League, which went to the polls in the counties carried by Moore was 81.2; in the eighteen counties carried by Whitney it was 61.9. Approximately 300,000 dry voters, the League declared, did not vote. (*American Issue*, New Jersey Edition, Dec. 1, 1925). Such statistics are of dubious value when it is pointed out that registration requirements are not the same in all counties. In communities of 5,000 or more, annual personal registration was required, whereas the smaller communities had permanent registration.

general charge, and a captain and ten canvassers were assigned to each precinct. For the first six months, attention was centered on registration. In registering, each person was asked to sign a pledge to go to the polls early in the morning and vote Oregon dry. More than 120,000 Neighborhood Visitors Reports were returned; 79,000 voters were registered in the closing three weeks, " either by being taken to the registrar, the registrar being taken to them en route, or by being gathered in groups at schoolhouses, picnics or meetings, and the notary taken there." The result was the adoption of the amendment by a majority of 36,840 votes.[44]

Oregon was easy compared to Ohio, but here, too, the League was victorious. Three times it had fought for state-wide prohibition without success. Finally, in 1918, it won by 25,000 votes. The organization that put this over was a model of political efficiency. A state campaign committee took charge of all the agencies interested. The state was divided into seven districts with a superintendent for each. There were also county managers, ward captains, precinct lieutenants and " key " men, responsible for a small number of votes. The county organizations went to work with a vim, doing personal work by calling upon managers, women, school children and everybody to make a last personal appeal to every voter in the county.[45] In addition, it was believed to be good tactics to organize voters into functional groups. There was a manufacturers' organization with S. S. Kresge at its head, a workers' group, a women's division, an organization of colored voters

[44] In 1910, the wet vote was 23 percent of the total possible vote; the dry vote was only 16 percent. Sixty percent of the voters stayed at home. In 1914, the wet vote constituted 24 percent of the total possible vote; the dry vote was 32 percent. Only 43 percent of the voters stayed at home. As its superintendent put it, the League " won in 1914 because drys, who usually loaf at home election day and kick the next day, went to the polls election day and boasted the next day." — Oregon Report, *Proceedings of the Sixteenth Convention of the Anti-Saloon League*, 1915, p. 502.

[45] Ohio Report, *Proceedings of the Nineteenth Convention of the Anti-Saloon League*, 1919, p. 303.

and a farmers' section led by the master of the state grange. " In fact," said the superintendent, " we had every thing organized except the brewery workers, and we disorganized them."

This elaborate structure was supplemented by publicity of every sort. One worker secured fifty automobiles and filled them with men and women who toured the state visiting homes and leaving literature, dry ballots and a personal appeal. Street car and newspaper advertisements and billboards, big and little, were used; $100,000 was spent on these items alone. In the midst of the influenza epidemic, which forced the League to cancel all its meetings three or four weeks prior to the election, and in the face of a reputed slush fund of $200,-000 put up by the liquor dealers, the League won the election. On a smaller scale similar tactics were employed everywhere in local option elections. The League took upon its shoulders the burden of the fight. From the circulation of election petitions to the enforcement of the law when adopted, the Anti-Saloon League made itself the factotum of the prohibition fight.[46]

Of course the Anti-Saloon League did not confine its activities to the defeat of pro-liquor laws and the securing of local option and state-wide prohibition. It was willing to compromise and work for other forms of restriction. A complete catalogue of the measures it favored cannot be given here. The League merely insisted that they be restrictive. " Legislation on the liquor question," said Superintendent Baker, " has revealed more hypocrites and heroes in public life than all other kinds of legislation combined in recent years. . . . Gothenburg systems, company schemes, dispensaries, license fees, high and low, minor and drunkard laws, Sunday and early closing enactments, have been the infant diseases through which the

[46] *American Issue*, Maryland Edition, March 14, 1908; *World Today*, Nov., 1910; *New York Journal*, Feb. 20, 1915; *New York Mail*, Nov. 10, 1915; *Home and State*, Texas, May 15, 1916.

great reform must pass on the way to a mighty typhoid — state and national prohibition — which is to revolutionize and purify our entire body politic. . . . The only solution of the saloon problem is no saloon." [47]

## The Wets' Nightmare

The effectiveness of the League tactics is recognized by all save the die-hards among the Prohibition Party who have been much broken up because they feel that the organization stole their party zephyr and made of it a non-partisan hurricane.[48] " While venality in politics has been the discouraging feature in popular suffrage, the Anti-Saloon League has built fires of moral conviction which have burned out the saloon even in places where the ballot has been most corrupt," [49] said one social worker. Perhaps the best testimony as to the effectiveness of the League comes from the liquor camp. " The Anti-Saloon League has learned well the game of politics and they are playing it skillfully." [50] " The League," says another wet journal, " is carrying on its work in every state in the union, secretly where it must do so, openly where it can work aboveboard. . . . To live, every saloon keeper must fight the Anti-Saloon League. That cannot be denied." [51] The matter is perhaps best summed up in the following, which the *Anti-Prohibition Manual* of the National Wholesale Liquor Dealers Association quoted approvingly:

The prohibition forces today are organized with a degree of efficiency attained by few movements in the history of the Republic. . . .

The power of that portion of public opinion which now supports the demand for national ‚rohibition is exerted upon Congress and

[47] *Proceedings of the Fourteenth Convention of the Anti-Saloon League,* 1911.

[48] D. L. Colvin, *Prohibition in the United States,* Chapter XXI.

[49] S. J. Barrows, president of National Prison Commission, " The Temperance Tidal Wave," *Outlook,* July 11, 1908.

[50] *Bonfort's Wine and Spirit Circular,* April 10, 1913.

[51] *National Liquor Dealers Journal,* quoted in *American Patriot,* May, 1913.

state political bodies and in elections through the Anti-Saloon League of America. The League organizes and manages every important prohibition fight made in the country, and maintains at Washington one of the most powerful lobbies ever seen at the national capital.[52]

[52] L. Ames Brown, " Prohibition's Legislative Efforts," *North American Review*, 1916, Vol. 204, pp. 589–93.

## CHAPTER V

## CONGRESS FEELS THE LASH

The activities of the Anti-Saloon League at Washington did not begin with the drive for national prohibition. The national legislative office was opened in 1899 under the direction of E. C. Dinwiddie. In a rather disreputable-looking old red brick building just across the street from the national capitol, the organization has its headquarters. From this vantage point Dinwiddie and, later, Wheeler watched, and at times directed, the temperance policies of the United States government. According to the United States Brewers' Association:

A national legislative agent with a force of subordinates was appointed to infest the lobbies of the capitol in Washington. Senators and Representatives who refused to do the League's bidding found they had to face bitter fights and personal abuse in party primaries and general elections.

When an Anti-Saloon League measure was pending on the calendar, the desks of the lawmakers would be deluged with " form " letters or telegrams from the " folks back home." [1]

The League lobbyists applied to Congress the methods that were in familiar use in the state legislatures. S. E. Nicholson, the League's veteran strategist, describes these methods:

The choosing of issues, the determination of policies, the introduction of bills, are not half the battle. Watching bills after introduction, lobbying before committees and among Congressmen, arranging for hearings in behalf of measures presented, are all a vital part of a national legislative program. Yet, even these . . . are mere incidents in the campaign. Back of all such endeavor there must be a nation-wide movement of public opinion, voicing itself in a

[1] *Year Book of United States Brewers' Association,* 1919, p. 10.

way that will be heard by every Congressman. Petitions are important if presented in sufficient volume; personal communications to members are still more effective, personal interviews are best of all, where the citizen can come face to face with his member and out of the fullness of his heart, make known his wishes for legislation as a true American sovereign. . . . The surest way to secure needed temperance legislation is for the sovereign voters, through well planned organization, to elect men as their representatives . . . who will write the laws upon the statute books.[2]

Politicians soon learned to reckon with this new force and were frequently at some pains to ingratiate themselves. R. D. Grier, Progressive candidate in the first Congressional district, Maryland, in 1912 wrote the League's superintendent, the Rev. Cyrus P. Keen:

I have learned that Hon. J. Harry Covington, the present Congressman from this district and the candidate of the Democratic Party for reëlection, has declared himself . . . in favor of the interstate shipment legislation desired by the Anti-Saloon League to enable the various states to enforce their liquor laws and prevent the police power of the state being held at naught by shipments made from outside under the protection of interstate commerce.

If elected I will favor the particular bill known as Senate Bill No. 4043 [the Kenyon bill] approved by the united forces which, under the direction of the Anti-Saloon League of America, are seeking this legislation.

" The average member of Congress," said one wet writer, " is more afraid of the Anti-Saloon League than he is even of the President of the United States. He does not hesitate to take issue with the chief executive of the country over important matters of state; but his courage vanishes into thin air when the whip of the Anti-Saloon League cracks a command." [3] The same writer speaks of the League as " the most

[2] *Proceedings of the Fourteenth Convention of the Anti-Saloon League,* 1911. See also *American Issue,* Maryland Edition, Feb. 22, 1908.
[3] Louis Seibold, " The Workings of Prohibition," a series of articles in the *New York World,* May, 1919.

potential political organization in the country." H. L.
Mencken in one of his politically lucid moments declared:
" Congress is made up eternally of petty scoundrels, pusillani-
mous poltroons, highly vulnerable and cowardly men: they will
never risk provoking the full fire of the Anti-Saloon League." [4]

But if the League succeeded in forcing Congress to obey orders by putting the fear of retirement in the breasts of politicians, there were some Congressmen who treated it with a
withering scorn. Ollie M. James, a Representative from Kentucky, was visited by a delegation which urged his support
for a League measure and intimated that it spoke for the majority of his constituents. " The stalwart Kentuckian listened
patiently until the spokesman of the dry delegation got through.
Straightening his brawny shoulders he said: ' I am naturally
glad to see any of my constituents. But if I thought for an in-
stant that you represented ten percent of them they could go
to hell, because I wouldn't represent any people who would
delegate you to speak for them.' " [5]

James came from a wet district. For those who came from
dry or doubtful areas it was another matter, and many fought
shy of the League as of the plague. " I have seen a member of
Congress," said former general superintendent Baker, " sup-
posedly friendly to temperance reform, duck his head and ac-
celerate his speed in the corridors of the national capitol when
about to meet representatives of the Anti-Saloon League." [6]

It is not proposed to examine here the history of all the
League's congressional measures.[7] Its two outstanding vic-

---

[4] *Prejudices, Fourth Series,* New York, p. 161.
[5] Seibold, *op. cit.*
[6] *Proceedings of the Nineteenth Convention of the Anti-Saloon League,*
1919, p. 31.
   A complete description of the temperance legislation passed by Congress,
for which the League claims credit, would fill a good-sized volume itself. Beginning in 1901, the League claimed credit for the following laws: Army Canteen Law, 1901; a law providing for saloon substitutes at army posts, 1902;
Act of March 3, 1903, prohibiting the sale of intoxicating liquor at immigration
stations; Soldiers' Home Canteen Law, 1906; an amendment to the Internal

tories were the securing of a law prohibiting interstate shipments of liquor into dry territory, and the submission of the
Eighteenth Amendment.

## Liquor and Interstate Commerce

The League very early perceived that state prohibition could
not be completely successful so long as liquor was shipped into
dry states under the protection of the commerce clause of the
Federal Constitution.  Kansas City, Kansas, could not remain
dry when it was possible to order liquor by telephone and have
it shipped in interstate commerce from Kansas City, Missouri.
In 1888 the Supreme Court held that common carriers were
required to receive shipments of liquor in interstate commerce
and that the consignee of such shipments had a right to receive
them.[8]  The drys responded to this decision with the Wilson
Act of 1890, which declared that liquor shipped in interstate
commerce became subject to local law upon arrival in the state.
This act was promptly sustained by the Supreme Court,[9] which
held that it did not constitute a delegation of Congress's power
to the states, but simply removed an obstacle to the state's
control of its own domestic property.  However, in 1898, it

---

Revenue Act of December 24, 1872, requiring a certified copy of the lists of
payers of internal revenue taxes to assist state prosecution of anti-liquor law
breakers, June 21, 1906; Oklahoma prohibition, 1906; prohibition enforcement in the Indian Territory, 1906; an anti-liquor code for Alaska, 1909;
appropriations for law enforcement in Alaska, 1908; prohibiting use of
mails for carrying intoxicating liquors, 1908; laws to enable Tennessee, Mississippi and Arkansas to arrange for effective measures against liquor sellers' re-
sorting to islands created by changes in the course of the Mississippi River,
1909; Penal Code amendments regulating C. O. D. shipments of liquor, 1909;
recognition of and participation in the International Congresses Against Alcoholism, beginning 1911; The Webb-Kenyon Law, 1913; anti-liquor law for
the District of Columbia (Jones-Works bill), 1917; war-time liquor legislation,
1917–18; prohibition for Hawaii, 1918; war-time prohibition, 1918; national
prohibition (in effect 1920); enforcement legislation — viz., Volstead Act and
supplementary legislation. — *American Patriot;* May and June 1916; *Proceedings of the Nineteenth Convention of the Anti-Saloon League,* 1919, pp. 234–54.
    [8] Bowman *v.* Chicago and North Western Railway Co., 125 U. S. 465,
1888; Leisy *v.* Hardin, 135, U. S. 100, 1889.
    [9] *In re* Rahrer, 140 U. S. 545.

was decided [10] that arrival meant delivery to the consignee where the contract of sale was entered into outside the bounds of the regulating state.[11]  This decision made the Wilson Act innocuous, for it was possible to ship liquor into prohibition territory by merely entering into a contract of sale before shipment, in which case the state law did not apply until actual delivery had been made.

The Anti-Saloon League sought legislation which would subject liquor shipped into the state to the same rules as liquor produced within the state, regardless of any previous contract or of the origin of the liquor shipment.  Such a law, the wets said, would be unconstitutional, since Congress could not divest articles of their interstate character so as to subject them to the state's police power.  In meeting this argument the League quoted the Rahrer case: " No reason is perceived why if Congress chooses to provide that certain designated subjects of interstate commerce shall be governed by a rule which divests them of that character at an earlier period of time than would otherwise be the case, it is not within its competency to do so."  The constitutional question was by no means clear, however, and many drys in Congress entertained grave doubts as to its being a legitimate exercise of congressional power.

The difficulty of enforcing state prohibition in the face of the flood of interstate shipments became the chief talking point of League speakers.  Congressman Hobson declared that nineteen million gallons of liquor were shipped annually into dry territory.  He proposed not only to divest liquor of its interstate character when shipped into dry states but also to prohibit its interstate transportation altogether.[12]

[10] Rhodes v. Iowa, 170 U. S. 412.

[11] This decision was followed later in American Express Company v. Iowa (196 U. S. 133, 1905); Adams Express Company v. Kentucky (206 U. S. 129, 1907) ; Heyman v. Southern Railway (203 U. S. 270, 1906) ; and Louisville and Nashville Railway v. Cook Brewing Co. (233 U. S. 70, 1912).

[12] *Proceedings of the Fourteenth Convention of the Anti-Saloon League,* 1911.  The Interstate Commerce Commission in 1911 reported that twenty

To the League the passage of an effective interstate shipment law was of the utmost importance. " Until the state can possess the same complete and exclusive jurisdiction over interstate shipments of liquor from the time they enter the state as it has over liquors manufactured within the state, there is certain to be difficulty and embarrassment in the enforcement of state laws on this question. . . . Under the guise of protecting a citizen in his right to use intoxicating liquor, the government guarantees the right of any citizen to import liquor without regard to the purpose of such importation. . . . Anyone who cares to run the risk of violating the state law may import liquors and have the delivery made under the Wilson Act." [13]

## A Fourfold Path

As the League viewed the problem there were four ways in which relief might be obtained: (1) by subjecting liquor to local jurisdiction upon its arrival within the state, both before and after delivery to the consignee; (2) by forbidding interstate shipments of liquor altogether; (3) by prohibiting interstate shipments of liquor when consigned to those who are not authorized by state law to dispose of them; (4) to amend the commerce clause to give Congress full power in the situation. The first of the alternatives alone seemed practicable. The contention of the wets that all such legislation was unconstitutional was met by the statement that the best way to settle the question was to pass the law and leave the question to the Supreme Court.[14]

---

million gallons of liquor were shipped annually into nine dry states. (*Congressional Record,* 62d Congress, 3d Session, p. 700; *American Issue,* Maryland Edition, Aug. 1911). Much of this was of poor grade and went to the South for negro consumption. (*Baltimore Sun,* June 24, 1911.)

[13] Nicholson, in *Proceedings of the Fourteenth Convention of the Anti-Saloon League,* 1911.

[14] In defense of the constitutionality of this proposal, the League attorneys cited the Palmer case (140 U. S. 562), Leisy *v.* Hardin (*supra*) and the

A bill embodying the League demands was introduced by Representative Hepburn of Iowa in 1902, just before Congress adjourned.[15] Early in the following session, the League saw to it that the bill was reported.[16] Under the watchful eye of the League lobbyist, " the inside work having been carefully looked after and the temper of the body become known, the measure passed [in the House] on January 27, 1903, without a division." [17] In the Senate the bill was referred to the committee on interstate commerce, but Chairman Elkins adjourned the committee before a report could be made.[18]

One serious criticism made of the original Hepburn bill was

---

lottery case, Champion v. Ames (188 U. S. 365, 1903). It was claimed that such a law did not constitute a delegation of power but merely removed an impediment to the enforcement of state laws by divesting liquor shipments of their interstate character. The wets cited Vance v. Vandercook (170 U. S. 45, 1898): " The right of persons in one state to ship liquor into another state to a resident for his own use, is derived from the Constitution of the United States and does not rest on the grant of the state law."

[15] This bill (H. R. 1531, 57th Congress, 1st Session) provided that all liquors shipped into a state, whether for " consumption, sale or storage," should, upon entering or upon arrival within the state, be subject to all the laws of the state or territory " to the same extent and in the same manner as though such liquids or liquors had been produced in such state or territory and shall not be exempt therefrom by reason of being introduced therein in original packages or otherwise." It was in the form of an amendment to the Wilson Act.

[16] " The bill was sleeping in the Judiciary Committee," said Mr. Dinwiddie, " when at our request Mr. Littlefield of Maine, who had successfully led our forces in the House in the anti-canteen struggle in 1900, had it referred to the subcommittee of which he was chairman and secured its unanimous recommendation to the full committee by whom it was . . . favorably considered and was reported to the House." The original bill had been amended by the committee so as to subject shipments of liquor to state law, immediately upon arrival, by adding the words, " before or after " actual delivery. In the debate, Bartholdt of Missouri denounced it because he said it " legalizes prohibition and nullifies the decision of the Supreme Court." Hepburn explained that the law would not prevent the importation of liquor for private consumption. Smith of Iowa, speaking for the bill, related some of his experiences as a district judge. He said that there had been times when as many as one hundred jugs of liquor were at one time in a single express office, sent by the consignor to himself as consignee. The liquor was then assigned to purchasers under bills of lading. So flagrant and extensive had these violations been under C. O. D. shipments that many express offices were little better than open retail saloons. — Congressional Record, 57th Congress, 2d Session, pp. 1327–59 ff.

[17] Proceedings of the Ninth Convention of the Anti-Saloon League, 1904, p. 31; also ibid., 1903, p. 84.

[18] Congressional Record, 57th Congress, 2d Session, pp. 1327–31 and 1359.

that it would interfere with shipments of liquor between wet states. To meet this objection the League, coöperating with Congressman Littlefield and others, drafted a new bill exempting from state control *bona fide* shipments of liquor in transit through a dry state. This measure was introduced in the next Congress by Hepburn and Senator Dolliver of Iowa.[19] The hearings on the bill dragged on from January to March, as repeated postponements were requested by the wets.

During the hearings before the House committee, Duncan B. Harrison, who represented the brewers, accused the League of misusing the franking privilege. The charge was widely quoted. The carelessness of the wets, however, saved the League's face. The League was sending out thousands of pieces of literature concerning temperance legislation. Much of the material dealing with the Hepburn bill consisted of speeches in the form of *Congressional Record* reprints. Many Congressmen saved themselves trouble by referring requests for information to the League, which mailed such reprints and other frankable matter under the Congressman's frank. There is nothing unusual about this; indeed, it is a common practice with pressure organizations of all sorts. Harrison, however, presented certain sealed, franked envelopes claiming that they contained non-frankable as well as frankable mail. Upon opening one of them there was found among other things a League envelope addressed to the same person, bearing cancelled postage stamps. It was apparent to the committee that the brewers or someone hostile to the League was attempting to impose upon them.[20]

When the bill was finally reported, less than three weeks before adjournment, there was little hope of its being reached in the regular calendar order. A special rule could be obtained only from the Rules Committee, of which the hostile Cannon

[19] *Congressional Record*, 58th Congress, 1st Session, H. R. 4072 and S. 1390.
[20] See Senate Documents 168–309, 58th Congress, 2d Session; *Proceedings of the Ninth Convention of the Anti-Saloon League*, 1904, p. 33.

was chairman. Another session had been lost. In the Senate
the bill fared no better. First a quorum of the committee could
not be had, then an offer was made to call another meeting of
the committee and recommend the bill for passage if the League
" would consent to an amendment proposed . . . by parties
unfriendly to the measure." Both Dolliver and Dinwiddie refused to bargain. Said the latter, " We preferred to go before
the people with our demand for an effective law." [21]

In the Fifty-Ninth Congress three bills on the subject appeared in the House and one in the Senate, but none of them
ever got beyond the committee stage, in spite of the petitions,
memorials and protests that poured in.[22]

The Sixtieth Congress was virtually swamped with proposals
for regulating this traffic. Nine such measures were introduced
in the Senate and twenty-six in the House, all by Congressmen
from the South and West. The dry voters were aroused and
were lighting fires of indignation under the political seats of
their estimable statesmen. The League was represented in the
House by Littlefield of Maine and in the Senate by Curtis of
Kansas. It was decided not to press for a report on the Littlefield bill during the first session. With Littlefield as chairman
of the subcommittee, it was believed that a favorable report
could be ultimately obtained " if sufficient pressure is kept on
the members of the Judiciary Committee." Everyone was
urged to write, telegraph or bring petitions to his Representative. Congress was made aware that the people were demanding action.[23] The League was accused of attempting to smother
Congress with letters on an endless chain plan.[24]

[21] *Proceedings of the Ninth Convention of the Anti-Saloon League,* 1904,
p. 34.
[22] *Congressional Record,* 59th Congress, 1st Session, pp. 115, 146, 1858,
3655; 2d Session, pp. 3258–63, 3961, 3396; also pp. 269, 1603, 1653, 2139, 7899.
*House Reports,* 6708 and 7115.
[23] *American Issue,* Maryland, Ohio and other editions, Jan. 18, 1908; *Congressional Record,* 60th Congress, 2d Session, pp. 3445–48, 3681, 3819.
[24] *The Journal,* Pittsfield, Mass., May 16, 1908.

In the House Judiciary Committee practically no progress was made. The committee listened to impassioned pleas from League lobbyists, but was unconvinced and refused to report the bill. But the League did not give up. In a letter to the editor of the *American Issue,* Nicholson said, " Mr. Littlefield attends all sessions of the committee and has virtually tied up all other legislation before that body. So long as the majority refuse to report out his measure the committee finds itself unable to transact any other business." In the same letter Nicholson appealed for more outside pressure on the committee.[25]  In the Senate the situation was not much more hopeful. The subcommittee reported adversely to the Judiciary Committee, declaring the proposed measure to be unconstitutional. Senator Knox of the committee then introduced, as an amendment to the revised penal code bill, a substitute regulating C. O. D. shipments of liquor in interstate commerce, and this was favorably reported.

Humphreys of Mississippi offered a similar substitute in the House. He objected to referring it to the Judiciary Committee where it would " sleep the sleep that knows no waking." He had no objection to the Committee on Interstate Commerce, but it seemed impossible to get the bill referred to that committee for, said Humphreys, " like the peace of the Lord the rules of the House passeth understanding." [26]

### *An Interview with " Uncle Joe "*

In the meantime — in May, 1908 — the Methodist General Conference met in Baltimore. Governor Hanly of Indiana introduced a resolution calling for the immediate passage of the Littlefield bill. This was adopted and a committee of twenty-five, including ministers, judges and governors, was appointed to wait on Speaker Cannon. Claiming to represent more than

---

[25] *American Issue,* National Edition, April 25, 1908.
[26] *Congressional Record,* 6oth Congress, 1st Session, p. 4569.

three million church members and some ten million people, they asked him to present their memorial to the House and urge the bill then pending. Cannon countered by asking those in the delegation who had read the bill to raise their hands, and only ten were able to do so. The Speaker smiled and went on to point out that many eminent lawyers in Congress, including himself, had serious doubt of its constitutionality. The petitioners insisted that such doubts should be resolved in favor of the " people " and that the Supreme Court should be permitted to decide. Cannon was uncharitable enough to quote from the testimony of Alvord, a League representative before the committee: " But I do not believe . . . that just to please somebody you ought to shove up propositions to the Supreme Court which you believe in your conscience and under your oath to be unconstitutional." He assured them that Congress was ready to do all it constitutionally could and urged them to push the Knox substitute regulating C. O. D. shipments. Until the states had removed the beam in their own eyes by prohibiting the *use* as well as the *sale* of liquor, he did not see how they could fairly ask Congress to go further than outlaw C. O. D. shipments to fictitious consignees. In short, Cannon insisted that Congress should be left to decide the question free from intimidation. Hanly replied, simply, " We wanted you to know our conviction on this question. We wanted Congress to know, for in the last analysis, the people make Congress." [27] W. H. Anderson subsequently characterized the meeting as "the most uncomfortable hour that Uncle Joe ever spent." [28]

*Outlawing C. O. D. Shipments*

Early in the second session, February 18, the House bill with the Humphreys amendment was debated and passed. The Senate disagreed with certain of the House amendments to

[27] *Congressional Record*, 60th Congress, 1st Session, Appendix, p. 176.
[28] *American Issue*, Maryland Edition, May 16, 1908.

other parts of the bill, and asked for a conference. The conference report was discussed in both houses, March 3, and agreed to. With the passage of the Knox-Humphreys amendment Bartholdt of Missouri expressed the " devout wish that the agitation for liquor legislation at the hands of Congress may have received a quietus . . . and that that amendment marks the line of demarcation beyond which Congress on that subject will not go." Langley of Kentucky, speaking for the League in the House, assured him that the C. O. D. amendment was only a step and that the drys had no notion of giving up the fight.[29] Although the League rejoiced at its passage and congratulated Knox and Humphreys, it was still unsatisfied. Half a loaf was better than none, but it was not at all sure that the whole loaf was not to be had.[30]

Speaker Cannon and the wet leaders of Congress were blamed for the failure of the sixtieth Congress to pass an effective law. When Cannon came up for reëlection the League set out to defeat him, but his machine was too strong for them. Little, therefore, could be expected from the sixty-first Congress with " Uncle Joe " still in the chair.[31] A further result of this fight was the selection of a new League leader in the House. Littlefield, who had urged Cannon's reëlection, was replaced by Miller of Kansas.[32] The Curtis-Langley bill, drafted by

[29] Briefly, the C. O. D. amendment made it illegal for any common carrier to deliver C. O. D. shipments of liquor to other than *bona fide* consignees, to collect the purchase price or any part thereof on or after delivery from the consignee, or to act in any manner as agent of the buyer or seller of such liquor; it made it illegal for anyone to ship liquor unless the package be labeled on the outside cover showing plainly the name of the consignee and the nature and quantity of its contents. Violations were punishable by fine or imprisonment or both. — *Congressional Record,* 60th Congress, 2d Session, pp. 3791, 455, 477, 519, 749, 1665, 2122, 2861.

[30] *American Issue,* New York Edition, March, 1909; *Proceedings of the Thirteenth Convention of the Anti-Saloon League,* 1909, pp. 34 ff.

[31] " The necessary fight against Speaker Cannon . . . precluded representatives of the League, as such, from receiving favors or even consideration from the existing management of the House." — *Proceedings of the Thirteenth Convention of the Anti-Saloon League,* 1909, p. 33.

[32] *Proceedings of the Thirteenth Convention of the Anti-Saloon League,* 1909, pp. 26 ff.

Wheeler, was chloroformed in committee, despite all the League's pressure.[33]

### The Webb-Kenyon Bill

The Democrats were in the saddle in the sixty-second Congress which assembled in April, 1911. With Champ Clark wielding the gavel, now somewhat shorn of its power, and the obnoxious Cannon removed, dry hopes revived. In the first session neither the League's McCumber-Webb bill, nor any of the eight others dealing with interstate liquor shipments got beyond the committee stage.[34] The fourteenth convention of the League assembled in Washington in December, 1911, soon after the second session opened. Nicholson, acting legislative superintendent, announced the intention of fighting every Congressman hostile to the League program. " Already," he said, " nearly a score of Congressmen opposed to this legislation have been elected to stay at home." General Superintendent Baker urged that state temperance legislation be momentarily neglected and all efforts concentrated on Congress:

The states are helpless to enforce their own laws because the Federal government persists in backing the speak-easy keeper and the blind-tiger keeper. If this present Congress, like its predecessors, refuses to hear the appeal of the people and give adequate relief, it is time to stop state legislation while we devote ourselves to the specific task of creating a Congress that will give relief. It is time our League attorneys and others . . . agree upon a bill that will be effective, and in their judgment constitutional . . . and let everybody get behind that bill and never stop . . . until it is a law upon the statute books.

33 See S. 2486 and H. R. 6169; *Congressional Record*, 61st Congress, 1st Session, pp. 2427 and 390. There was considerable debate over prohibition in Hawaii. The demand for such legislation was confined almost exclusively to the Anti-Saloon League. A bill providing for prohibition in the island by act of Congress was dropped when numerous Hawaiian organizations protested. Congress contented itself with referring the subject to the Hawaiian people. — *Congressional Record*, 61st Congress, 1st Session, pp. 1358, 34, 103, 390, 2013, 2347; 2d Session, pp. 3993, 945, 4029, 3876, 138, 577, 1517, 3132, 3264, 4920-24, 5107; *Congressional Record*, 61st Congress, 1st Session, pp. 1060-66, 164-65.
34 *Congressional Record*, 62d Congress, 1st Session, pp. 518, 1201.

The people have fought too long to tolerate a makeshift measure; they will forgive us if the measure should prove unconstitutional, but they will hold to strict account any man or set of men, in or out of Congress, who make themselves responsible for an inefficient measure.[35]

Suiting the action to the word, a special conference was called to draft such a measure. Nearly two hundred delegates, representing thirty-nine states and twenty-six organizations, attended this conference. The committee appointed to draw up a bill included, among others: the Rev. A. J. Barton, League superintendent of Texas; F. S. Caldwell, an Oklahoma attorney; former Governor Hanly of Indiana; Superintendent Nicholson; Senator Charles Curtis; Senator McCumber; Congressman Webb; and Margaret Dye of the W. C. T. U.[36] The bill[37] agreed upon was introduced by Senator Kenyon and Congressman Sheppard. Several other bills were introduced, including one by Congressman Webb. The Senate committee,

[35] *Proceedings of the Fourteenth Convention of the Anti-Saloon League,* 1911.

[36] *Proceedings of the Fourteenth Convention of the Anti-Saloon League,* 1911.

[37] This bill (H. R. 16214–S. 4043) is sufficiently important to include here in full. It read: " *Be it enacted,* That the shipment or transportation in any manner or by any means whatsoever of any spirituous, vinous, malted, fermented, or other intoxicating liquor of any kind, including beer, ale, or wine, from one state, territory or district of the United States, or place noncontiguous to but subject to the jurisdiction thereof, into any other state, territory, or district of the United States, or place noncontiguous to but subject to the jurisdiction thereof, or from any foreign country into any state, territory, or district of the United States or place noncontiguous to but subject to the jurisdiction thereof, which said spirituous, vinous, malted, fermented or other intoxicating liquor is intended, by any person interested therein, directly or indirectly, or in any manner connected with the transaction, to be received, possessed or kept, or in any manner used, either in the original package or otherwise, in violation of any law of such state, territory, or district, of the United States, or place noncontiguous to but subject to the jurisdiction thereof, enacted, in the exercise of the police powers of such state, territory, or district of the United States, or place noncontiguous to but subject to the jurisdiction thereof, is hereby prohibited; and any and all contracts pertaining to such transactions are hereby declared to be null and void, and no suit or action shall be maintained in any court of the United States upon any such contract or contracts, or for the enforcement or protection of any alleged right based upon or growing out of such contract or contracts, or for the protection in any manner whatsoever of such prohibited transactions."

after extensive hearings, reported the Kenyon bill favorably.[38] Congress was bombarded with appeals from the drys, protests from the wets and threats from both sides. Armfuls of arguments, legal and moral, petitions galore and sacks of mail poured in. The legislatures of five states memorialized Congress to pass the legislation.[39]

The debate in the Senate began on December 16, 1912. Some of the ablest men in that body participated. McCumber, Borah, Kenyon and Sheppard spoke in its behalf.[40] Sanders of Tennessee, speaking for the bill, roundly denounced the mail-order liquor business, waxing indignant at appeals from such dealers urging him to oppose the Kenyon bill. He quoted one letter:

Allow me to write you in behalf of our business. Chattanooga is the second largest mail-order whisky center in the South and if the Kenyon bill passes . . . it means that our business will be practically destroyed.

We certainly will appreciate anything that you can do for us. . . .

P. S. We have 150 white employees here in our store in Chattanooga. This will give you some idea of the magnitude of the mail-order business out of Chattanooga.[41]

Aside from this there was an effort to insert an amendment to provide that nothing in the bill should make illegal the shipment of liquor into a state for personal or family use. It was

[38] Sen. Doc. 448, 62d Congress, 2d Session; *Congressional Record,* 62d Congress, 3d Session, pp. 2796–2805. The bill was reached April 15, 1912, and after several unsuccessful attempts, on August 16, Senator Kenyon succeeded in securing a unanimous consent agreement to consider the bill upon the opening of the third session. — *Congressional Record,* 62d Congress, 2d Session, pp. 10994, 11053.

[39] *Congressional Record,* 62d Congress, 3d Session, pp. 3272, 3305, 2766, 2871, 2889, 2428, 2525, 2870, 1761, 2253.

[40] Senator Root expressed his sympathy with the efforts to curb this illicit traffic, but doubted its constitutionality. He further expressed the hope, interesting in the light of his later views, that " The time may come, and I shall be glad to see it, when the people of the United States will be ready to act as a whole in suppression of this traffic." — *Congressional Record,* 62d Congress, 3d Session, p. 2915.

[41] Although Tennessee had prohibited the sale of intoxicating liquor within the state, there was no law prohibiting its manufacture and exportation to other states. — *Congressional Record,* 62d Congress, 3d Session, pp. 700 ff.

replied that this was unnecessary since only shipments intended for a purpose illegal under the laws of the state were outlawed; where state law did not prohibit the use of liquor, and few states did, such shipments would be unaffected anyway.[42]

Pressure from outside had a telling effect. Stone [43] of Missouri declared that he intended to vote for the measure because of the flood of letters and telegrams he had received asking him to do so. The liquor lobby at the capital reported:

On December 16, 1912, the day set for a vote on the Kenyon interstate shipment bill, the galleries of the United States Senate were filled to overflowing with enthusiastic advocates of the measure.

Every state in the Union had its temperance workers on hand to encourage by their presence Senators Kenyon, McCumber and Sanders in their efforts to convince by prepared arguments, the other members of the United States Senate that the bill should be passed and become law whether constitutional or not. Your committee is of the opinion that both the Kenyon-Webb and Jones-Works bills are in danger of passage on account of the whip hand the Anti-Saloon League seems to be holding over the heads of the members of Congress.[44]

In the House the Webb bill was reported on February 7, 1913, with a recommendation that it pass.[45] Here too, the pressure was evident. Webb cited a long list of religious and reform organizations that had petitioned for the bill, claiming that they represented more than thirty-five million constituents. Sabbath of Illinois replied that the legislation was being forced upon the country by " narrow-minded and prejudiced persons . . . who are seeking to force their views and belief upon the country as a whole." [46]  A Kentucky member fulminated:

---

[42] *Congressional Record,* 62d Congress, 3d Session, pp. 2690, 2921.

[43] *Ibid.,* p. 2917.

[44] *Report of Congressional Committee of National Liquor League,* Jan. 21, 1913.

[45] H. R. 17593; House Report 1461; *Congressional Record,* 62d Congress, 3d Session, pp. 2762, 2788-2865.

[46] *Ibid.,* pp. 2835-36.

It is admitted by the Anti-Saloon League of America, in asking for this legislation, that the great mass of legislation which they have spread upon the statute books in the various states is an absolute failure. . . . This sham and pretense of a prohibition law is about to be written upon the statute books of the nation because the leaders of the Anti-Saloon League have so decreed. This House stands ready, if they will give the word, to write upon the statute books of this country a real prohibition law.

A Wisconsin opponent declared:

The campaign in favor of this legislation has been a long and bitterly contested one. For over ten years every resource of a clever and persistent lobby has been used to influence the membership of this House in favor of this most iniquitous legislation. Salaried agents and organizers . . . have been instructing various churches, organizations, clubs and individuals in all kinds of methods of reaching their Congressmen and Senators, and seeking by petition, letter and frequently by open threat to influence members in favor of this sort of legislation.[47]

The pressure, however, was by no means one-sided. Bartholdt of Missouri, chafed by the tyranny of the League, read a protest from the German-American Alliance which he claimed represented two million citizens.[48] The drys answered by pointing to the barrage of the wets:

For months every member's mail has been flooded by the voluminous briefs of the Wholesale Liquor Dealers Association, the Model License League, the Liberty League, and every organization in the liquor business in this country . . . warning us that this legislation is unconstitutional. Great God! has the time come when honorable members rise on the floor and engage in partnership with the views of the liquor traffic of this country and their legal hirelings in their interpretation of the fundamental law of our fathers?[49]

A circular of The David Wise Co., distillers, deplored the names of "beer drivers and stablemen and brewery roust-

---

[47] *Congressional Record,* 62d Congress, 3d Session, Appendix, p. 913.
[48] *Ibid.,* p. 2816.
[49] *Congressional Record,* 62d Congress, 3d Session, p. 2835.

abouts " in wet petitions and urged instead that the wets " get as many well-known and prominent citizens as you can to write to your United States Senators protesting against the passage of this bill." [50]   Said a prominent liquor paper:

Congress convenes December 3.   On December 16, the Kenyon bill, S. 4043, will be made the special order of business.   This bill is the most dangerous measure ever aimed at the liquor traffic.   What have you done to defeat it?   Your Senator and your Congressman are your representatives and must listen to your protest.   This bill must be killed.   It will not die unless Senators and Congressmen are made aware of the strong opposition to it. . . .   The passage of the Kenyon bill will be the biggest victory ever won by the Anti-Saloon League.   What are you going to do about it? [51]

The Democrats were accused of driving the legislation through at the crack of the whip.

It is plain that the bill is to be railroaded through today.   The Democracy is in the saddle and feeling its oats; that party is bent on riding roughshod over all the caution and sagacity which kept the Republican Congresses for lo, these many years from doing violence to vested rights and the fundamental law of the country.[52]

The criticisms that were made in the Senate were repeated in the House — that it was an unconstitutional delegation of power and that it failed to protect legitimate shipments of liquor for personal use.

Davis of West Virginia proposed an amendment for this purpose denying that such shipments were protected in the proposed bill.   Impugning the sincerity of the League's attitude, he quoted Dinwiddie's testimony before the committee, that it was a man's constitutional right to receive liquor in interstate commerce for his personal use, and then cited a letter sent to all members, in which Dinwiddie had said:

[50] *Congressional Record*, 62d Congress, 3d Session, p. 2899.
[51] *Bonfort's Wine and Spirit Circular*, Nov. 25, 1912.
[52] Bartholdt of Missouri, *Congressional Record*, 62d Congress, 3d Session, p. 2816.

Besides an attempt to put on a penalty clause our friends are asked to be on guard against a provision to exempt imported liquors for personal use. We contend this is purely a state matter. Such a clause is against the real policy and underlying principles of the bill. It will shackle and hobble the states while the whole intent of the measure is to unfetter them. It will legalize the introduction of liquors for personal use when that whole question should properly be left to state control.

We earnestly urge the friends of this legislation to resist to the very last any effort to attach a " personal use " clause to the bill, a plan which the liquor interests have been urging for ten years past.[53]

However inconsistent this may seem at first blush, the contradiction is more apparent than real. Dinwiddie recognized that until the states had exercised their police power to the extent of outlawing the use of liquor as well as its manufacture and sale, the right to receive such liquor for personal use was protected by the commerce clause. It had been so held by the Supreme Court. At the same time, to put such an exemption in the proposed law, while it could not deprive the states of their police power to prohibit the use of liquor, would result in unnecessary confusion.

When on February 8, 1913, the Webb bill came to a vote, it passed easily, 239 yeas and 64 nays. All attempts to safeguard personal use were defeated.[54] The measure was not quite identical with the Kenyon bill [55] and there was some fear that the House would pass the Webb bill, the Senate the Kenyon bill, and both would be smothered in conference. To prevent this, the Senate accepted the Webb bill as a substitute for the Kenyon bill and it was submitted for executive approval.[56]

There was some surprise when a few days later President Taft on the advice of Attorney General Wickersham vetoed

[53] *Ibid.*, p. 2824.  [54] *Ibid.*, p. 2866.
[55] The Senate committee had amended the bill adding a section making all interstate liquor shipments subject to state law immediately upon entering the state. It was felt this would cause confusion and litigation since the first section prohibited all shipments for the purpose of violating state laws.
[56] *Ibid.*, p. 2924.

the bill as unconstitutional. Vigorously condemning the theory that Congress should pass laws and let the Supreme Court decide as to their constitutionality, he reasserted the doctrine, which goes back at least to Andrew Jackson, that the President and Congress as well as the Court are bound to interpret and obey the constitution.[57]

There might have been some difficulty in surmounting this veto, but within a week the Supreme Court unwittingly entered the situation with its decision in the white slave case, which the drys asserted settled the question.[58]  The Senate promptly passed the measure over the President's veto by a vote of 63 to 21.[59]  The House, with equal readiness and even more decisively, repassed the bill, 246 to 95.  The Anti-Saloon League had won a major victory.  The wets were fully aware of its significance:

> The passage of the Webb-Kenyon bill, its veto by President Taft and its victory over the veto by more than two-thirds majority apparently mark the climax of a movement that has been active for half a century.  If the Supreme Court declares the act unconstitutional, it does not change the impressive fact that in the face of the united effort of all branches of the alcoholic liquor trade, the National Congress voted for the bill.[60]

The lamentations of the wets were equalled only by the hosannas of the drys:

> The victory of the Webb-Kenyon-Sheppard bill withdrawing the Federal protection from the liquor trade in its nullification of state laws prohibiting the sale of liquors within its territory was undoubtedly due, preëminently, to the Anti-Saloon League.  That is a fact. The Anti-Saloon League organized the movement, saw its develop-

[57] *Congressional Record*, 62d Congress, 3d Session, p. 4293.  The League had insisted that Congress should pass the law, leaving the question as to its constitutionality entirely to the court.

[58] Hoke and Economides *v.* United States, 227 U. S. 308; Hoke *v.* United States, 227 U. S. 316, 1913.

[59] *Congressional Record*, 62d Congress, 3d Session, pp. 4297–99.

[60] George Muller, statistician, United States Brewers' Association, in *National Liquor Dealers' Journal*, April 2, 1913.

ment, watched its struggle and danger points, used the telegraph freely and with effect, brought to bear the necessary pressure of men and argument, and won one of the greatest victories in the history of temperance reform.[61]

The wets fully expected the law to be declared unconstitutional.[62] They even claimed that the League shared their view.

But the Anti-Saloon League, the most arrant organization of canting hypocrites and jesuitical grafters the world has ever known, has neither desire nor expectation that the Webb law shall be anything but a makeshift and a stop-gap, a football for hypocrites to kick hither and yon until it is sent clear over the fence by the court of final resort.

Four years elapsed before the law came directly before the Supreme Court. At length, on January 8, 1917, it was completely sustained.[63] The Attorney General and the Department of Justice, relying upon the opinion of former Attorney General Wickersham as to the invalidity of the law, declined to defend it before the court. The government's case therefore was presented by Wheeler, the League's general counsel.[64] Many opponents of the legislation were deeply grieved. One writer pronounced it tyranny, " whether it comes from the hands of a monarch, the voice of a mob, or the vote of the majority." [65] The Anti-Saloon League, of course, rejoiced. Congressman Webb, speaking to the League's convention that year, said:

[61] *Central Christian Advocate,* April 2, 1913.
[62] *Barrels and Bottles,* April 19, 1913.
[63] Clark Distilling Co. *v.* Western Maryland Railroad, 242 U. S. 311, 1917. For a discussion of the act from a legal point of view see: Lindsay Rogers, " Unlawful Possession of Liquor," *Columbia Law Review,* 1916, Vol. XVI, pp. 1–17; also the same author's " Life, Liberty and Liquor," *Virginia Law Review,* 1919, Vol. VI, pp. 156 ff. An extensive bibliography is given by T. R. Powell. " Decisions of the Supreme Court, 1914–17," *American Political Science Review,* 1918, Vol. XII.
[64] Wheeler, "Inside Story of Prohibition," *New York Times,* March 28, 1926. See *New York Herald,* Jan. 10, 1917.
[65] J. W. Emerson, " Against Webb-Kenyon Law " [a letter], *Outlook,* Feb. 14, 1917, Vol. 115, p. 284.

They called me a cornfield lawyer because I said it was constitutional, but I tell you. . . . I felt absolutely safe for the destiny of that great measure in the hands of the great Supreme Court of this country and, thank God, my faith has not been disturbed. . . . It [the decision and the law] is the first and greatest blow that the liquor interests of the country ever received right " between the eyes."

I believe the year 1917, . . . so far as prohibition activities and victories are concerned, is the greatest year in the history of the world.[66]

[66] *Proceedings of the Eighteenth Convention of the Anti-Saloon League,* 1917, p. 87.

# CHAPTER VI
## ARMAGEDDON

The natural climax of the League's work was the movement for national prohibition. In a measure, this had been its goal from the beginning. Having driven the traffic out of school and church districts, the League had demanded county prohibition on the theory that, unless the whole county was dry, it would be impossible to enforce liquor laws in dry areas within the county. State-wide prohibition was then sought in order to make county prohibition effective. By 1913 the League became convinced that state prohibition could succeed only in a dry nation.[1]

The campaign for national prohibition was formally launched at its national convention in that year. Wheeler, at that time superintendent of the Ohio League, greeted the delegates:

We welcome you . . . to the launching of the most beneficent and far-reaching movement since the civil war. As Moses said to the children of Israel that they should go forward, just so the time has come for the moral forces of this great nation to march on against the last bulwarks of the enemy. A great national evil has been localized and quarantined. Over two-thirds of the saloons of

[1] In 1913 nine states, having an aggregate population of 14,600,000, had state-wide prohibition. In thirty-one other states with local option laws 26,-000,000 people were living under no-license. Three with a population of 3,700,-000 had prohibition except in those sections where a majority vote had set it aside; two had prohibition for all territory outside cities and villages. Congress had abolished the saloon in military forts and on reservations, in the navy, soldiers' homes, and the national capitol building, and had shown its dry leanings by overcoming the President's veto of the Webb-Kenyon Act. A survey of Congress showed that a substantial majority came from dry constituencies. The League claimed that more than fifty percent of the people and seventy-one percent of the area of the United States were under prohibitory laws. It was felt that the time had come to drive the traffic to its last stand. — *Year Book of the Anti-Saloon League*, 1913; E. H. Cherrington, *Evolution of Prohibition*, pp. 319–20.

America are now in ten states. They are localized more today than
slavery was when the last stage of the conflict was reached. The
people are growing restless. Like the muttering of a great storm you
can hear the determined demand from every quarter to attack the
enemy all along the line for national constitutional prohibition. I
do not know how you may feel about this, but I would die rather
than run from such a conflict.[2]

It was a formidable gathering, with representatives from
every state in the union. Ministers, judges, social workers,
scientists, Senators, Congressmen, governors and the League's
own leaders trained in pulpit and politics, all dedicating themselves to a final assault upon the bulwarks of evil. They were
conscious of the difficulties they had to face. "Victory demands idealism, plus an army," declared Bishop Wilson, the
president. "As Moses approached with unsandaled feet that
bush of flame and caught the word of God, so come we to this
hour and in its solemn hush we read and recognize the divine
hour for a new advance — Prohibition for all our land. . . .
Members of the convention, we turn our faces toward the future. The host you represent has wrought well. Today the
cry is forward."

John G. Wooley reached the peak of eloquence in address-
ing the convention on "The Call of an Epoch":

The meeting is the Constitutional Convention of the Churches of
America in national action against the crime of crimes. . . . That
business must go. Day and night we will pursue it, locally and at
large. We will crowd it to the ropes. We will not break away in
the clinches. And when it lies dying among its bags of bloody gold
and looks up into our faces with its last gasp and whispers, "Another million of revenue for just one breath of life," we will put the
heel of open-eyed national honor on its throat and say "NO! Down
to Hell and say we sent thee thither!"[3]

The liquor trade itself seemed to realize that it was the dawn
of Armageddon:

[2] *Proceedings of the Fifteenth Convention of the Anti-Saloon League,*
1913, p. 14.                          [3] *Ibid.,* p. 29.

To us there is the handwriting on the wall and its interpretation spells doom. The liquor business is to blame. It seems incapable of learning any lesson of advancement or any motive but profit. To perpetuate itself it has formed alliances with the slums. . . . It deliberately aids the most corrupt political powers. . . . There are billions of property involved . . . but when the people decide that the truth is being told about the alcoholic liquor traffic the money value will not count. . . .[4]

## The Great Remonstrance

Following the convention a council of one hundred, later the National Temperance Council, was organized. It united all the leading temperance organizations. At the same time the League created a committee of one thousand men, which, with a similar committee of women, appointed by the W. C. T. U., was to march to the capitol and present to both houses of Congress a resolution providing for the submission of a constitutional amendment.

These " grand " committees joined forces in Washington December 10, 1913. Four thousand men and women wearing the white ribbon of temperance formed for the parade. Except for a six-year-old boy and a four-year-old girl, who were in the lead, youth was conspicuously absent. But as they moved down Pennsylvania Avenue, jeered at by their enemies, cheered by their friends, they did not falter. A few dropped out along the way, but the majority, many of them grown gray and infirm in the long campaign, marched doggedly on to the strains of " Onward, Christian Soldiers." Arrived at the steps of the capitol, they were met by Senator Sheppard and Congressman Hobson to whom they intrusted their petition.

Later the same day the resolution was introduced by Sheppard in the Senate.[5] The Judiciary Committee, to which it was

---

[4] *National Liquor Dealers' Journal,* Sept. 10, 1913.
[5] The text of the resolution follows:
*Whereas,* exact scientific research has demonstrated that alcohol is a narcotic poison, destructive and degenerating to the human organism, and that its

referred, never reported it. In the House it fared better. Hoping for immediate consideration the drys thronged the capitol on the day following the parade. Hobson, presenting the resolution to the House, warned his party that an accounting was at hand. " If the Democratic Party can only live by joining the liquor interests to debauch the American People, then in God's name let it die." Bartholdt of St. Louis rose to suggest that the House move out of Washington to avoid pressure from the drys. Turning to the crowded galleries he shouted, " Never mind! You may intimidate village councils and members of state legislatures and even some Congressmen, but you can not cow or intimidate me." And, turning to his colleagues, " I predict that not one of you who vote for it will ever come back to tell the tale." [6]

---

distribution as a beverage or contained in foods, lays a staggering economic burden upon the shoulders of the people, lowers to an appalling degree the average standard of character of our citizenship, thereby undermining the public morals and the foundation of free institutions, produces widespread crime, pauperism and insanity, inflicts disease and untimely death upon hundreds of thousands of citizens, and blights with degeneracy their children unborn, threatening the future integrity and the very life of the nation; *Therefore be it resolved:* By the Senate and House of Representatives of the United States of America in Congress assembled (two-thirds of each House concurring therein), that the following amendment of the Constitution be, and hereby is proposed to the States, to become valid as a part of the Constitution when ratified by the legislatures of the several States as provided by the Constitution.

ARTICLE . . .

Sec. 1. The sale, manufacture for sale, transportation for sale, importation for sale, and exportation for sale, of intoxicating liquors for beverage purposes in the United States and all territory subject to the jurisdiction thereof are forever prohibited.

Sec. 2. Congress shall have power to provide for the manufacture, sale, importation, and transportation of intoxicating liquors for sacramental, medicinal, mechanical, pharmaceutical or scientific purposes, or for use in the arts, and shall have power to enforce this article by all needful legislation.

*Congressional Record*, 63d Congress, 2d Session, p. 615, S. J. R. 88. The resolution was drafted by a committee composed of Wayne Wheeler; F. S. Caldwell of Oklahoma City, author of the Webb bill; Judge W. A. Covington of Mississippi; ex-Governor Hanly of Indiana; Judge W. A. Campbell of West Virginia; J. F. Burke of Michigan; and Superintendent Baker. — *American Patriot*, Jan., 1914.

[6] *Congressional Record*, 63d Congress, 2d Session, pp. 736–45.

### Plans Are Laid

The next day in the League's offices, just across from the capitol, the drys planned their campaign. They resolved on three modes of attack: (1) an intensive drive in the states for new dry territory; (2) a fight for dry Congressmen in every district where a reasonable chance of winning offered; (3) a fight for more dry Senators. To accomplish these ends a special headquarters committee had been created by the convention. The fight began at once.[7]

Congress was all but buried in an avalanche of communications from the people back home. The wires were hot with messages. The local leagues spurred on the church folks, and it seemed that the flood of public opinion had broken on an unsuspecting Congress. A partial list of endorsed petitions contained the names of 9296 organizations with a total membership of 3,358,586.[8]

### The Debate

The Judiciary Committee of the House reported Hobson's resolution without comment, May 9, 1914, and on December 22 it came up for debate. The galleries were again so crowded that the Speaker warned, " There are going to be ten mortal hours of speech making here today and some of it, perhaps, will be rather lively, and the chair asks members to help keep order, and the people in the galleries, too." Long slips of paper containing the names of over six million petitioners hung from the balconies, and on both sides of the Speaker's chair Hobson had placed numerous charts showing the progress of prohibition. Kelly of Pennsylvania began by insisting that the passage of the resolution was in the nature of a referendum to the people

[7] *American Patriot*, Jan., 1914.
[8] *Congressional Record*, 63d Congress, 2d Session, p. 8626. See also pp. 4716, 5646, 7354, 8273, 8691, 11162, 11218, 11437, 11673, 12005, 12130, 12064, 12519, 12662–64, 12782, 13356 for some dry petitions and pp. 6217 ff. for some from the wets.

on prohibition.   Anticipating the argument that a minority in thirty-six states could amend the Constitution, he pointed out that one-fortieth of the voting population living in thirteen states could prevent its adoption.   He also added that Patrick Henry had opposed ratification of the Constitution on this very ground.   " It is a most fearful situation," Henry had said, " when the most contemptible minority can prevent the alteration of the government, even when most oppressive."   Lenroot of Wisconsin objected to submission because it would keep the question more surely in politics, since an amendment once submitted could, he said, be ratified at any time in a hundred years. Lindbergh of Minnesota asserted that passage of the resolution would give the people an opportunity to settle the question once for all: " Today we are called upon to record our votes in favor of the preservation and not the destruction of our race — to save the boys and girls who will become the future citizens and rulers of our country."   Hobson, as the chief protagonist of the drys, met the assaults of the children of darkness with one of his best " Great Destroyer " speeches.   More than six million people had petitioned for submission, " ten times as many as ever petitioned any government in the history of the world.   Twelve thousand organizations have passed official resolutions."   So thoroughly had the League done its work.

The wets ransacked the arsenal of a half century's temperance agitation.   Underwood, their leader, dwelt upon the danger of governmental consolidation, the loss of a tremendous revenue, and the futility of prohibition.   " And yet," he said, " in an idle hour, cloaked in the robe of temperance because all men believe in temperance, a faction has arisen in the republic that would tear down the very fabric of the government itself and destroy the foundation stones on which it rests. . . . Prohibition is a tyrannous scheme to establish virtue and morality by law."

Calling the League the legitimate heir of the Know-Nothing Party and its grandchild the A. P. A., Oglesby of New York said:

The Anti-Saloon League has adopted the methods of the Caesars and threatens us with proscription . . . if we Republicans and Democrats do not bow to its will. The legislative superintendent of the League who watches over this Congress published to the world the warning, " The graves of many state legislators and members of Congress can be seen along our line of march."

Vollmer of Iowa reached the empyrean of wet eloquence and invoked the spirits of " George Washington, the brewer; Thomas Jefferson, the distiller; Abraham Lincoln, the saloon keeper; and Jesus of Nazareth who turned water into wine."

When the vote was about to be taken, Mann of Illinois proposed that ratification be by conventions in the states. The League spokesmen objected that this additional obstacle served no good purpose, offering the specious reason that the same people who chose the legislatures would choose the delegates. The amendment was defeated, as was a substitute offered by Morrison, which would completely prohibit the interstate transportation of liquor. He commented on an objection Dinwiddie had made that Congress already had power to do this, saying that if this was so, " the duty rests upon the Anti-Saloon League to write such a statute into the body of our Federal laws." He added: " It is a matter of common knowledge that the Anti-Saloon League controls the vote of a majority of the members of Congress." Hobson proposed an amendment giving Congress or the states power of enforcement " independently or concurrently," which was agreed to, and the resolution thus amended came to a vote. The roll-call stood 197 in the affirmative and 190 in the negative. Lacking the necessary two-thirds, the resolution failed.[9]

[9] *Congressional Record*, 63d Congress, 3d Session, 1914, pp. 495-616. An analysis of the vote on the Hobson resolution may be found in Appendix A.

## The Real Battle Begins

In a sense the result was a victory. This was the first time that a full debate on prohibition had taken place in the House of Representatives. Under the circumstances the result was encouraging. Here were the floor leaders of both parties, the chairman of the Rules Committee, and inferentially the President, arrayed against the resolution. That it was not overwhelmingly defeated was due in large measure to the pressure directly applied by the League, and to the victories it had won in the fall elections. The League had conducted a vigorous campaign. A special campaign committee had been appointed in June which, through the local organizations, kept in touch with the political situation in every part of the country. Records of candidates were minutely scrutinized. All were asked to state their views, and the word went down the line to support or politically execute. The League did not enter a contest where the possibility of victory was too remote, but wherever there was a reasonable chance the organization planted its guns and waged incessant war. Twenty thousand speakers were sent out to urge the selection of dry candidates. The publishing plant at Westerville worked night and day. Pamphlets, dodgers, bills and posters, literally by the hundreds of thousands, were broadcast.[10]

The temperance movement was in full tide. Arizona, Colorado, Oregon, Virginia and Washington adopted prohibition. Local option victories were recorded in Connecticut, Illinois, Vermont, Wisconsin, Kentucky, Maryland, Michigan and Minnesota. Three political parties in Idaho pledged the submission of state-wide prohibition. In dry Kansas a candidate for governor who stood for resubmission was defeated almost ten to one. League candidates were elected to the Senate in Kentucky and Illinois.[11]

[10] Wheeler, "Inside Story of Prohibition," *New York Times*, March 29, 1926.          [11] Cherrington, *Evolution of Prohibition*, pp. 337–40.

When the next League convention met at Atlantic City in 1915, the European war had been in progress almost a year. The agitation in England for curtailment of the liquor traffic was highly commended and when Lloyd George was quoted as saying, "We are fighting the Germans, the Austrians, and Drink: and the deadliest of these is drink," the cheers rang out like hosannas. The United States not being as yet a combatant, it was too early for the League to begin its campaign on the trade as pro-German, although there were hints of it.

Hobson, defeated for the Senatorship in Alabama by Underwood and now free to devote his energies to leading the dry hosts, outlined for the convention "The Grand Strategy of the Fight." Only an extensive summary can do justice to the plan of attack which this modern Joshua proposed:

Make general use of the government frank in sending out dry speeches and other documents.

Request all papers and periodicals to decline liquor advertisements, and see that the friends of temperance back up the request.

Seek the enfranchisement of women everywhere.

Incorporate in the campaign the adult Sunday school, Christian Endeavor, Epworth League and others, and assign them specific duties.

Call the Salvation Army into action.

Make the coming year noted in religious history for revivals and turn their full force into the liquor fight.

Organize special sections for labor unions, foreign voters and business men.

Make the amendment the sole ultimate objective. "We control or can control in forty states, therefore this method absolutely insures our final victory. . . ."

Give the states equal and joint power with Congress in the matter of enforcement. This will provide against any claim of disturbing the balance of power between the Federal government and the states.

Stress the fact that the amendment is confined to *sale* and touches nothing relating to *use*. . . . Never relax in cutting all liquor's connections with moral forces, "Personal Liberty," the "Sanctity of the Home," "Home Rule," "States' Rights," . . . "keeping liquor always in its sordid nakedness of drugging and destroying humanity for filthy lucre."

Develop local fights so as to produce the best effect upon the national field. Furious onslaughts in such enemy citadels as New York and Pennsylvania will seriously cripple the aid that would otherwise be given to liquor forces in pivotal states and districts.

The amendment is to be the paramount issue in all future national elections.

Oppose all candidates who fail to give a public pledge endorsing the amendment.

Require a similar pledge of candidates for any county or state convention or delegates to any national convention.

Take the offensive everywhere. Attack! Attack! Attack! [12]

Listen to the prophetic outpouring of the Rev. Ira Landrith, of Nashville, Tennessee, who called himself a preordained and predestined Presbyterian:

God wants to kill the liquor traffic through His organized omnipotence, the Church of God, and I believe that the Church of God at its weakest and its worst is better than any other institution on earth at its strongest and best. . . . The liquor traffic must die, and we are here to pronounce your sentence, O King Alcohol! . . . You call yourself a king and yet you lift your red fangs, wet with the heart blood of the hundred thousand men you have murdered this year, and looking into the resolute faces of American churchmen and prohibitionists you plead, Mercy! Mercy! . . . But you die! You die on or before the Fourth of July, 1920, the public welfare requiring it.[13]

Nor did the wets entirely disagree. " The saloon is doomed," said Colonel Gilmore in *Bonfort's Wine and Spirit Circular*.[14]

The submission of a prohibition amendment could only be had from a dry Congress. The vote on the Hobson resolution in 1914 indicated to the League the states in which a concerted effort to elect dry Congressmen would be necessary. The Rep-

[12] *Proceedings of the Sixteenth Convention of the Anti-Saloon League,* 1915, pp. 97–103.    [13] *Ibid.*, p. 279.
[14] Quoted in *Literary Digest*, March 27, 1915. See also *National Enquirer*, Aug. 31 and Dec. 28, 1916.

resentatives from twelve states had voted solidly for the resolution. A majority of the members from each of sixteen other states were favorable. A majority of the members from each of twelve states were unfavorable, and seven state delegations had voted solidly against the resolution. The Nebraska delegation divided evenly. The elections of 1914 had resulted in considerable gains, but the League was by no means sure of the required two-thirds.

### Damning the Sin, Not the Sinner

Following Hobson's suggestion, the League's resolution in the sixty-fourth Congress was so worded as to prohibit only the sale of intoxicating liquor.[15] In the Senate it was amended by striking out the words " for sale " after " manufacture," " transportation " and " importation," and adding a clause prohibiting exportation. Fearing that the amended resolution might be construed as applying to the *use* as well as the *sale* of liquor and thus take on the character of sumptuary legislation, the League's representatives abandoned it.[16]

Senator Sheppard did not like the amendment as it came from the committee. " I am not a prohibitionist," he said, " in the strict sense of the word. I am fighting the liquor traffic. I am against the saloon. I am not in any sense aiming to prevent the personal use of alcoholic beverages." [17]

### Prohibition for the District of Columbia

The League had another reason for being content to lay aside national prohibition for the time being. There were prospects

[15] *Sec. 1.* That the sale, manufacture *for sale*, transportation *for sale* and importation *for sale* of intoxicating liquors for beverage purposes in the United States and all territories subject to the jurisdiction thereof, and the exportation thereof are hereby prohibited.
*Sec. 2.* The Congress and the States shall have power independently or concurrently to enforce this article by all needful legislation.
[16] *Congressional Record*, 64th Congress, 2d Session, pp. 669 and 3118 (Senate Joint Resolution 55 and House Joint Resolution 84).
[17] *Indiana Daily Times*, Jan. 15, 1917.

of a real prohibition law for the District of Columbia. A bill embodying the wishes of the League was introduced by Senator Sheppard on December 7, 1915.[18] Following the usual plan of damning the tool but excusing the user, this bill outlawed the *traffic* in intoxicating liquors, but made no provision for outlawing their personal *use* — in fact, permitting importation for this purpose. The original bill had also forbidden the exportation of alcohol as well as its importation. It so happened that there was a yeast factory in the District which exported large quantities of grain alcohol. Mr. Corby, its owner, was a devoted prohibitionist and friend of the League. When attention was directed to the matter a conference of League officers was called and its attorney announced, " The Sheppard bill will be amended so as to exempt the manufacture of pure grain alcohol " for other than beverage purposes.[19] Accordingly, Sheppard offered an amendment permitting the manufacture and exportation of alcohol for " lawful " purposes. Senator Smoot, insisting that " if we are going to have prohibition we ought to have it in fact," offered a substitute which would have stopped the importation and exportation of liquor altogether. Senator Reed of Missouri added: " Now if it is the theory of the authors of this bill that liquor is a product that poisons the souls and bodies of men . . . and if they propose to prohibit it in the District of Columbia, they ought not to provide that the District should be kept as a place where the raw materials can be manufactured that will destroy men and women in other states." No exception should be made for Corby or anyone else. Reed too proposed to prohibit the manufacture of alcohol in, or its exportation from, the District of Columbia.[20]

[18] *Congressional Record*, 64th Congress, 1st Session, pp. 90, 1665; 2d Session, pp. 1059, 4558.
[19] *Washington Times*, Jan. 30 and Feb. 2, 1916.
[20] *Congressional Record*, 64th Congress, 2d Session, 1916, pp. 370, 367–69, 469.

The League was further embarrassed by a proposal of Senator Underwood's for a referendum of the people of the District on the question. The League's objections to this were neither sound nor plausible and the amendment was only defeated by a tie vote. " I do not doubt for a moment," said Underwood, " that without influence, without a lobby behind it, without threat of political disaster for men who vote against it, this bill would have no chance whatever of passing . . . unless the people of the District . . . were first given an opportunity to vote on it." [21] Apparently the lobby was as powerful as Underwood believed it to be, for all amendments excepting those proposed by Sheppard were defeated and the bill passed by a vote of 55 to 32.

In the House the bill had moved more slowly. A majority was favorable but the District committee which had the bill in charge was hostile. As March 4 approached, Congress was absorbed with the problems of preparedness and foreign relations, with the country on the verge of war. These issues did not cause the League to be any less active in behalf of its own program. The leaders of the House had promised the League's legislative committee that " in the event of dilatory tactics by the wets, a special rule would be granted " setting apart a day for debate and fixing the hour for a vote. This was done on February 28, 1917, four days before adjournment, and the bill was adopted. Contrary to predictions, it was signed by the President.[22]

### Reed Bone-dry Amendment

Senator Reed was bent on driving the drys to the very periphery of aridity. In the same session, when the League was urging a bill to exclude liquor advertisements from the mails,

---

[21] *Ibid.*, pp. 477, 485 and 555.
[22] *Ibid.*, 2d Session, p. 4558; *Proceedings of the Eighteenth Convention of the Anti-Saloon League*, 1917, p. 151. An analysis of the House vote on the District of Columbia bill may be found in Appendix B.

he suggested an amendment to prohibit entirely the shipment of intoxicating liquors into dry territory. This forced the drys to consider prohibition of the *use* of, as well as the *traffic* in, alcoholic beverages. The amendment was adopted in both the Senate and the House and fell like a bomb into the League camp. Dinwiddie expressed dislike for such fanaticism but urged Congressmen and Senators to vote for it.[23] It is difficult to say whether Reed caught the League off guard or whether that organization called his bluff. In speaking of the amendment later, Baker said:

Reed, the Missouri joke, sat down with Tom Gilmore, the Kentucky joke, and worked out the bone-dry amendment in the hope of dividing the prohibition forces, and when hoisted with their own petard, they have the effrontery to claim credit for the only real prohibition, when everybody knows they are sorry they did it.

In any event it was a blow, since in the future the question of personal use could not so easily be sidestepped. Congressman Morrison described what happened:

During the sixty-third Congress the power of the Congressional lobby [i. e., the Anti-Saloon League] became supreme in both houses. . . . In the sixty-fourth Congress it had arranged for a special rule in the House of Representatives to bring the Hobson resolution up for consideration and action. Like a " bolt from the blue " the Reed amendment defied the almightiness of the congressional lobby and passed the Senate before the lobby could get its machine into effective action. The lobby followed the Reed amendment to the House and fought it there, but the spell was broken. The members of the House rejoiced at their newly discovered power to think and act for themselves, and passed the Reed amendment by a vote of three to one. . . . This episode constrained the lobby to abandon the special rule for consideration of the Hobson resolution.[24]

[23] *Congressional Record,* 64th Congress, 2d Session, pp. 1093–1102, 1192–1238, 1302–1488.
[24] *Congressional Record,* 64th Congress, 2d Session, Appendix, pp. 733–42.

### Foundations of Victory

The League had staked its hopes on the elections of 1916. The reëlection of Wilson was expected and it was feared that the Democrats would be against the amendment. No effort was made to commit the presidential candidates. The main desideratum was a dry Congress. " Back in the field we got busy again," said Wheeler. " All the energy we put into the 1914 campaign boiled and bubbled with hotter fire in the campaign of 1916. We laid down such a barrage as candidates for Congress had never seen before, and such as they will, in all likelihood, not see again for years to come. . . . On election night the lights burned late in our Washington office. Elsewhere our state workers were getting the returns. . . . We knew late election night that we had won. Many hours before the country knew whether Hughes or Wilson had triumphed, the dry workers throughout the nation were celebrating our victory. We knew that the Prohibition Amendment would be submitted to the states by the Congress just elected." [25]

The congressional election was not the only straw in the wind. In the two years 1915 and 1916, nine additional states entered the prohibition column. These were Alabama, Arkansas, Iowa, Idaho, South Carolina, Montana, South Dakota, Michigan and Nebraska, making a total of twenty-three dry states. Local option elections continued to harass the worried trade in a dozen states.[26]

Diplomatic relations with Germany had been severed February 3 and the President urged a policy of armed neutrality. " Twelve willful men " determined to talk the proposition to death and the sixty-fourth Congress expired in the arms of this filibuster. The new Congress was convened April 2 to declare war. The League felt confident that it could command

[25] *New York Times*, March 30, 1926.
[26] Colvin, *Prohibition in the United States*, p. 435; *Year Book of the Anti-Saloon League*, 1915, 1916.

"WET" AND "DRY" COUNTY MAP OF THE UNITED STATES
JANUARY 1, 1904

WHITE — PROHIBITION TERRITORY
BLACK — LICENSE TERRITORY

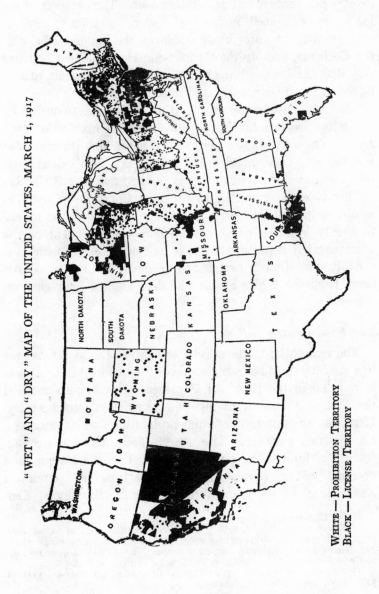

"WET" AND "DRY" MAP OF THE UNITED STATES, MARCH 1, 1917

WHITE — PROHIBITION TERRITORY
BLACK — LICENSE TERRITORY

enough dry votes to put prohibition over. The prospect of doing so was enhanced by the need for conservation of food resources and the unfortunate union of the liquor traffic with the Germans, notably the German-American Alliance. It was now that the League brought into play its propaganda linking liquor with pro-Germanism and treason.[27]

When the Democratic caucus of the House met to outline its legislative program for the special session, the prohibition issue arose. The wets in the caucus served notice that if prohibition was included they would desert their party. This determination was not shaken when it was pointed out that if the Republicans were permitted to organize Congress, prohibition would be included anyway. As a compromise, it was agreed that only legislation recommended by the President or the administrative departments was to be considered. Feeling reasonably sure that a prohibition recommendation would not come from the White House, the drys trained their guns on the Senate.[28]

## The Food Control Bill

The real battle of the special session, so far as the League was concerned, came over the Lever food control bill. It was introduced in the House of Representatives in pursuance of the President's policy of guarding the nation's food supply. Here was an opportunity to put prohibition over at once as a conservation measure. The use of foodstuffs in the manufacture of liquors had long been decried by the League as a criminal waste. When the bill came from the committee amendments by the score were proposed.[29]  Barkley of Ken-

[27] See Chapter II, pp. 67 ff.
[28] *Congressional Record*, 65th Congress, 1st Session, 1917, pp. 1709, 4627, 3571, 1827, 1726, 1828, 1829; *Proceedings of the Eighteenth Convention of the Anti-Saloon League*, 1917; Carver, *Government Control of the Liquor Business in Great Britain and the United States*, New York, 1919, pp. 152–65.
[29] *Congressional Record*, 65th Congress, 1st Session, pp. 3094–96, 3311–12, 3425, 3487, 3906, 4583, 4713, 1663–67.

tucky discovered that by striking out certain clauses and phrases in the bill, it would constitute a prohibition against the use of foodstuffs in the manufacture of intoxicating liquors. He moved to so amend it. On a *viva voce* vote the motion was declared lost. A show of hands was asked and it was again declared lost. A roll call was then demanded and the motion carried.[30] In the Senate the bill was attacked from two sides. The finance committee had drawn the new revenue bill on the basis of the *status quo* and had counted on $325,000,000 from the tax on liquor. The wets attacked the liquor clause of the food control bill as confiscatory and unconstitutional, and threatened to prevent the enactment of the entire program unless the clause applying to beer and wine was stricken out. Senator Lodge denounced " the effort to impose general prohibition on the country by confusing it with the question of the conservation of food." Hardwick of Georgia quoted the *New York World* as saying " If the time ever comes when morality in the United States must depend upon the work at Washington of a pretentious lobby, pious and paid, the Declaration and the Constitution will have been written in vain." On the other hand, pressure from home was continually felt. Senator Pomerene presented petitions from over 130 organizations in Ohio alone, demanding war-time prohibition.[31]

## Wilson Appeals to the League

The matter had apparently reached an impasse when President Wilson sent for Senator Martin of Virginia, Democratic floor leader, and recommended that the bill be modified. Martin in turn sought the ear of the legislative committee of the League. The League's own press release stated:

On last Thursday [i. e., June 28] the legislative committee of the Anti-Saloon League of America, which was in session with the

---

[30] *Ibid.*, pp. 4961, 3544, 3792–3834, 3847–3903, 3937–91, 4131–90.
[31] *Ibid.*, pp. 4196, 4356, 4403–67, 4509–5367; *Proceedings of the Eighteenth Convention of the Anti-Saloon League*, 1917, pp. 151–57.

national committee of the League in Washington, was summoned to the office of United States Senator Martin of Virginia, the Democratic floor leader of the Senate. On arrival at his office we were informed that the President had just sent a messenger to him to ascertain, in view of the prolonged threatened filibuster by the representatives of the liquor interests in the Senate, if we would not consent to strike from the food administration legislation, now pending in the Senate, " beer and wine," as he was anxious that the legislation be speedily enacted. . . . The appeal was made in the name of patriotism. We asked if the appeal had been made to the other side and were informed it was no use, as Senator Penrose of Pennsylvania and his type declared they would filibuster all summer before it should pass, unless beer and wine were exempt. Knowing as we did that that traffic always puts personal gain over patriotism we informed the Senator that if the President would put his request in writing, thus assuming the responsibility, we would give the matter careful consideration.[32]

The League was unwilling to instruct its friends in Congress to make concessions until assured that the President realized and recognized that responsibility for the delay rested with the wets and that the credit for immediate passage of the food bill would be given to the League. Nor were the officials of the League willing to place themselves in the position of retreating before the enemy when victory was so close at hand. To place the affair in the proper light, the President was to write a letter to the legislative committee requesting their consent to the passage of the bill and stating, or at least intimating, that the delay was caused by the wets. President Wilson at first shied from putting such a request in writing. He finally consented, and wrote a letter to the League legislative committee. A carbon copy was sent to Senator Martin. This letter was not satisfactory to the Anti-Saloon League, and Martin requested the President to write a letter setting forth more specifically his request and reasons for it. The second letter follows:

[32] *New York Times*, July 1, 1917. See also *Proceedings of the Eighteenth Convention of the Anti-Saloon League*, 1917, p. 155.

June 29, 1917.

My dear Mr. Cannon:

I am very glad to respond to the request of Senator Martin, the Democratic floor leader in the Senate, that I give to your Legislative Committee an expression of my opinion with regard to the wisest and most patriotic policy to be pursued toward the food administration legislation now pending in Congress.

I regard the immediate passage of the bill as of vital consequence to the safety and defense of the nation. Time is of the essence, and yet it has become evident that heated and protracted debate will delay the passage of the bill indefinitely if the provisions affecting the manufacture of beer and wine are insisted upon.

In these circumstances I have not hesitated to say to members of the Senate who have been kind enough to consult me that it would undoubtedly be in the public interest in this very critical matter if the friends of these provisions should consent to their elimination from the present measure. Feeling that your committee is actuated by the same patriotic motives which inspire me, I am confident that these considerations will seem to you as they seem to me, to be imperative.

With much respect, sincerely yours,

Woodrow Wilson.

To this letter the committee of the League replied:

June 30, 1917.

To the President,
The White House, Washington, D. C.
Sir:

We have earnestly considered the statement in your letter of yesterday to the legislative committee of the Anti-Saloon League of America, that in the face of the present food crisis you are greatly concerned lest the passage of the food administration legislation now pending in Congress be jeopardized by a heated and protracted debate upon certain sections of the bill relating to the manufacture of foodstuffs into intoxicating liquors.

We are aware of the threats made by the friends of beer and wine in the Senate, of an indefinite and protracted filibuster against these provisions of the bill. We beg to advise you that as patriotic Americans, determined to uphold you as commander-in-chief of the army and navy in the present war, we will not, for our constituency, offer any obstruction to the prompt passage of the Food Control Bill.

Of course we cannot presume to indicate to members of Congress what action they should take in view of this request from the President of the United States. They will doubtless act in accordance with their convictions of duty.

We are glad that your request applies only to the pending food administration legislation. It will be our purpose to urge the passage of the legislation prohibiting the waste of foodstuffs in the manufacture of beer and wines at the earliest possible date, either in the form of a separate bill or in connection with other war legislation.

We assure you of our purpose as patriotic American citizens, to coöperate in every possible way in the winning of the great war in which our nation is engaged.[33]

Sincerely and respectfully yours,

P. A. Baker,
*General Superintendent*

Edwin C. Dinwiddie,
*Legislative Superintendent*

James Cannon, Jr.,
Arthur Barton,
Wayne B. Wheeler,
*Legislative Committee*

This letter was received by the drys as a defeat and by the wets as a threat. Senator Vardaman of Mississippi replied to an appeal from his home state to support the bone-dry measure:

The good old ship Prohibition . . . was submarined day before yesterday by the President of the United States. It is now lying on the bottom beneath about forty fathoms of beer and wine. . . . I am afraid some of the officers of the crew deserted before it went down. Will do my best to save the wreck. But it is my deliberate judgment that no power on earth except the people can raise it.[34]

This revelation of the power of the League in the legislative councils of the nation aroused the wets, and they pictured the

[33] *New York Times*, July 1, 1917. See also *Proceedings of the Eighteenth Convention of the Anti-Saloon League*, 1917, p. 4585.   [34] *Ibid.*, p. 5081.

decline of democratic government and the rise of a puritanical oligarchy. The *Cincinnati Enquirer* [35] summed up this feeling editorially:

For brazen effrontery, unmitigated gall, superlative egoism, transcendent audacity, supreme impudence, commend us to the legislative committee of the prohibition lobby that has throttled war legislation and has delayed the nation's preparations for the great conflict in which it is engaged. . . . Here we have the President of the United States under orders to an officious and offensive lobby.

While the League did not " presume to indicate what attitude members of Congress should take," its declaration was sufficient so to grease the legislative slide that the food control bill, minus the beer and wine provision, passed August 10. In conference the bill was amended so that the manufacture of foodstuffs into distilled spirits was prohibited and the President was given authority to extend the restriction to beer and wine when he should deem it necessary.[36]

## The Prohibition Amendment

Whether the League had made a deal with the Senate leaders, whereby the passage of the food control bill was to open the way for a vote on submission, it is impossible to say. According to the League's statement, the stand which its legislative committee had taken toward that bill had so commended itself to the Senate that " the day after its reply to the President, several Senators announced their intention of voting for the resolution to submit the national prohibition amendment." [37]

A resolution providing for such an amendment [38] had been

[35] July 10, 1917; see also *Washington Post,* July 2, 1917.

[36] *Ibid.,* pp. 5367, 5767, 5927; *Proceedings of the Eighteenth Convention of the Anti-Saloon League,* 1917, p. 156.

[37] *Proceedings of the Eighteenth Convention of the Anti-Saloon League,* 1917, p. 156.

[38] *Congressional Record,* 65th Congress, 1st Session; see Senate Joint Resolutions, 3, 17, 22, 29, 35, 74, and House Joint Resolutions 2, 10, 20, 35, 40, 44, 45.

reported favorably June 11. The familiar objection was raised that submission would keep the liquor question in politics for fifty years. Wheeler, who was in his customary place in the Senate gallery, was sent for by Senator Harding, who met him in the lobby. The League had supported Harding in his first campaign for the Ohio legislature, and they were old friends. "You fellows ought to agree to have some limitation put on the time for ratification," Harding said. Wheeler replied that he was not sure of the legality of such a proposition. He was assured that such a provision would mean three or four votes for submission, and Harding suggested that the period for ratification be five years. Wheeler consulted a list of the states to learn in how many there would be two chances at ratification within that period. In one or two states there was some doubt of two chances, so he proposed that the period be extended to six years and this change was made. Borah and others believed any limitation to be unconstitutional, but the amendment was accepted and the resolution passed, August 1, by a vote of 65 to 20.[39] In the House, however, it did not seem expedient to press the matter in the short time before adjournment, and it was allowed to go over until the regular session.

Congress reassembled December 3. Within a week the proposed amendment was reported and December 17 set for the debate. Meanwhile the League's eighteenth convention met in Washington. Victory was close at hand; four states had adopted prohibition within the year, bringing the total to twenty-seven. This was no time to ground arms. "You have got to marshal, in the lower house of Congress within the next few days, 290 out of 435 votes if all are present and voting," warned a speaker who called himself a "lobbyist for Jesus Christ." "My appeal to you is that you strengthen the hands of your committee in this city, that you fortify your Third

[39] *Congressional Record*, 65th Congress, 1st Session, 1917, pp. 52, 5587–5665; Wheeler, *New York Times*, March 31, 1926.

House." One League official boasted that he had seen to the sending of nine hundred telegrams in one day to Congressmen during the previous session. Wheeler insisted that the amendment must be passed in that session of Congress. His reason is interesting: " We have got to win it now because when 1920 comes and reapportionment is here, forty new wet Congressmen will come from the great wet centers with their rapidly increasing population." So much was the Anti-Saloon League concerned with the will of the majority.[40]

As the time for consideration of the resolution in the House approached, the wets lamented the fact that a secret ballot could not be taken. " Every Congressman knows," said the *Washington Times*,[41] " that if the ballot on the constitutional amendment were a secret ballot, making it impossible for the Anti-Saloon League bosses to punish disobedience, the amendment would not pass."

The great day at length arrived and the House moved to a consideration of the resolution. The debate developed no new ideas on either side. The familiar chords were struck. The drys again advanced the absurd claim that submission was a referendum, to which a North Carolina member retorted, " We are not mere automatons to register the will of the Anti-Saloon League." But what the drys lacked in argument they made up in organization.

There was a demand that some time be allowed the liquor

[40] *Proceedings of the Eighteenth Convention of the Anti-Saloon League,* 1917, p. 75.

[41] Dec. 14, 1917. On Friday, December 7, 1917, a letter was sent to all members of Congress which declared: " The Anti-Saloon League of America has retarded the national preparedness for more than a year and produced unheard-of disorganization in all branches of commerce and supply. . . . Every step toward preparedness was literally purchased from the Anti-Saloon League organization by yielding the privilege of destroying by legislative sabotage the nation's resources and revenue. . . . What are the works of the I. W. W. compared with the machinations of the League corporation? Prohibition is war on American industries and an aid to our enemies." To all of which the League replied contemptuously, " And this letter is from the German-American Brewers led by C. J. Hexamer, the Kaiser's representative in America." — *Proceedings of the Eighteenth Convention of the Anti-Saloon League,* 1917, p. 153.

interests to adjust their affairs, before the amendment took effect. " There was no good answer to this argument so we traded jackknives with them," said Wheeler. " We agreed that we would stand for a year's time after ratification before the amendment should become effective if, on the other hand, they would add a year's time to the six years voted by the Senate as the time limit for ratification. That gave seven years for ratification and one year for the amendment to take effect." [42]

These changes were made and the enforcement section altered. The resolution was adopted by a vote of 282 to 128 — a majority well over the necessary two-thirds. The following day, December 18, the Senate concurred in the House amendment, 47 ayes to 8 nays.[43] The proposed amendment was offered to the states in the following form:

Sec. 1. After one year from the ratification of this article the manufacture, sale or transportation of intoxicating liquors within, the importation thereof into, or the exportation thereof from the United States and all territory subject to the jurisdiction thereof for beverage purposes is hereby prohibited.

Sec. 2. The Congress and the several States shall have concurrent power to enforce this article by appropriate legislation.

Sec. 3. This article shall be inoperative unless it shall have been ratified as an amendment to the Constitution by the legislatures of the several States, as provided in the Constitution, within seven years from the date of the submission hereof to the States by the Congress.

### Ratification

The next hurdle was ratification. The League felt sure that it could count on states with prohibition laws to ratify promptly. Twenty-seven states had such laws. This left nine non-prohibition states to be brought into line. Only twelve states held regular sessions of their legislatures in 1918. Of these, eight

[42] Wheeler, *New York Times*, March 31, 1926.
[43] *Congressional Record*, 65th Congress, 2d Session, 1917, pp. 422–70, 478. An analysis of the House vote on submission may be found in Appendix C.

### TABLE IV

RATIFICATION OF PROHIBITION AMENDMENT BY STATE LEGISLATURES

| STATE | SENATE | | | LOWER HOUSE | |
|---|---|---|---|---|---|
| | Date | Yea–Nay | | Date | Yea–Nay |
| (1) Mississippi........ | Jan.  8, 1918 | 28–5 | | Jan.  8, 1918 | 93–3 |
| (2) Virginia........... | Jan. 10, 1918 | 30–8 | | Jan. 11, 1918 | 84–13 |
| (3) Kentucky......... | Jan. 14, 1918 | 28–6 | | Jan. 14, 1918 | 66–10 |
| (4) South Carolina.... | Jan. 18, 1918 | 28–6 | | Jan. 28, 1918 | 66–29 |
| (5) North Dakota..... | Jan. 25, 1918 | 43–2 | | Jan. 25, 1918 | 96–10 |
| (6) Maryland......... | Feb. 13, 1918 | 18–7 | | Feb.  8, 1918 | 58–36 |
| (7) Montana.......... | Feb. 19, 1918 | 35–2 | | Feb. 18, 1918 | 77–8 |
| (8) Texas............. | Feb. 28, 1918 | 15–7 | | Mar.  4, 1918 | 72–30 |
| (9) Delaware.......... | Mar. 18, 1918 | 13–3 | | Mar. 14, 1918 | 27–6 |
| (10) South Dakota..... | Mar. 19, 1918 | 43–0 | | Mar. 20, 1918 | 86–0 |
| (11) Massachusetts..... | Apr.  2, 1918 | 27–12 | | Mar. 26, 1918 | 145–91 |
| (12) Arizona........... | May 23, 1918 | 17–0 | | May 24, 1918 | 29–3 |
| (13) Georgia........... | June 26, 1918 | 34–2 | | June 26, 1918 | 129–24 |
| (14) Louisiana......... | Aug.  6, 1918 | 21–20 | | Aug.  8, 1918 | 69–41 |
| (15) Florida........... | Nov. 27, 1918 | 25–2 | | Nov. 27, 1918 | 61–3 |
| (16) Michigan.......... | Jan.  2, 1919 | 30–0 | | Jan.  2, 1919 | 88–3 |
| (17) Ohio.............. | Jan.  7, 1919 | 20–12 | | Jan.  7, 1919 | 85–30 |
| (18) Oklahoma ........ | Jan.  7, 1919 | 43–0 | | Jan.  7, 1919 | 90–8 |
| (19) Maine............. | Jan.  8, 1919 | 29–0 | | Jan.  8, 1919 | 122–20 |
| (20) Idaho............. | Jan.  8, 1919 | 38–0 | | Jan.  7, 1919 | 62–0 |
| (21) West Virginia...... | Jan.  9, 1919 | 27–0 | | Jan.  9, 1919 | 78–3 |
| (22) Washington........ | Jan. 13, 1919 | 42–0 | | Jan. 13, 1919 | 93–0 |
| (23) Tennessee......... | Jan.  9, 1919 | 28–2 | | Jan. 13, 1919 | 82–0 |
| (24) California......... | Jan. 10, 1919 | 24–15 | | Jan. 13, 1919 | 48–28 |
| (25) Indiana........... | Jan. 13, 1919 | 41–6 | | Jan. 14, 1919 | 87–11 |
| (26) Illinois............ | Jan.  8, 1919 | 30–15 | | Jan. 14, 1919 | 84–66 |
| (27) Arkansas.......... | Jan. 14, 1919 | 34–0 | | Jan. 13, 1919 | 93–2 |
| (28) North Carolina..... | Jan. 10, 1919 | 49–0 | | Jan. 14, 1919 | 93–10 |
| (29) Alabama........... | Jan. 14, 1919 | 23–11 | | Jan. 14, 1919 | 64–34 |
| (30) Kansas............ | Jan. 14, 1919 | 39–0 | | Jan. 14, 1919 | 121–0 |
| (31) Oregon............ | Jan. 15, 1919 | 30–0 | | Jan. 14, 1919 | 53–3 |
| (32) Iowa.............. | Jan. 15, 1919 | 42–7 | | Jan. 15, 1919 | 86–13 |
| (33) Utah.............. | Jan. 15, 1919 | 16–0 | | Jan. 14, 1919 | 43–0 |
| (34) Colorado.......... | Jan. 15, 1919 | 34–1 | | Jan. 15, 1919 | 63–2 |
| (35) New Hampshire..... | Jan. 15, 1919 | 19–4 | | Jan. 15, 1919 | 221–131 |
| (36) Nebraska.......... | Jan. 13, 1919 | 31–1 | | Jan. 16, 1919 | 98–0 |
| (37) Missouri.......... | Jan. 16, 1919 | 22–10 | | Jan. 16, 1919 | 104–36 |
| (38) Wyoming.......... | Jan. 16, 1919 | 26–0 | | Jan. 16, 1919 | 52–0 |
| (39) Wisconsin......... | Jan. 16, 1919 | 19–11 | | Jan. 17, 1919 | 58–35 |
| (40) Minnesota........ | Jan. 16, 1919 | 48–11 | | Jan. 17, 1919 | 92–36 |
| (41) New Mexico........ | Jan. 20, 1919 | 12–4 | | Jan. 16, 1919 | 45–1 |
| (42) Nevada............ | Jan. 21, 1919 | 14–1 | | Jan. 20, 1919 | 33–3 |
| (43) Vermont........... | Jan. 16, 1919 | 26–3 | | Jan. 29, 1919 | 155–58 |
| (44) New York......... | Jan. 29, 1919 | 27–24 | | Jan. 23, 1919 | 81–66 |
| (45) Pennsylvania....... | Feb. 25, 1919 | 29–16 | | Feb.  4, 1919 | 110–93 |
| (46) New Jersey........ | Mar.  9, 1922 | 12–4 | | Mar.  7, 1922 | 33–24 |
| | | 1,309–340 | | | 2,975–1,023 |

ratified. Seven states called special sessions to ratify, making a total of fifteen by January 1, 1919. In that month twenty-nine additional states ratified. In less than fourteen months the required number of states had accepted it. Rhode Island and Connecticut alone failed to approve. According to the provisions of the amendment, on January 16, 1920, one year after the ratification by the thirty-sixth state, national prohibition became a part of the fundamental law of the land.

The celerity with which the amendment was ratified took the wets by surprise. " The grip held by the Anti-Saloon League over the state legislatures was never better illustrated than in the manner in which these bodies obeyed the command to ratify," the brewers said. " In vain were suggestions made that the lawmaking bodies were without instructions from the people on this most important question. In vain were efforts made to have the sentiment of the electorate tested by referendum voting. In all but three states in the Union, the machinery of the prohibition autocracy worked smoothly, mercilessly and swiftly, and scarcely a year elapsed after the proposed article was submitted when it was announced that the requisite number of legislatures had acted favorably and national prohibition had been imbedded in the Constitution of the United States." [44]

The result was never in doubt. Only in New York, Pennsylvania and Illinois was the vote at all close. In six states — Kansas, Utah, Wyoming, South Dakota, Idaho and Washington — it was unanimous in both houses. In several others there was no dissent in one house. More than eighty percent of the members of the forty-six state legislatures were recorded in favor of the amendment. It is not unreasonable to assume that public opinion was pretty generally favorable.

The major battles were in Illinois, New York and Wisconsin. The Illinois League campaigned in every election district in the

[44] *Year Book of the United States Brewers' Association*, 1919, p. 18.

state with the result that a dry majority was returned to the house, which voted for ratification 84 to 66. In the senate, under the system of county representation, the dry rural counties were dominant and the amendment was approved two to one.[45]

The fight in New York was more dramatic. " Ratification by New York was the hardest blow struck the liquor traffic. It destroyed forever the plea that it was not fair for small states to put national prohibition over the large states. . . . It was won by out-guessing and out-generaling the foe, by organization, by hard hitting and merciless fighting. . . . To win, it was necessary to build the greatest permanent Anti-Saloon League organization ever built in any state. . . ."[46]

The victory in New York was considered of more importance than merely adding another state to the list of those ratifying. It marked the fall of the chief stronghold of the liquor interests in America. The ratification fight found New York with twenty dry cities and 650 dry towns out of a total of 932.[47] The dry sentiment was found chiefly in the up-state rural districts. The cities, especially New York, were notoriously wet. Tammany was opposed to prohibition in any form. The state's congressional delegation was wet. Out of forty-three members in the lower house of Congress, only thirteen voted for submission. In the election of 1918, Governor Whitman was defeated for reëlection by Smith, but the League claimed a dry legislature. The Democrats had declared against ratification; the Republicans avoided the question. The League attributed Whitman's defeat to the failure of his party to declare itself.

[45] Of the 102 counties in the state, 55 were entirely dry, 46 were partly dry, and only one was wholly wet. Out of 1160 cities and villages, 917 were dry and only 243 were wet. Outside of Chicago, 77 percent of the population of the state was living in dry territory. — *Year Book of the Anti-Saloon League,* 1925, pp. 87 ff.; *Christian Science Monitor,* June 6, 1918.
[46] Anderson's Report *Proceedings of the Nineteenth Convention of the Anti-Saloon League,* 1919, p. 296.
[47] *Year Book of the Anti-Saloon League,* 1925, p. 121.

" In some cases the Anti-Saloon League had to oppose not only the Democrats and the wet interests but the Republican organization. . . . The Anti-Saloon League advised the governor's managers and backers that they were in danger of defeat, but instead of heeding, they did their utmost to keep the League out of the campaign. . . . After doing all that could be done for the governor . . . the Anti-Saloon League then turned in and saved the legislature, in spite of double-dealing and incompetence on the part of the political managers." [48] Twenty-nine Republicans, a working majority, were returned to the senate. Of these, twenty were either committed to ratification or came from dry districts and could be expected to vote dry. In the lower house a favorable vote was certain. The Republicans had 94 members, the Democrats 54 and the Socialists 2, and on January 23, by a strict party vote, the assembly ratified, 81 to 66.

The danger spot was the senate. With only twenty sure votes out of a total of fifty-one, and with nine Republicans doubtful, there was but one way to make sure of victory.[49] Ratification must be made a party issue, and this became the object of the League strategy.

As the fight narrowed down it seemed important to the drys to secure the vote of Senator Whitley of Rochester. Progress along that line, however, was slow. Whitley didn't even want to see the Anti-Saloon League men. Finally, S. E. Nicholson, one of the League workers, went to New York and saw Will Hays . . . and secured from Mr. Hays a letter of introduction to George W. Aldrich, the Republican boss of Rochester.[50]

[48] During the 1918 campaign Anderson estimated that " representatives of the Anti-Saloon League of New York traveled three-quarters of a million miles, made fifty thousand personal calls and addressed over five thousand meetings at which they spoke to over half a million people." In addition the League sent out over a million communications by mail and circulated the equivalent of fifty million book pages of literature. To which might be added the newspaper publicity which the League got, up to a hundred million copies. — *American Issue*, New York Edition, June 14, 1919.

[49] Anderson, *Ratification Certain if the People Insist* (pamphlet), 1919.

[50] Wheeler, *New York Times*, April 1, 1926.

Nicholson appealed to Aldrich on the ground that it would be politically unwise for the Republicans in New York not to ratify. New-York could not defeat the amendment, since thirty-six states had already ratified, but he urged New York Republicans to get on the wagon if they wanted to play in the band. Aldrich appealed to Whitley, who agreed to enter the caucus. The caucus voted to make prohibition a party measure, and on January 29, by a vote of 27 to 24, the senate ratified.

Governor Smith had urged that the question be submitted to the people, and the League has been sharply criticized for refusing to allow this. The League claimed that this came with poor grace from the wets who for years had denied the people this privilege. It also insisted that the Constitution of the United States specifically requires ratification by the legislature.[51]

The organization for ratification in Wisconsin was equally efficient. R. P. Hutton became superintendent in June, 1917, leaving sixteen months to prepare for the primary elections, which took place in September, 1918. It was believed that the results of the Republican primary would tell the tale. "We used a million book pages of literature per month," said Hutton. "We put on a country schoolhouse campaign. . . . We put factory experts to speak in the factories and got the com-

[51] Anderson, *New York Times*, Sept. 4, 1921. When in 1916 the League had been fighting for its optional prohibition referendum bill, the attorney for the New York State Brewers' Association had said, " Under our form of government, the people vote on the liquor question just as they do on all other questions when they elect members of the legislatures whose duty it is to make laws to govern all kinds of human activity. There is no more reason why the people should vote directly on the question of granting a license to sell liquor, than on that of granting a license to a druggist or a certificate to a doctor or on the manner in which a butcher or bakery shop be conducted. . . . The theory of state and Federal government does not contemplate that the people of any state or locality should meet and pass laws." The League's position was equally inconsistent with their 1916 stand when they insisted " that every voter in New York has an inherent right, which he should be permitted to exercise, to vote on the liquor question." It makes considerable difference whose ox is being gored.

panies to pay the men for listening. We built up a Council of One Thousand to back us — business and labor leaders. . . . We enlisted the Hemlock Hardwood Lumber Association in its entirety. We sold the factories billboards and posters which were changed bi-weekly, and a monthly educational scientific tract in tabloid form which went into the pay envelopes. We organized the drys in every county. We helped to select dry legislative candidates who could get votes. We listed the two-thirds of our voters who habitually failed to vote in the primary, divided them into blocks of five, put a dry corporal over each five, and got 138,000 of these stay-at-homes to the polls on the primary day, September 3, knowing who was the dry candidate for senate and assembly, and absolutely pledged to vote for them. We staged the biggest demonstration in Madison the state has ever seen. We ratified! and in the archives at Washington, Wisconsin was one of the thirty-six! We put it over." [52]

[52] *Proceedings of the Nineteenth Convention of the Anti-Saloon League,* 1919, p. 322.

# CHAPTER VII

## THE WIDOW'S MITE

Reform organizations, even those devoted to the Lord's work, cannot, like the Children of Israel in the desert of Paran, rely upon manna from heaven. They must have money.

The Anti-Saloon League began very modestly. There were no millionaires to sign checks in six figures to put the organization on its feet. The early founders of the League, with one or two exceptions, were ministers. They were men of small means. Money had to come, if at all, from small subscribers. The story goes that in the first campaign in Ohio in 1895, Russell, after borrowing to the limit of his credit, pawned his watch to buy stamps. At the organization meeting at Oberlin in 1893, $513 a year was subscribed for three years. Oberlin not only gave birth to the League, but nursed it during those early years with gifts aggregating a thousand dollars annually. By May, 1894, eight thousand dollars had been raised through some three hundred local committees. It was a puny start, but it gave the leaders courage to carry on.[1]

The League's earliest guardian angel was E. W. Metcalf of Elyria. Through Metcalf, A. I. Root, president of the Root Bee Company, his friend and fellow church member, became interested. Up to 1913 the Root Company had contributed upwards of thirty thousand dollars to the League. From such humble beginnings the Anti-Saloon League prospered until at the height of the campaign for national prohibition it was spending about $2,500,000 a year.[2]

[1] Cherrington, *History of the Anti-Saloon League*, pp. 18, 21.
[2] W. B. Wheeler, "The Inside Story of Prohibition," *New York Times*, March 29, 1926.

*Rockefeller and the League*

As its prosperity increased, the League was charged with being a corrupt, corporation-controlled political lobby. Colonel Gilmore of the Model License League declared that he had seen a list of six corporation heads, each of whom contributed a hundred thousand dollars to the Anti-Saloon League.[3] He furnished no evidence, and the League denied it. Captain William Backus, a veteran Ohio brewer, charged that the Anti-Saloon League was maintained with Rockefeller money:

> Invariably, the Anti-Saloon League members of the assembly can be counted on to do the right thing for the Standard Oil Company in this state. . . . Rockefeller, through his daughter, Mrs. McCormick of Chicago, is backing the Anti-Saloon League of America to the extent of $350,000. If it were not for Rockefeller, the Anti-Saloon League would go out of business.[4]

He offered no proof. The entire yearly income of the Anti-Saloon League at that time was scarcely $500,000. Stories of Rockefeller's gifts are legion. " It is reported that John D. Rockefeller has secretly given $5,000,000 to fight the saloons." [5] " John D. Rockefeller has given $500,000 to the Anti-Saloon League . . . to start newspapers in several states . . . to attack the liquor traffic. . . ." Eastern brewers alleged that these contributions were for the purpose of keeping the saloon question " before the public to detract attention from the methods of the Standard Oil Company." [6] Later it was charged that Rockefeller contributed $15,000,000 to the ratification fight in New York.[7]

Such smoke does not necessarily indicate fire, but it is acknowledged that the Rockefellers contributed substantially to

[3] *American Issue*, Maryland Edition, May 30, 1908.
[4] Memorandum in files of United States Brewers' Association. See also *Detroit Free Press*, July 4, 1908.
[5] *New York Evening Journal*, Jan. 21, 1910.
[6] *Trade News* of Sioux Falls, South Dakota, Feb. 15, 1910.
[7] *New York American*, March 26, 1923. The same paper carried a statement from Anderson denying this charge and placing the contribution at $75,000.

the Anti-Saloon League. In 1910 a list of all Rockefeller donations up to and including that year showed that the League had received a total of $100,000.[8] In 1919 John D. Rockefeller, Jr., declared that " within a period covering twenty years these contributions have amounted to only $350,323.67.[9]

What prompted Mr. Rockefeller to contribute? Was it because of his Baptist reformist background? Was it because he believed prohibition to be good business? Was it to secure political power? Perhaps it was a combination of these reasons. There is an early statement of John D. Rockefeller, Jr., that " the cause of temperance is in keeping with the belief of both my father and myself." He explained his contributions after the adoption of the Eighteenth Amendment thus:

> To fail in the observance and enforcement of such a law strikes at the very foundation of orderly government and is in that way an attack upon civil liberty, for in a republic there can be no freedom for the individual if there is no respect for and enforcement of the laws which have been enacted in a manner prescribed by the people themselves in the constitution which they have adopted.[10]

Other motives were sometimes alleged. In 1910, M. S. Poulson, League superintendent in Nebraska, was reported as saying:

> John D. Rockefeller's representative offered to subscribe a substantial sum to the Anti-Saloon League if we would promise to stop our fight against Speaker Cannon and the men who, with him, have been holding up temperance legislation at Washington. . . . We refused the money and told the representative we didn't want it.[11]

A California paper quoted him further:

[8] *Chicago Record Herald*, Oct. 18, 1910. Earlier in the same year the *Newark Evening News* (Mar. 3, 1910), a wet paper, in an article on " Leading American Philanthropists," gave a similar list showing the League item as $350,000. Rockefeller alone, of the men included, is recorded as a League contributor.

[9] Letter to the editor of the *St. Louis Post Dispatch*, Sept. 29, 1919. This statement was repeated on April 13, 1920.

[10] *New York Evening Post*, April 4, 1921.

[11] *Globe and Commercial Advertiser*, Lincoln, Jan. 8, 1910.

Mr. Rockefeller was informed he did not have enough money to buy us off. . . . We are not opposing these men politically, but when they deliberately block the way to needed reforms and go so far as to try to buy us off, why the Anti-Saloon League intends to go into the home districts and expose them to the utmost. . . . I have become convinced from the tactics of such men as Rockefeller that they are subservient to the trusts. Cannon is a dangerous evil in our national affairs, and he and his supporters must be routed if the cause of temperance is to receive any impetus at Washington. There is not enough money in the Rockefeller coffers to buy us away from our fight for reasonable interstate liquor shipment legislation. . . . I believe the Anti-Saloon League should join in the present struggle to defeat the purpose of the Cannon-Aldrich combine.[12]

## Big Business Aids

The Anti-Saloon League never became a one-man organization. Rockefeller's contributions,[13] important as they were, do not explain a fund of $2,500,000. Where did it all come from? There are, of course, many stories of huge slush funds donated by business men convinced of the economic soundness of prohibition. On March 31, 1924, Congressman Dyer of Missouri inserted in the *Congressional Record* a letter from a joint committee representing the American Federation of Labor, charging that " The League is spending $2,500,000 a year. . . . The big contributors of money constitute the real power behind the Anti-Saloon League." In support of these charges he cited a letter [14] of S. S. Kresge which is sufficiently interesting to reproduce in full:

[12] *The Herald*, Los Angeles, Jan. 9, 1910. It was also said that when Governor Herrick of Ohio was defeated by J. M. Pattison, with the backing of the League, " Rockefeller was so grieved that he withdrew his contribution for a year." — *Detroit Free Press*, July 4, 1908, quoting C. R. Mabee, a former League employee.

[13] The importance of the Rockefeller contributions to the New York League is reflected in the statement made by Anderson in 1923, when Rockefeller withdrew his support, that the League should be made independent of large contributors so that " no such unhappy chance as the appointment of a hostile Rockefeller representative [Fosdick] can ever again jeopardize the work of the League." *New York American*, March 26, 1923.

[14] *Congressional Record*, 68th Congress, 1st Session, pp. 5290–92.

Mr. Charles L. Knower,
St. Louis, Mo.
Dear Mr. Knower:

This message is sent because of your interest in " good business."

A committee of 55 persons, called the manufacture and business committee of the Anti-Saloon League of America, began eight years ago to help the National Anti-Saloon League win and hold prohibition. A good many have assisted us. *League men say our aid has been an essential factor for success.* Now we are in the hot fight to uphold flag and law and finish the job. More help is needed. We need you!

Besides the state organization the national division of the Anti-Saloon League under separate budget, has 200 employees who keep the organization everywhere strong and by voice and print do tremendous educational service. In its legal, legislative and law enforcement departments it stimulates and backs up enforcement of the law throughout the nation. Additional contributions are urgently required for current expenses and for special work for 1924 now begun, including the big convention at Washington in January, for publicity and public sentiment.

Even if you assist this work in your own state, it is increasingly and vitally necessary that those who have a business interest like the members of this committee and you shall strongly help the national organization also. Knowing from close touch the national efficiency and needs, besides helping in the Michigan League, I have personally given during the past year $10,000 to the National League as a " good business investment."

Your assistance was never more needed than right now. Please give personal and special attention to this and send a check for $1000, $500, $250, or $100, which will suitably indicate your desire to keep the liquor " bloodsucker " off decent trade. Read the enclosed copy of Roger Babson's letter [15] to Mr. Russell, the secretary of this com-

---

[15] The Babson letter cited by Mr. Kresge says in part: " The great improvement in business which followed the war, and is so clearly shown by the Babson Chart, was very largely the result of the influence of prohibition. . . ." (From files of the Anti-Saloon League of New York.)

Discussing the sources of the Anti-Saloon League's finances, the 1919 *Report of the United States Brewers' Association* gives the following: (1) Pledge system. (2) Contributions from " Captains of Industry." (3) Special sums raised at conventions and other gatherings. (4) Legacies of the " faithful." Explaining the contributions of business men, this report assigns as reasons, the belief, among other things that prohibition would result in (a) more efficient workers, (b)

mittee, and then mail your check to Foster Copeland, treasurer, or to S. S. Kresge, chairman, in the enclosed envelope. Our committee will appreciate your coöperation.

Yours for the protection of law,

S. S. Kresge,

Chairman, Manufacture

and Business Committee.

The Anti-Saloon League has steadfastly refused to divulge the names of its principal contributors. This attitude has been adopted for a variety of reasons. Large contributors frequently requested or required that their names be kept secret. Business men and manufacturers who made contributions did not want to risk the danger of political and economic reprisals from the enemies of the League. " Many a man hates the liquor traffic," said Mr. Anderson, " and wants to oppose it, who does not feel called upon to stand out alone as a target for the abuse of the saloon and its allies. The Anti-Saloon League offers a way in which that man can count effectively against the saloon without becoming known. We sacredly guard the names of our contributors." [16] In asking that the names of contributors be kept secret by the committee investigating campaign expenditures in June, 1926, Wheeler gave as his reason the annoyance which besets persons known to have made large contributions to any cause.[17] There is considerable evidence that the brewers systematically made war on business men who supported the cause of prohibition.[18]

---

workers willing to accept less pay since they would no longer be able to spend their money for liquor, (c) improved shop conditions.

[16] *American Issue,* Maryland Edition, Oct. 17, 1908.

[17] *United States Daily,* June 28, 1926.

[18] See Chapter X.

While it is impossible here to list any considerable number of the larger contributors to the Anti-Saloon League funds, some names have been made public. Among those who have at one time or another contributed in amounts of over $500 may be listed John D. Rockefeller, Jr.; S. S. Kresge; A. Z. Blair, Portsmouth, Ohio; Robert Young, Columbus, Ohio; Alexander Neffs, Neffs, Ohio; Summerfield Baldwin, Baltimore, Maryland; D. C. Boyd, Galion, Ohio; Samuel Dunlap, Circleville, Ohio; James N. Gamble, of the Proctor and Gamble

The belief that prohibition means sober workmen and an increased buying power, due to the release of money formerly spent on drink, is one obvious motive for business men's support. According to the League's critics, however, this was not the only motive. For example, in 1908, the *Sacramento Union* charged that manufacturers and business men were supporting the Anti-Saloon League so that when prohibition was achieved the loss of revenue so occasioned " will prove the continued necessity of a high protective tariff." [19]

By 1910 the League was frankly appealing to manufacturers and business men. In December, 1911, Purley Baker, then general superintendent, said: " The League must have more money; it cannot continue to rely entirely on contributions from servant girls and neighborhood janitors." Appealing to the rich to donate as they give to schools and colleges, " some of them of doubtful moral standards," he said, " the one supreme need is more literature, more postage, more stenographers. . . . We have about 350 men now in the field. In the next five years we should have a thousand, and men of the finest type stand ready to offer themselves as fast as they can be assured that the reward of their consecration is not starvation." [20]

Similar sentiments were expressed in Anderson's Bluebook of the League.[21] " Large gifts are especially valuable in the early stages of the work because they make it possible to seize

Co., Cincinnati, Ohio; A. F. Root, Medina, Ohio; E. W. Metcalf, Elyria, Ohio; J. R. Sayre, Sayerville, New Jersey; V. Everett Macy, New York City.

The author does not wish to be misunderstood as defending secrecy with regard to these contributions. Political morality would be improved by complete publicity. However, in view of the political morals of the time and the nature of the prohibition fight, arousing as it did such bitter animosity, the League has been no worse than hundreds of other pressure organizations. Those interested may find an additional list of League contributors in Appendix D.

[19] *Sacramento Union*, March 27, 1908.

[20] *Proceedings of the Fourteenth Convention of the Anti-Saloon League,* 1911.

[21] *The Church in Action Against the Saloon*, p. 50. This manual for League workers was in some respects the League's most important publication.

strategic opportunities and reap the full fruits of years of preparatory work, to start new lines of work and enlarge the 'plant.' " But such large contributions were few and far between. According to Wayne Wheeler:

Ninety percent of the money came from persons who had pledged themselves to send us from 25 cents to $2.00 a month. In only one case . . . did the national organization receive so much as $25,000 a year from a single source and only five persons contributed $10,000 a year or more. I am sure that none of the state organizations fared better. The money came from little people of the country, just as the prohibition sentiment came from them.[22]

*The Widow's Mite*

Considerable interest has centered about the names of the larger contributors and their motives. The circumstances and motives of humbler donors have received scant attention. Many touching stories have been told of drunkards' wives, of newsboys and children who have contributed to the League funds out of gratitude for its work in executing old John Barleycorn. A widow who donated ten dollars annually to the cause, wrote the following:

I am a widow with another family to help, a widowed niece who is bedridden, with three boys all tubercular and one blind, and a sister with heart trouble. Needless to say, it all came through drink. Father fell downstairs 2:00 a. m. and killed himself while drunk . . . Thus you see that until I see my way clear I cannot increase my pledge.[23]

A little boy with fewer troubles but equal sincerity sent in the following letter with his contribution:

I am only a little boy (10) ten years old. That's why I give so little. My father is dead, and we are very poor, Mother, little Sister and I. I am a tither and try to be as good as Father was.[24]

[22] Wheeler, " The Inside Story of Prohibition," *New York Times,* March 29, 1926. [23] *American Issue,* New York Edition, May 10, 1924.
[24] *American Issue,* New York Edition, March 11, 1922.

An aged subscriber wrote:

When I agreed to aid the Anti-Saloon League for five years, it did not occur to me that I might not be here that long, so I wish to pay up my dues as fast as I can. I am sending you ten dollars now and hope to send the remainder ere long.

I am almost eighty-eight years old and I do not expect to be here many years longer, but I want to be square here when I leave.[25]

Frank Kent of the *Baltimore Sun,* after a study of the League in 1922, placed the number of its contributors at seven hundred thousand.[26] During the 1926 convention of the League, Raymond Robbins, asked by a *Chicago Tribune* reporter where the Anti-Saloon League got its money, said:

I know where some of its resources come from. Some of them come from the mothers and wives thankful for the fact that because of the Anti-Saloon League they have sober husbands, food and shoes for their children and better furniture for their homes. . . . Some more of it comes from grateful employers who bear testimony . . . to the increased efficiency and regularity of labor, the larger power of production in their shops, the lessened injured material and broken machinery that comes through the sober workingmen of the United States. . . . Some of it comes from those bankers of America, grateful for the tremendous increase in the savings of the people.[27]

In reporting the League convention in 1925 for the *New York World,* the Rev. Sam Small, a former dry worker, said: "The gifts of rich men were negligible always and still are, in the grand total of League resources. The millions came from men and women from ocean to ocean who subscribed not more than fifty cents per month, year by year." [28]

It is impossible to say definitely what proportion of the League income comes from these various sources. Contribu-

---

[25] *American Issue,* New York Edition, Sept. 9, 1922.
[26] Letter to the author.
[27] Memorandum in files of Anti-Saloon League of New York.
[28] *New York World,* Nov. 6, 1925. This statement is significant, since Dr. Small has repudiated the Anti-Saloon League and prohibition, and cannot consequently be accused of seeking to whitewash the organization.

butions range all the way from ten cents to twenty-five thousand dollars.[29]  The number of persons who give more than a hundred dollars are few in proportion to the number of small contributors.  When in the Maryland local option campaign of 1908 the League spent twenty thousand dollars, it was stated that " This money has been given by a half dozen men who gave several hundred dollars each, about five persons who gave from fifty to one hundred dollars, and about four thousand men and women who contributed annually from one to twenty-five dollars, the average being about four dollars." [30]  This instance may be considered typical.

In the foregoing discussion no effort has been made to separate the finances of the national League from those of the state branches.  It must be borne in mind that, although they derive their incomes in essentially the same manner and from the same source, the finances of the national and state Leagues are kept quite distinct.  The size of the contributions to the national League may be indicated by the fact that from 1911 to 1925 it received only two subscriptions of ten thousand dollars or over.  Barely two percent of the income was in amounts of a hundred dollars or more.  Only a small fraction of the contributions exceeded a thousand dollars.  Generally speaking, therefore, over the period 1911 to 1925, approximately 98 percent of the income of the national League was received in amounts of less than a hundred dollars.  In those state Leagues from which reports could be obtained, contributions were distributed as indicated in Table V.

### The Pledge Plan

The backbone of the League's financial structure has always been the contributions solicited through the churches.[31]  The

---

[29] H. M. Chalfant, " The Anti-Saloon League — Why and What? " *The Annals of the American Academy of Political and Social Science*, Sept. 1923.

[30] *American Issue*, Maryland Edition, Oct. 2, 1909.

[31] Some money was raised in meetings outside the churches, but the amount

TABLE V

SIZE OF CONTRIBUTIONS TO STATE LEAGUES

| STATE | $1,000 OR MORE | $100–$1,000 |
|---|---|---|
| Arkansas | None | None |
| Connecticut | None | 3 percent |
| Illinois | No records | No records |
| Kansas | One in 1925 | None |
| Louisiana | None | Five in three years |
| Mississippi | None | None |
| Nevada | None | None |
| New Jersey | 22 percent | 8 percent |
| North Carolina | None | 10 percent |
| Oklahoma | None | Very few; two of $500 in 1909 |
| Pennsylvania | One only | 1911–19, very few 1920–25, about 3 percent |
| South Carolina | None | One only |
| South Dakota | None | 10.5 percent |
| Tennessee | One per year for five years | Six in five years |
| Virginia | 3 percent | Not over twenty-five |

custom in coöperating churches is to set aside each year one regular Sunday service for the presentation of the League's work, by a trained representative. This plan has the double advantage of enabling the League to secure revenue and at the same time carry on its propaganda. But the primary purpose of such meetings, or "field days" as they are called, is the raising of funds. The League uniformly declines invitations to speak where the subscription privilege does not accompany the invitation.[32] "Let no church open its doors merely for the sake of having a League speaker come in and preach a tem-

was small — *viz.*, Mississippi, 5 percent; Nevada, about 20 percent; New Jersey, 1 percent; North Carolina, 10 percent; Oklahoma, about 4 percent; South Carolina, about 2 percent; South Dakota, about 2 percent. The proportion raised as the result of personal solicitation is almost negligible, as are also the contributions from corporations, only two of the fifteen states reporting any revenue from this source.    [32] Anderson, *The Church in Action*, p. 56.

perance sermon. That is the least and most insignificant element involved." [33] At the conclusion of the service, pledge envelopes are distributed. A copy of such a pledge follows.

*Subscription Envelope*

---

To carry forward the work of the

ANTI-SALOON LEAGUE OF NEW YORK

" The Church in Action Against the Saloon "

M ...........................................................

Street ......................................................

City or Village .............................................

   Church ..................................................

---

|  |  |
|---|---|
| Date ....................... | If a voter write<br>" V " in this square |

| | |
|---|---|
| $500  *per month* | FOR ONE YEAR * I will pay toward the |
| $100  *per month* | support of the Anti-Saloon League of New |
| $ 50  *per month* | York the sum per month indicated by my |
| $ 25  *per month* | $\times$ mark payable *every three months in* |
| $ 10  *per month* | *advance.* |
| $  5  *per month* | |
| $  1  *per month* | One dollar of the above subscription of 33c. |
| 75c. *per month* | or more, is intended to pay my annual sub- |
| 50c. *per month* | scription to the *American Issue,* New York |
| 33c. *per month* | Edition. |

---

* For five years if marked in this square.

---

State Headquarters, 16th Floor, 906 B'way
New York City.

---

The pledge took the form of an envelope within which was enclosed a blank check form as follows:

[33] *American Issue,* Maryland Edition, Jan. 8, 1910.

Town where your bank is located ............. Date..........
Write name of your own bank ........................ Bank

### PAY TO THE ORDER OF THE ANTI-SALOON LEAGUE OF NEW YORK

16th Floor–906 B'way, New York City

($..........) ................................... Dollars.
(Sign here) ..............,......................................
(Address) ...................................................

After the pledges are in, the subscription department of the state or national League, as the case may be, sees that they are actually paid. Loose offerings are also taken, but yield small results compared to the pledge system. " All other plans for financing . . . the League have failed, and success everywhere has been in exact proportion to the willingness of the churches to profit by experience and to operate fully on this tested basis." [34] Notwithstanding the increased accounting expense, League officers preferred receiving ten thousand dollars from ten thousand individual subscribers to receiving the amount in one budgeted sum. This may seem poor finance, but it is certainly sound psychology.[35]

[34] Anderson, *The Church in Action*, p. 52. To the pledge envelope is attached a small pencil, the " big stick " that beat the life out of the liquor traffic. The brewers published photographs of the Anti-Saloon League subscription card as pictures of their chief enemy.

[35] The League has been vigorously denounced at times for collecting money on a commission basis. Although there have been instances of collectors in the employ of the League working on a commission basis, they have been few. (See statement by Congressman J. McLemore, *Congressional Record*, 65th Congress, 1st Session, pp. 6283–87; also, *American Issue*, Maryland and Ohio Editions, Aug. 22, 1908.) The most notorious case was that in New York when Anderson was superintendent. Convinced that church subscriptions would never yield enough to permit the undertaking of the elaborate program he had outlined, he proposed a separate extension department. This plan was not designed to replace church pledges but to reach the large numbers of Catholics and Jews and those of no church who opposed the liquor traffic. During its first year, 1918–19, this department produced $100,000 in subscriptions. It continued until 1923 when Anderson was sent to state's prison (see p. 236). — *American Issue*, New York Edition, June 14, 1919.

Many of the churches, in the interest of more careful accounting, endeavored to put their income and expenses on a budget basis.  Under such a plan a definite amount would be set aside for the League, obviating direct appeals to the congregation.  The Anti-Saloon League did not relish this:

> The general application of this budget rule would inevitably kill the League by instantly paralyzing its efficiency . . . the officials of the budget class of churches will seldom appropriate . . . more than a small fraction of the amount that would be contributed by the members themselves if they were given an opportunity. . . . Even if the lump contribution were larger, it would not accomplish as much in the promotion of the cause as a smaller sum made up of subscriptions which establish a vital contact and develop a sense of personal responsibility on the part of the individual members. It gets some money but it enlists no men.[36]

The budget plan, it was said, was merely an excuse for excluding the League altogether, or for giving it a limping support.  " There are some dozens of churches that have taken this position and on the average they are today giving less than one-fourth as much financial support as they did before the budget came into existence." [37]   Where, in spite of protest, the budget was adopted, the Anti-Saloon League claimed exemption from it, declaring that the war against liquor was an emergency campaign.  " This is the church's biggest job — her biggest fight.  She ought to put it at the top of the program instead of at the bottom." [38]

### Finances of the National League

Usually the state Leagues pay a portion of their collections into the national treasury, besides purchasing their supplies from the American Issue Publishing Company.  The propor-

[36] Anderson, *The Church in Action*, p. 53.
[37] *American Issue*, Illinois Edition, May 31, 1912.
[38] Anderson, *The Church in Action*, p. 54.

tion which the states contribute varies from one to ten per cent of their collections.[39]

During the years 1911 to 1919, the years of the League's greatest prosperity, between eighty and ninety percent of the national League's income came from pledges secured at its own field days in the churches. The balance came from state contributions and individual subscriptions solicited or volunteered apart from church meetings. Prior to 1912, the national League had no systematic method of soliciting and collecting funds. In that year a subscription department was organized. Table VI presents a summary of the work of this department between 1912 and 1923.

The national League, as has been indicated, raised this money as a rule through direct appeals to church congregations and dry audiences in public meetings. The number and distribution of such meetings, over the period 1914 to 1922 are shown in Table VII.

[39] PAYMENTS MADE TO NATIONAL LEAGUE BY STATE BRANCHES

| State League | Year | Total Receipts | Paid to National Anti-Saloon League |
|---|---|---|---|
| Iowa............ | 1921 | $47,032.83 | $4,000.00 |
| Iowa............ | 1922 | 50,636.14 | 6,000.00 |
| West Virginia..... | 1920 | 16,587.12 | 305.00 |
| New York........ | 1920 | 347,313.41 | 9,999.96 |
| Illinois........... | 1925 | 178,976.78 | 13,150.00 |

— *Report of Senate Committee Investigating Campaign Expenditures*, June, 1926, Senate Report 1197, 69th Congress, 1st Session, pp. 1363, 1427 ff. and 1887 ff.

TABLE VI

NATIONAL ANTI–SALOON LEAGUE FUNDS
PLEDGED AND COLLECTED UP TO JAN. 1, 1923

| FUND | AMOUNT | | | PERCENT | | |
|---|---|---|---|---|---|---|
| | Pledged | Collected | Canceled | Col- lected | Can- celed | Receiv- able ¶ |
| A. Special * | $100,236 | $80,883 | $9,495 | 80 + | 9 | 10+ |
| B. 1912 | 52,200 | 36,199 | 11,178 | 69 | 21 | 10 |
| C. † 1913 | 211,645 | 150,905 | 23,691 | 71 | 11 | 18 |
| D. † 1914 | 732,671 | 360,789 | 250,437 | 49 | 34 | 17 |
| F. 1915 | 808,223 | 333,709 | 338,846 | 41 | 41 + | 18 |
| H. 1916 | 820,418 | 313,957 | 439,968 | 38 | 53 | 12 |
| LL. ‡ 1916 | 37,059 | 17,583 | 16,852 | 47 | 46 | 7 |
| K. 1917 | 1,657,262 | 520,561 | 842,338 | 31 | 50 + | 19 – |
| M. 1918 | 2,041,417 | 568,724 | 1,029,853 | 27 | 50 | 23 |
| *Total* to 1918 § | *$6,461,131* | *$2,383,310* | *$2,962,658* | *36* | *45* | *19* |
| O. 1919 | $4,063,820 | $838,668 | $1,194,870 | 20 | 28 | 52 |
| R. 1920 | 3,468,941 | 451,741 | 661,422 | 13 | 19 | 68 |
| Special 1921 | 1,517,217 | 208,593 | 164,677 | 13 | 10 + | 77 |
| Special 1922 | 640,313 | 75,764 | 18,511 | 11 + | 2 + | 87 |
| TOTALS | $16,151,422 | $3,958,076 | $5,002,138 | 24 | 30 + | 46 |

* Fund A, Special, 1914. For enlarging the plant of the American Issue Publishing Company and inaugurating a daily paper (merged with the weekly *American Issue,* Jan. 1, 1917).

† Funds C and D. These were funds secured after the League had definitely declared for national prohibition. It was agreed that after all expenses incident to the subscription campaign were paid, the balance should be expended in the interest of national prohibition, half through the state leagues and half through the national Anti-Saloon League. — Cherrington, *Report to Executive Committee of the Board of Directors of the Anti-Saloon League of America,* Jan. 12, 1924.

‡ Lincoln-Lee Legion Fund. The Legion was the League's total abstinence unit (see p. 64). A special drive for its support was made in 1916.

§ The 1918 pledges were the last completely due at the time of this record, showing over 35 percent of the amount pledged actually paid in.

¶ The League regards all accounts as receivable unless the pledge is canceled by the maker. After the lapse of a certain time a portion of the unpaid accounts are turned over to the state Leagues for collection. There are no reports of collections thus made. The percentage shown here represents pledges retained by the national organization.

TABLE VII

MEETINGS HELD UNDER THE AUSPICES OF THE SUBSCRIPTION
DEPARTMENT OF THE NATIONAL ANTI-SALOON LEAGUE

| STATE | 1914 | 1915 | 1916 | 1917 | 1918 | Total |
|---|---|---|---|---|---|---|
| Alabama | | | 10 | | 236 | 246 |
| Arizona | | | | 45 | | 45 |
| Arkansas | 4 | 54 | | 154 | | 212 |
| California | 39 | | | | 2 | 41 |
| Colorado | 19 | | | | | 19 |
| Connecticut | | 24 | | | | 24 |
| Delaware | 1 | | | | | 1 |
| District of Columbia | 18 | | | 56 | 2 | 76 |
| Florida | | 6 | 112 | 50 | 140 | 308 |
| Georgia | | 16 | | 383 | 256 | 425 |
| Idaho | | 3 | 31 | 56 | 33 | 123 |
| Illinois | 466 | 44 | 2 | 2 | 13 | 527 |
| Indiana | | 57 | 21 | | | 78 |
| Iowa | 11 | | 23 | | 13 | 47 |
| Kansas | 15 | 85 | 1 | 473 | 118 | 692 |
| Kentucky | 52 | 2 | | | | 54 |
| Louisiana | | 63 | 101 | 48 | 83 | 295 |
| Maine | | | | | 110 | 110 |
| Massachusetts | 291 | 47 | 53 | | | 391 |
| Michigan | 153 | | | 161 | 10 | 324 |
| Minnesota | 1 | 1 | | | 395 | 397 |
| Mississippi | | | 217 | | 174 | 391 |
| Missouri | 11 | 107 | 8 | 11 | | 137 |
| Montana | 8 | 83 | | 64 | 35 | 190 |
| Nebraska | 8 | | | 235 | 151 | 394 |
| Nevada | 1 | | | | | 1 |
| New Hampshire | | 28 | | | | 28 |
| New Jersey | 1 | 64 | | | | 65 |
| New Mexico | 3 | | | | 39 | 42 |
| New York | 4 | 175 | 747 | 65 | 23 | 1014 |
| North Carolina | 17 | 15 | 47 | | 357 | 436 |
| North Dakota | 2 | | | 1 | 2 | 5 |
| Ohio | 4 | 45 | | | | 49 |
| Oklahoma | 3 | | | 314 | 62 | 379 |
| Oregon | 18 | 29 | | 1 | 226 | 274 |
| Pennsylvania | 7 | 93 | | | | 100 |
| Rhode Island | 18 | | | | 12 | 30 |
| South Carolina | | 68 | | 208 | 140 | 416 |
| South Dakota | | 34 | | | 5 | 39 |
| Tennessee | | | | 182 | 201 | 383 |
| Texas | 7 | 45 | 19 | 196 | 4 | 271 |
| Utah | | 2 | | 74 | | 76 |
| Vermont | | | 21 | | | 21 |
| Virginia | | 78 | 226 | 167 | 120 | 591 |
| Washington | 28 | 4 | | 203 | 16 | 251 |
| West Virginia | 1 | 2 | | | | 3 |
| Wisconsin | 2 | | 18 | | | 20 |
| Wyoming | 6 | | | 1 | | 7 |
| Totals | 1219 | 1274 | 2657 | 3150 | 1748 | 10,048 |

For the years 1919 to 1922 the totals only are given: 1919 — 3994; 1920 — 2604; 1921 — 2347; 1922 — 786.

For the entire period, 1914 to 1922, the total number of meetings held was 19,779.

Special funds were occasionally raised. For example, in 1926 an appeal was made in connection with the primary elections.[40] This money, about $11,000, was received by the League treasurer at Westerville and sent to Wheeler at Washington. It went into a so-called library fund out of which payments were made in connection with the primary elections.

[40] CONTRIBUTORS TO SPECIAL PRIMARY FUND, 1926.

| | |
|---|---:|
| J. H. Baker, Baltimore, Md. | $500.00 |
| E. A. Laitner, Treas., Detroit, Mich. | 2500.00 |
| Charles M. Cox, Melrose Highlands, Mass. | 500.00 |
| Rufus Bates, Treas. Cong. Church, Weymouth, Mass. | 1000.00 |
| H. C. Stockman, Birmingham, Ala. | 100.00 |
| Robert Treat Paine, Boston, Mass. | 100.00 |
| W. C. Scott, Melrose Highlands, Mass. | 100.00 |
| Samson Brothers Co., Toledo, Ohio. | 250.00 |
| Wm. A. Harbison, Pittsburgh, Pa. | 250.00 |
| J. N. Klock, Treas., Benton Harbor, Mich. | 200.00 |
| F. A. Evans, Treas., Philadelphia, Pa. | 250.00 |
| W. H. Cowles, Spokane, Wash. | 200.00 |
| Dr. H. A. Kelly, Baltimore, Md. | 100.00 |
| G. W. Loan, Grafton, W. Va. | 100.00 |
| W. H. Griffith, Bridgeport, Conn. | 100.00 |
| Alice D. Lodge, Grosse Point Farms, Mich. | 100.00 |
| F. M. Jackson, Birmingham, Ala. | 250.00 |
| C. O. Blood, Lynnfield Center, Mass. | 1000.00 |
| Charles S. Huston, Coatsville, Pa. | 500.00 |
| Robert Treat Paine, Boston, Mass. | 100.00 |
| B. S. Pearsall Co., Elgin, Ill. | 100.00 |
| W. T. Raleigh Co., Freeport, Ill. | 100.00 |
| E. C. Jameson, Chicago, Ill. | 500.00 |
| W. A. Rogers, New York City | 100.00 |
| Fillmore Condit, Long Beach, Cal. | 250.00 |
| Mrs. George Wupperman, New York City | 500.00 |
| W. B. Wheeler, magazine article | 500.00 |
| Balance in original library fund | 1.29 |
| Received in amounts less than $100 | 758.00 |
| TOTAL | 10,959.29 |

—*Report of the Senate Committee on Campaign Expenditures*, June 1926, Senate Report 1197, 69th Congress, 1st Session, pp. 1382–87. Exhibit No. 175-B.

*The Publishing Company*

The finances of the American Issue Publishing Company deserve mention here. When this concern was incorporated in 1909 only $1000 of its authorized capital stock of $10,000 was paid in. The company, however, had in August, 1924, according to Dun's reports, assets of $422,229 and liabilities of $95,555, or a net worth of $348,754. Its land, buildings, machinery and equipment were valued at $149,197. During almost twenty years of existence no dividends have ever been paid.[41]

All the state Leagues and the national League purchase literature and supplies from the publishing company.[42] The corporation has prospered notwithstanding the fact that printed matter is supplied practically at cost. The earnings since organization have been $321,717.70.[43]

[41] *Ibid.*, pp. 1327–54. See above, p. 12, and footnote, p. 221.

[42] California, Alabama and one or two other states publish their own papers, but all purchase supplies of some kind from the publishing company at Westerville.

[43] The latest available financial statement of the American Issue Publishing Company follows:

STATEMENT AS OF JUNE 30, 1925

*Current Assets*
Liberty bonds, bills receivable, etc. ............................ $130,127
*Working Assets*
Printed stock, work in process, supplies ........................ 67,743
*Deferred Assets*
Prepaid insurance, Encyclopedia, Lincoln-Lee .................. 74,204
*Fixed Assets*
Land, buildings, machinery, furniture and fixtures .............. 148,198

Total Assets ......................... $420,272

*Current Liabilities*
Bank overdrafts, mortgage, bills payable ...................... $ 69,814
*Reserves* ...................................................... 12,827
*Fixed Liabilities*, long-time notes ................................. 6,000
*Present Worth*, capital stock and surplus ........................ 331,631

Total Liabilities ...... $420,272

—*Report of Senate Committee Investigating Campaign Expenditures,* June, 1926, Senate Report 1197, 69th Congress, 1st Session, pp. 1332, 1457–60.

EXPENDITURES [44]

Wheeler, in 1926, estimated the total amount spent by dry agencies during some thirty years at about $35,000,000. This, he said, represents the expenditures of all the dry agencies campaigning for prohibition.[45] Some idea of the amount spent by the national and state Leagues can be obtained from Table VIII.

TABLE VIII

RECEIPTS AND EXPENDITURES OF THE NATIONAL ANTI-SALOON LEAGUE AND TWENTY-THREE STATE LEAGUES *

| UNIT | GROSS, 1920–25 | | YEARLY AVERAGE | |
|---|---|---|---|---|
| | Receipts | Expenditures | Receipts | Expenditures |
| National Anti-Saloon League .......... | $3,444,623 | $3,430,286 | $574,104 | $571,714 |
| New York ......... | 1,856,826 | 1,927,063 | 308,471 | 321,177 |
| New Jersey ........ | 412,390 | 407,874 | 68,731 | 67,979 |
| Ohio .............. | 900,865 | 882,397 | 150,144 | 147,066 |
| Indiana............ | 392,789 | 386,174 | 65,465 | 64,362 |
| Illinois............. | 1,369,220 | 1,356,434 | 228,203 | 226,070 |
| Wisconsin .......... | 418,689 | 418,689 | 69,781 | 69,781 |
| Kansas ............ | 139,794 | 137,943 | 23,299 | 22,990 |
| Connecticut........ | 21,687 | 21,679 | 3,614 | 3,613 |
| Kentucky .......... | 110,434 | 117,781 | 18,405 | 19,630 |
| Virginia............ | 249,061 | 247,254 | 41,510 | 41,209 |
| South Carolina ..... | 28,840 | 28,840 | 4,806 | 4,806 |
| Florida ............ | 71,764 | 71,773 | 11,960 | 11,962 |
| Rhode Island....... | 67,036 | 66,768 | 11,172 | 11,128 |
| Iowa .............. | 308,457 | 301,408 | 51,409 | 50,234 |
| Vermont........... | 67,642 | 65,287 | 11,273 | 10,881 |
| West Virginia ...... | 89,022 | 79,022 | 14,837 | 13,170 |
| Massachusetts....... | 294,108 | 296,478 | 49,018 | 49,413 |
| Oklahoma.......... | 45,274 | 44,666 | 7,545 | 7,444 |
| North Carolina ..... | 105,740 | 93,082 | 17,621 | 15,513 |
| Alabama............ | 129,338 | 126,813 | 21,556 | 21,135 |
| Missouri........... | 269,990 | 262,134 | 44,998 | 43,689 |
| Nebraska .......... | 62,625 | 59,553 | 10,437 | 9,925 |
| Maryland .......... | 246,575 | 245,856 | 41,095 | 40,976 |
| Total ......... | $11,102,789 | $11,075,253 | $1,850,364 | $1,846,875 |

* *New York Times*, Aug. 3, 1926; *United States Daily*, July 3, 1926. The New York League in 1920 had approximately 50,000 regular contributors, who in that year gave about $348,000.

[44] A partial summary of the income and expenditures of the National and fourteen State Leagues may be found in Appendix E.

[45] Wheeler, " Inside Story of Prohibition," *New York Times*, June 24, 1926.

Table IX shows the year-by-year variation in the expenditures of ten state Leagues.

### TABLE IX
#### EXPENDITURES OF STATE LEAGUES BY YEARS, 1920–25[4]

| STATE | 1920 | 1921 | 1922 | 1923 | 1924 | 1925 |
|---|---|---|---|---|---|---|
| Kansas ....... | $41,091 | $51,899 | $37,988 | $30,838 | $27,976 | |
| Indiana....... | 51,800 | 44,851 | 53,241 | 54,237 | 61,547 | $51,498 |
| Massachusetts. | 57,655 | 45,246 | 41,683 | 54,230 | 46,464 | 51,200 |
| Iowa ......... | 47,360 | 50,330 | 49,553 | 45,711 | 41,464 | |
| New Jersey ... | 67,073 | 56,909 | 65,390 | 66,904 | 69,929 | 57,205 |
| North Carolina | | 15,005 | 14,965 | 15,727 | 16,454 | 6,931 † |
| Wisconsin..... | 70,103 | 57,886 | 65,232 | 65,064 | 58,251 | 48,885 |
| Illinois........ | 105,701 | 224,835 | 181,297 | 203,578 | 217,924 | 193,097 |
| Oklahoma..... | 6,659 | 6,859 | 6,885 | 7,373 | 7,243 | 2,987 |
| North Carolina | | 2,068 | 4,992 | 6,877 | 7,540 | 7,363 |

* *United States Daily,* Aug. 3, 1926.      † As of Sept. 30, 1925.

### TABLE X
#### APPORTIONMENT OF EXPENDITURES
#### ANTI–SALOON LEAGUE OF NEW YORK *

| | 1920 | 1921 | 1922 | 1923 |
|---|---|---|---|---|
| Salaries (staff workers and special workers).................. | $142,762 | $134,567 | $119,911 | $104,026 |
| Labor and clerk hire.......... | 52,481 | 58,295 | 54,240 | 55,809 |
| Travel and hotel expenses...... | 48,355 | 44,981 | 32,620 | 26,286 |
| Printing and stationery........ | 27,518 | 17,882 | 8,460 | 9,239 |
| Publication, *American Issue*.... | 17,467 | 29,722 | 26,778 | 22,160 |
| Postage..................... | 15,972 | 14,212 | 11,381 | 11,477 |
| Rent, four offices............. | 12,983 | 12,650 | 13,092 | 13,248 |
| To National Anti-Saloon League | 10,000 | 14,667 | 3,600 | 14,400 |
| Telephone and telegraph....... | 3,002 | 2,681 | 2,251 | 2,073 |
| Office expense................ | 4,636 | 2,219 | 1,736 | 390 |
| Depreciation, furniture and equipment ................ | 2,730 | 2,789 | 2,595 | 2,364 |
| Literature and supplies ........ | 2,251 | 461 | 1,281 | 1,159 |
| Janitor service, etc. .......... | 2,010 | 2,315 | 2,535 | 1,684 |
| Newspapers, periodicals........ | 933 | 1,075 | 935 | 886 |
| Special meeting............... | 914 | 409 | 1,145 | 1,028 |
| Miscellaneous................ | 4,035 | 9,771 | 3,387 | 5,872 |
| Total.................. | $348,049 | $348,696 | $285,947 | $274,308 |

* *Jamestown Post,* New York, Oct. 4, 1923.

The character of pressure groups as of individuals can frequently be understood from the manner in which they spend their money. The Anti-Saloon League of New York spends more than any other state League. Table X reveals the purposes for which expenditures are made.

The national League spends over half a million dollars each year. We have seen something of the manner in which this money is raised; we have yet to inquire for what it is spent. In the first place the costs incident to subscription campaigns must be met. Procuring the subscriptions to the national League's four million dollar fund in 1919 involved outlays such as:

|  | Cost for Year | Cost per Meeting |
|---|---|---|
| Salaries of speakers,* etc. ............. | $168,495 | $42.20 |
| Expenses of speakers ................ | 97,797 | 24.40 |
| Literature for meetings .............. | 56,718 | 14.20 |
| Rentals for meetings ................ | 30,383 | 7.60 |
| Office overhead, 25% ................ | 10,735 | 2.70 |
| Total........................ | $363,828 | $91.10 |

* The average yearly salary per speaker was about $2100, plus $1200 for expenses.

This table indicates a rather high cost per meeting and a total cost of almost ten percent of the $4,000,000 pledged. The latest report indicates a probable shrinkage of $2,000,000 in this sum, making the cost twenty percent. This would not be unusual in charitable or subscription organizations.

The average cost per meeting for the 19,779 meetings held by the subscription department, 1914 to 1922, was about sixty-five dollars, distributed somewhat as follows: salaries to speakers, agents and others, thirty-three dollars; traveling expenses for speakers and agents, seventeen dollars; literature and hall rentals, six and eight dollars respectively. Table XI shows the average salaries of persons employed in connection with these subscription campaigns.

Practically all expenditures are accounted for in the first instance by the subscription department. Table XII summarizes the operations of that department during the League's third decade.

TABLE XI

SALARIES OF PERSONS EMPLOYED AT SUBSCRIPTION MEETINGS*

| FUND | CAM-PAIGN | NUMBER OF PAID REPRESENT-ATIVES | TOTAL SALARIES | TOTAL TRAVELING AND HOTEL EXPENSES | COST PER REPRE-SENTATIVE | |
|---|---|---|---|---|---|---|
| | | | | | Salary | Expenses |
| A. | 1914 | 15 | $5,074 | $2,355 | $339 | $157 |
| B. | 1912 | 11 | 3,251 | 1,464 | 295 | 133 |
| C. | 1913 | 15 | 19,468 | 7,033 | 1,300 | 469 |
| D. | 1914 | 12 | 31,416 | 14,354 | 2,618 | 1,196 |
| F. | 1915 | 54 | 45,957 | 17,695 | 851 | 328 |
| LL. | 1916 | 6 | 1,496 | 1,031 | | |
| H. | 1916 | 44 | 60,481 | 33,858 | 1,624 | 941 |
| K. | 1917 | 44 | 88,426 | 47,005 | 2,010 | 1,068 |
| M. | 1918 | 62 | 83,419 | 47,351 | 1,345 | 764 |
| O. | 1919 | 80 | 168,495 | 97,797 | 2,106 | 1,222 |
| R. | 1920 | 72 | 124,848 | 70,093 | 1,734 | 975 |
| Special | 1921 | 64 | 78,039 | 54,094 | 1,219 | 845 |
| Special | 1922 | 50 | 28,355 | 23,397 | 567 | 468 |

* This table includes salaries of speakers, field agents, date makers, advance men, lecture bureau managers, personal solicitors, department superintendents, etc. The salaries and expenses indicated are in connection with these special subscription campaigns and must not be confused with salaries of permanent league officials or special speakers.

## Salaries

Special speakers were employed at various times, and received substantial fees. It was in this connection that " William Jennings Bryan worked for humanity for $250 a day and expenses, spot cash," as the *New York World* [46] expressed it. Bryan received $11,000 from the League in 1919.[47] Former Congressman Richmond P. Hobson, the Spanish War hero, was another platform favorite. Between 1914 and 1922 he re-

[46] March 1, 1920.      [47] *United States Daily*, July 3, 1926.

ceived $171,250.[48]  W. E. Johnson ("Pussyfoot") in the same period received $18,807.  John F. Kramer, former Federal prohibition director, lectured for $7,500 a year.  The fees of the Rev. Sam Small amounted to $32,655.[49]  Malcolm Patterson, former governor of Tennessee, was paid $42,211.

TABLE XII

DISBURSEMENTS OF SUBSCRIPTION DEPARTMENT
OF THE NATIONAL ANTI-SALOON LEAGUE, 1912–22

| | |
|---|---:|
| Salaries of speakers, field agents, date makers, personal solicitors, advance men, lecture bureau managers and department superintendents | $740,708 |
| Traveling and hotel expenses of these | 419,352 |
| Special literature used at meetings | 178,216 |
| Hall rentals and local publicity | 117,863 |
| League periodicals sent to special lists during state campaigns (invoiced at cost), including the *American Patriot, National Daily, American Issue, New Republic* and state periodicals | 621,621 |
| Postage, telephone, etc. | 262,488 |
| Office, clerical, bookkeeping and secretarial staff | 256,621 |
| Printed matter used in collections | 109,988 |
| Miscellaneous items, office overhead, etc. | 151,430 |
| Industrial Service Department | 2,076 |
| Old Building and Equipment Fund (Fund A) | 11,251 |
| Funds distributed to state Leagues, Speakers Bureau and departments of national League | 584,098 |
| Emergency advances to state Leagues administered as departments of national League (Alabama, Arkansas, District of Columbia, Florida, Idaho, Georgia, Kansas, Louisiana, Massachusetts, Minnesota, Mississippi, Montana, North Carolina, Nebraska, New Mexico, Oklahoma, Oregon, South Carolina, Tennessee, Texas, Virginia, Washington and Wyoming) | 943,923 |
| Payments for literature to be sent to states under Chicago Plan * | 24,568 |
| 1922 Budget allotment | 77,031 |
| Total disbursements | $4,501,234 |

* The Chicago Plan was an arrangement under which the state leagues agreed to contribute a definite percentage of their income to the national League and the latter undertook to aid impecunious state Leagues.

Most of the speakers received much less.  It does not necessarily impeach the sincerity of Bryan and Hobson to remark that at such salaries they could afford to be sincere.  Roughly

[48] In 1919 and again in 1920 his fees exceeded $30,000.
[49] *United States Daily*, July 3, 1926, and *New York Times*, July 3, 1926. Fees paid to other speakers may be found in Appendix F.

speaking, salaries paid to speakers varied according to their ability to get subscriptions. "The Hero of the Merrimac," "the most kissed man in America," as Hobson was called, and Bryan, with his stirring eloquence, had sufficient color, apart from the merits of the campaign, to succeed in drawing crowds for a financial ballyhoo.[50]

Considerable criticism has been directed at public officials, such as Upshaw, Hobson and others, who received compensation from the Anti-Saloon League while in the public service. There has been no intimation that their services to the League seriously interfered with their public duties. The sole danger involved in such activity lies in the possibility of corruption. There is no suggestion that the men here mentioned would have voted differently or used their influence against temperance legislation but for the pay thus received.

[50] Congressman Upshaw of Georgia presents an amusing illustration of the way some of these speakers appraised their own worth. He spoke at a League meeting in Washington, D. C., in 1924. In reporting the meeting to M. G. Kelser, the League field manager, he said:

"My dear Mr. Kelser:

"Sing the Doxology and turn a few somersaults if you want to in celebration of our very fine rally at Immanuel Baptist Church last Sunday night. I turned over to Wheeler's office the cards amounting to a little over $1100 in subscriptions and about $50 in cash and checks. . . .

"I think you will have to shell down the corn and admit that your Georgia friend made a pretty good speech on America's greatest battle. . . ."

At the side of the letter he wrote: "Remember this $1168 collection cost you no advertising — only $1 taxi. In sending check, 'let your conscience be your guide.'" The letter was signed, "Yours, very dry, W. D. Upshaw."

In commenting upon Upshaw's service to the superintendent of the League in Colorado, where the redoubtable Georgian was seeking speaking dates, Kelser later said: "Upshaw is inclined to think of himself a little more highly than he ought, when it comes to the matter of remuneration for his services." (*Report of the Senate Committee on Campaign Expenditures,* June, 1926, Senate Report 1197, 69th Congress, 1st Session, pp. 1399–1401.)

There is some evidence that Hobson himself was paid more than his services were worth. One League superintendent told the author that on Hobson's first visit he was worth more than they paid him as a subscription getter; that on his second he was probably worth his salary, but that if he spoke a third time in the same place, he positively did damage to the temperance cause. He further remarked that Hobson's plea could be made effectively only to the uncritical and that an analysis of almost any of his speeches would show them to be tissues of fallacies and non-sequiturs. This opinion has been corroborated in conversations which the author has had with others high in the League's councils.

Upshaw, when asked if he accepted money from the Anti-Saloon League while he was a member of Congress, replied: " Of course I get paid for my time, but I never allow my engagements to interfere with my work in Congress. . . . I justify being paid on the same ground that a preacher accepts pay for Sunday service." [51] Other members of Congress — for example, Willis and Fess — were very careful to accept nothing beyond expenses for speaking while holding office,[52] notwithstanding the fact that fees to public officials for speaking are not without precedent.[53]

J. G. Wooley,[54] Prohibition candidate for President in 1900 and afterward with the League, advised, " This is a big fight for a big stake, for big men and big money. . . . Search out big, brainy haters of the traffic. Pay them relatively as the steel trust pays. Give them adequate equipment and demand adequate results." Bryan and Hobson, at least, received " steel trust " salaries. A reform movement, emphasizing its own moral and religious character, conducted on steel trust principles cannot fairly complain when it is judged by those standards. It is no defense to reply that the brewers and liquor dealers were paying salaries as large, or larger. The brewers were business men defending their property interests and making scant claim to be judged by any but business standards. The League claimed to represent the churches. It was crusading for civic purity and its methods must be judged by the standards it set for itself. When one recalls the giving by invalid women and orphaned children, these large salaries seem a trifle incongruous.

[51] *New York World*, April 21, 1926.
[52] *Report of Senate Committee Investigating Campaign Expenditures*, June, 1926; Senate Report 1197, 69th Congress, 1st Session, p. 1397.
[53] Members of Congress who received pay in varying amounts from the League were: Upshaw, Democrat, of Georgia; Cooper, Republican, of Ohio; Jones, Republican, of Washington; Barkley, Democrat, of Kentucky; Lowry, Democrat, of Mississippi; Robinson, Republican, of Indiana. — *New York Times*, June 18, 1926.
[54] *American Issue*, Indiana Edition, May 7, 1912.

A further contrast appears when we compare the fees of these special speakers with the salaries of the permanent employees of the League. Wheeler at no time received more than $8000 a year; and Cherrington, the manager of the publishing company, receives a like amount. The aggregate salaries of the twelve active officers at the national headquarters in 1924 amounted to $52,161, an average of $4350. These officers give all their time to League work and make nothing " on the side." Aside from the general manager, the four most important employees of the American Issue Company receive salaries between $3000 and $4000.[55]

Other officers of the League, with their salaries, are as follows:

General superintendent ................ $7,000
Associate general superintendent ........ 6,500 — 7,000
State superintendents [56] ................ 2,400 — 8,000
Assistant state superintendents ......... 1,500 — 4,000
District superintendents .............. 2,000 — 4,500
Legal advisers (State) [57] .............. 2,500 — 6,000

## THE LEAGUE AND THE CORRUPT PRACTICES ACTS

It will be remarked that in the foregoing expenditures none are labeled " political," although League officials have time and again admitted that they were in politics. It has been the avowed purpose of the organization since its beginning to elect drys and defeat wets. It is consequently puzzling to find the League, when asked to give an account of its political ex-

[55] *Report of Senate Committee Investigating Campaign Expenditures,* June, 1926, Senate Report 1197, 69th Congress, 1st Session, 1366–68.
[56] Davis of New York is the only one receiving $8000.
[57] In a few instances legal advisers are paid more than $4000, notably in New York, where O. S. Poland's salary is $6000.

penditures, insisting that it is not a political organization but an educational and scientific society.

Broadly viewed, the entire outlay of the League may be regarded as political. The League spends money to educate men and women to vote dry, as the regular parties spend money to educate people to vote the Republican or Democratic ticket. It is true, the Anti-Saloon League rarely puts forward a candidate of its own. Its policy is to support those candidates of other parties who are "satisfactory." If a political organization be viewed narrowly as one which selects its own candidates for public office, the Anti-Saloon League may properly escape being so designated.

Numerous demands have been made that the League file returns under the Federal Corrupt Practices Act. This act requires all "political committees" to file with the clerk of the House of Representatives a detailed statement of all receipts of a hundred dollars or more. Political committees are defined as "all committees, associations, or organizations which shall in two or more states influence the result, or attempt to influence the result, of an election at which Representatives in Congress are to be elected." [58]

In 1920 the clerk of the House of Representatives sent Wheeler a copy of the Corrupt Practices Act. It has been claimed that this constituted an official declaration by the clerk of the political nature of the Anti-Saloon League, so as to bring it within the provisions of the law. This is not true. Clerk William Tyler Page, in testifying before a House committee in 1924, explained his action: " Now in 1920, having observed that, in that presidential campaign, certain organizations for some reason or other had not filed with the clerk of the House any statement under this law, perhaps feeling themselves exempt from its provisions on account of the character of the organizations, and knowing that certain organizations were

[58] *United States Statutes at Large*, 1911, Chapter 33.

acting politically, I obtained as nearly as possible from the Library of Congress a list of such organizations and sent them copies of the law without comment. My duties under this law are purely ministerial. It is not for me to say whether an organization politically active comes within the purview of the law or not." [59]

This reminder raised the issue within the League, and in consequence it filed two statements of expenditures. They were certified to by Wheeler as " Treasurer of the Campaign Committee of the Anti-Saloon League of America," and included expenditures in the following districts:

*First Report, October 22*

| | |
|---|---|
| Indiana | Fourth and Fifth Congressional Districts |
| Iowa | Eleventh District |
| Texas | Sixteenth District |
| Minnesota | Seventh District |
| New Hampshire | First and Second Districts |
| New York | First, Second and Forty-second Districts |
| Pennsylvania | Tenth, Twentieth, Twenty-second, Twenty-fifth, Twenty-eighth and Thirty-eighth Districts |
| Maryland | First and Sixth Districts |

*Second Report, October 29*

| | |
|---|---|
| Minnesota | Seventh Congressional District |
| Ohio | Fifth District |
| Maryland | Eleventh District |
| Pennsylvania | Twenty-fifth and Twenty-eighth Districts |
| New York | Fortieth, Forty-first and Forty-second Districts |

The total expenditures of the national League in the interests of dry candidates in 1920, as shown by these reports, were $3,492.47.[60] In filing its reports, the League stated:

[59] *Hearings of Committee on Election of President*, Feb. 21, 1924, pp. 1–13. Quoted in J. K. Pollock, *Party Campaign Funds*, New York, 1926, p. 195.
[60] Report in the files of the clerk of the U. S. House of Representatives.

We respectfully protest any obligation on the part of the Anti-Saloon League of America to file this report under the above law, as the activities of the League are educational, scientific and charitable rather than political, as intended by the law. We file this report, therefore, under protest, covering those contributions and expenses only in connection with the national organization in the election of Congressmen, as indicated in the report.[61]

Since 1920 the League has continued to file a statement under protest. During a congressional hearing, Wheeler was asked why the organization made any return at all. This colloquy ensued:

Mr. Wheeler: According to the interpretation that many people place upon that law, it was never intended to cover a committee that was not a political committee. I have said to our national organization that when we spend any money in trying to influence the election or defeat of a member of Congress, I thought that it was a better plan for our national organization to file an account of that expense.

I have stated that we do not believe that we are within the provisions of that law: but, rather than be subjected to the criticism that we were evading the law, I have filed that report. . . .

Mr. Husted: Have you any objection to the filing of the report?

Mr. Wheeler: No.

Mr. Tinkham: Why that protest if you have no objection?

Mr. Wheeler: It is only a question of whether the law covers us. If the law does not require it, then naturally it is just that much extra work to do it. No organization or committee would do it if the law did not require it. And then the question comes, does the law require it? Where there is a doubt, I think an organization which stands for law enforcement should resolve that doubt in favor of the law until it is otherwise settled.[62]

It is perhaps not too much to say that in failing to make returns for the years 1910 to 1918 the national organization certainly violated the spirit of the Corrupt Practices Act and possibly the letter.

[61] Report in the files of the clerk of the U. S. House of Representatives.

[62] Extracts from *Hearings before Subcommittee on Appropriations*, House of Representatives, 67th Congress, 2d Session, 1922, pp. 467 ff.

The obligation of the state Leagues to file under the federal act depends upon whether the Anti-Saloon League be viewed as a single unit with subordinate branches or as an aggregation of independent local organizations. If the latter view is taken, and such a view is not wholly unreasonable, the Federal law would not apply, since the state Leagues do not make expenditures in two or more states. The bulk of their money is raised and expended wholly within the state.[63]

It may be pointed out that such an interpretation of the law might easily defeat the whole purpose of the Corrupt Practices Act. If a national organization which itself spends little or nothing is required to report, while the state organization, through which large sums are spent, does not report, the law may be effectually nullified.[64]

On the other hand, an equally cogent case can be made out for regarding the League as a unit. It has been previously pointed out that the states received financial aid from the national body. Advances so made are not usually accounted for in the reports filed by the national League. The political significance of this aid and the close articulation of these organizations is illustrated by a statement of Superintendent Shields, of the Tennessee League: "A number of Congressmen who hold the balance of power and pile up majorities in Congress come from southern and western states, where money for organization and educational purposes is scarce. They have always had to have help from the national League. From this office [in Washington] legislation is initiated, a constant watch is kept on the actions of Congress, and when opposition appears, danger signals are flashed to every state in the Union." [65]

The fact is that regardless of their structural independence,

---

[63] See statement of Wheeler in *Hearings before Subcommittee on Appropriations*, 1922, p. 467.

[64] See *Congressional Record*, 67th Congress, 2d Session, 1922, pp. 5015–24.

[65] Quoted by Congressman Tinkham, *Congressional Record*, April 4, 1922, 67th Congress, 2d Session, pp. 5015–24.

the state Leagues function, when need arises, as agents of the national League, and the latter is their agent at Washington. The following paragraphs are from a circular letter written by Arthur J. Davis, executive secretary of the campaign committee of the Massachusetts Anti-Saloon League, on June 10, 1922:

> These are crucial days, not only for Massachusetts, but for the whole country. On November 7 come the congressional elections, the elections which determine whether or not the Volstead Act will be modified so as to practically nullify the Eighteenth Amendment.
>
> Dry Congressmen must be elected. If wet legislators are sent to Washington, our cause will be set back half a century. . . .
>
> To meet this situation, we need $60,000. We should have more, but will make this do. . . .

The Rev. W. C. Shupp, superintendent of the Anti-Saloon League of Missouri in 1922, was even more explicit:

> The Anti-Saloon League is now building the strongest organization it has ever had in Missouri. . . .
>
> We should have for the work mapped out $60,000 or more. We expended $49,000 in the last prohibition campaign and then we ran short about $5000.
>
> Our organization will fight Senator James A. Reed and other candidates who have furnished wet leadership. . . .
>
> This will include Senators, Congressmen, prosecutors, and members of the legislature . . . in fact, wet candidates who have anything to do with legislation or enforcement of the liquor laws.[66]

Wheeler admitted that "on the whole it would work for good" to have complete publicity of all contributions and expenditures of every organization seeking to influence elections, but added, "I do not think it necessary . . . in the states where they have their own state laws governing the conduct of the organizations in the states . . . that they should have to file another report here with reference to the election or defeat of candidates for Congress."[67]

[66] *St. Louis Globe Democrat*, April 11, 1922.
[67] *Hearings before Subcommittee on Appropriations*, 1922, p. 472.

Some of the state Leagues were apparently in doubt, for in 1920 West Virginia, Iowa, Maryland, Missouri, Wisconsin and Oregon made returns to the clerk of the House of Representatives.[68]

The meaningless character of a national report without the corresponding state reports, is indicated by the national statement filed December 1, 1920, showing the expenditure of $3492. The Wisconsin report, filed at Washington a month previous, showed a total of $10,028 in the same elections.[69] Again in 1922 the statement of the national organization showed $2559 spent in the primary elections in twelve states, including —

| Illinois | $102 | Ohio | $450 |
|---|---|---|---|
| Indiana | 77 | Oklahoma | 50 |
| Iowa | 13 | Pennsylvania | 180 |
| New Jersey | 500 | Other expenses | 318 [70] |

The items listed speak for themselves as to their political nature:

Sixteenth district of Illinois, $100 for printing, postage and organization work against candidate William E. Hull; $510 to George B. Safford of Minneapolis for printing, postage and organization work in fifth district against John R. Coan; seventh district for A. J. Volstead; eighth district for O. J. Larson; newspaper material, seventh district.

The expenditures made by the League in Volstead's district aroused the ire of Tinkham and other wets. Asked by

[68] In commenting on this fact, Wheeler said: " I take it for granted that some of them felt that they would file that report even though it was not necessary. They may have been in doubt about it. . . . Others, on the advice of those who looked into this law, were just as clear that there was no occasion for doing so, and I think that they were clearly in the right on that." (*Hearings before Subcommittee on Appropriations*, 1922, p. 473.) It may be added that no protest was made by the state Leagues that filed.

[69] The Ohio League reported expenditures of $5769 (statement filed with the Secretary of State of Ohio, November 12, 1920). This, however, included expenditures in behalf of state candidates as well as Congressmen.

[70] This report also contained the names of contributors of $100 or more, listing: S. S. Kresge of Detroit, $1000; A. Z. Blair of Portsmouth, Ohio, $500; Robert Young of Columbus, Ohio, $500; Samuel Dunlap, Circleville, Ohio, $500; D. C. Boyd of Galion, Ohio, $500; Alexander Neff, Neffs, Ohio, $500; S. Baldwin of Baltimore, $250; a total of $3750.

Hill of Maryland, a fellow-wet, if he thought "it proper that a gentleman [Wheeler] who becomes treasurer and spends money to assist in the election of members of Congress, should at the same time be a legislative agent and go before this same member of Congress [Volstead], in whose election he has assisted, to ask for legislation for his employer corporation," Tinkham replied: "It seems to me highly reprehensible that a man should allow his campaign expenses to be paid in part by any organization whatsoever which he knows in advance is coming before the committee upon which he sits as a member. . . ."[71]

Whatever its ethics, the situation is not novel. Manufacturers and business associations have long contributed to the campaign expenses of members of Congress, and their agents have subsequently appeared before these members in support of legislation. The danger of contributions by corporations has been recognized by Congress in prohibiting them. Unfortunately for the accuracy of Congressman Hill's query, the National Anti-Saloon League is not a corporation. At other times Hill and Tinkham are found insisting that the League is a political committee as much subject to the Federal Corrupt Practices Act as the Republican national committee or the campaign committee of the American Federation of Labor. Granting this, would it be any more reprehensible for the Anti-Saloon League to appear before members of Congress, whose election it has furthered, than it would be for Republican leaders and agents of the American Federation of Labor? Their argument pushed to its logical conclusion would ban all expenditures by organizations interested in influencing electoral results, although few organizations would spend money on elections if they were not interested in legislation.

The state committees of the national parties rarely make a return under the Federal act. If the State Anti-Saloon Leagues

---

[7] *Congressional Record*, April 4, 1922, 67th Congress, 2d Session, pp. 5015–24.

are to be regarded as integral parts of the national organization, it would seem only fair that such an interpretation should be applicable to the state committees of the Republican and Democratic parties as well. Tinkham in a speech in 1922 denounced the League for its failure to comply with the law. Asked if he believed that the Federal Corrupt Practices Act applied to the state committees of the Republican and Democratic parties, he replied that if the state and national committees are interlocked as those of the Anti-Saloon League are, the state organizations should report. Mann of Illinois thereupon retorted, " If the Massachusetts Republican Committee is not interlocked with the National Republican Committee, then I do not understand its purpose." [72]

One of the reasons given by Wheeler for claiming exemption for the state Leagues from the Federal act was the fact that they account for their expenditures to their respective states.[73] But their obligation, even under local laws, was contested by some of the state organizations.

In the State of New York the election law requires the treasurer of every political committee which, in connection with any election, receives or expends any money, to file a sworn statement of all receipts, expenditures and liabilities.[74] The term " political committee " is defined as:

Any committee or combination of three or more persons coöperating to aid or to promote the success or defeat of a political party or principle or any proposition submitted to vote at a public election; or to aid or take part in the election or defeat of a candidate for public office; or to aid or take part in the election or defeat of a candidate for nomination at a primary election or convention.

[72] *Congressional Record,* April 4, 1922, 67th Congress, 2d Session, pp. 5015–24.

[73] A complete list of the state Leagues making a return under the various state laws is not available. From nineteen state superintendents who replied to an inquiry of the author, it appears that only seven report, viz.: New York, Massachusetts, Connecticut, Nevada, New Jersey, Ohio and Wisconsin.

[74] Election Law, Section 321; Chapter 16, Consolidated Laws of New York, Section 320.

[The statute expressly declares that the term " political committee " shall not apply to] any committee or organization for the discussion or advancement of political questions or principles without connection with any election.[75]

The Anti-Saloon League of New York, believing itself to be exempted by this last provision, did not file any statement of its expenditures. In March, 1917, the New York Court of Appeals had held that the Home Rule Tax Association, which was formed for the purpose of defeating a proposed tax amendment to the state constitution, and which had spent money to that end, was a political committee within the meaning of the election laws and hence required to make a return.[76] Relying upon this decision, an action was brought in March, 1923, to require the Anti-Saloon League to make a return. In answer the League declared that it was a body corporate and not a committee or combination of three or more persons and that it was an organization for the discussion and advancement of political questions and principles without connection with any election. On the hearing in the lower court, it developed that the proceeding had been brought against the " Anti-Saloon League of New York," whereas the League had, in 1905, incorporated as " The New York Anti-Saloon League." In May, 1913, without following the procedure prescribed, the officials of the Anti-Saloon League had changed the name to " The Anti-Saloon League of New York." As the League claimed to be operating under the charter to the New York Anti-Saloon League, the proceeding was defective and the petitioners had been misled by the change in name. However, the trial court ruled that it was the same corporation; it was a continuance of the original corporation *de facto* if not *de jure*. The court further ruled that the League could not claim exemption as a corporation and that it was an association of three or more

---

[75] Election Law, Section 320.
[76] Matter of Woodbury *v.* Home Rule Tax Association, 174 App. Div. 569; affirmed without opinion, 220 N. Y. 675.

persons within the meaning of the election law. It was shown that the Anti-Saloon League had taken an active part in the primary and general elections of 1922 " by the printing and distribution of publications, bulletins, circulars and letters, by public addresses made to qualified electors directly referring to the record and qualifications of candidates for nomination and election and by assistance rendered in the organization and direction and by activities of workers at the polls." Consequently it was ordered to file a statement of expenditures for the elections of 1922. "The law," said the court, " is predicated upon the fundamental truth that publicity will never hurt a good cause and has destroyed many bad ones." [77]

An appeal was taken to the Appellate Division of the Supreme Court in New York, which affirmed the order of the lower court, but modified it by inserting the name " The New York Anti-Saloon League " in the place of " The Anti-Saloon League of New York." [78]

At length the case reached the Court of Appeals, New York State's court of last resort. In July, 1924, the court (one judge dissenting) reversed the inferior court, holding that the substitution of the " New York Anti-Saloon League " for the " Anti-Saloon League of New York " had brought into the case an " entirely new party."

The court went on to declare that the Anti-Saloon League was a corporation and not a political committee. " It seems to us quite impossible," said the court, " to describe a corporation as a ' committee ' or a combination of three or more persons." It therefore was under no obligation to file under the provisions of the Election Law.

This decision, however, was not without its darker side for the League:

[77] Matter of Vannier v. Anti-Saloon League of New York, 120 Misc. 412; 198 N. Y. S. 605.

[78] 207 App. Div. 870, 1923. In September, 1923, the Anti-Saloon League complied with the Corporation Law and amended its title to that of " Anti-Saloon League of New York."

We think that the evidence taken in the proceeding easily would have permitted the Judge before whom the same was heard to find that said " New York Anti-Saloon League " did collect and expend moneys for the purpose of influencing said election. . . . We think the evidence amply justified the finding that it had gone beyond the activities for which it was organized and that it has collected and expended money for the purpose of influencing elections; and that under its former superintendent [Anderson] there were occasions when it did not hesitate to expend money in one form or another to encompass the defeat of those who incurred its disapproval.

Such conduct places it between two statutes to one of which, at least, it must yield obedience. Section 44 of the General Corporation Law (Consolidated Laws, Chapter 23) under the penalties of the criminal law prohibits any corporation, except one organized or maintained for political purposes only, to " directly or indirectly pay or use any money or property for any political purpose whatever." Of course this corporation insists that it was not organized for " political purposes " only, and therefore on its own claim, it is not exempt from the provisions of that statute. But if, in some manner, it should be held that it might expend money in connection with elections to promote the success or defeat of candidates, we think it would encounter the provisions of Section 322, subdivision 2, Election Law, pertaining to filing statements of such expenditures.[79]

To meet this dilemma the Anti-Saloon League of New York, when it takes part in a political campaign, now acts through a campaign committee.[80] The expenditures made by this committee are small in comparison with the total expenditures of the League. In 1924 they were scarcely $3000. Whatever may be said of its conduct in the past, there is no question that since the above decision the Anti-Saloon League of New York has watched its step closely, and passed the spirit to the letter of the law.

[79] 238 N. Y. 457, 1924.
[80] Wherever the League is incorporated — namely, in Massachusetts, South Dakota, Pennsylvania, Kansas and Illinois — a similar device is employed. In New Jersey the League is incorporated, but election expenditures for publicity are specifically authorized provided the advertisement or document specifies by whom the expenditure is made.

## CHAPTER VIII

## MONEY CHANGERS IN THE TEMPLE

The first concern of the Anti-Saloon League, the declared enemy of immorality and corruption, should certainly have been to keep its own skirts clean. But its work was carried on by mere mortals whose footsteps frequently falter. Perhaps it was the proximity of iniquity. Perhaps it was the organization's own prosperity. Certain it is that money changers did creep in.

It is not proposed to review every case where corruption was charged. It may well be imagined that an organization handling large sums of money, employing, in the course of thirty years, thousands of different individuals, might fail to maintain its pristine purity. There can be no doubt of the honesty and sincerity of the early leaders of the League. However much one may dislike their principles, however much one may condemn their tactics, their morality stands beyond reproach. But this cannot be said of all, and if there is rejoicing in heaven at the repentance of one sinner, there must have been hallelujahs in hell at the stumblings of these men of God.

The League was fighting a powerfully intrenched foe. Its battle was against great odds. The liquor traffic, with fabulous wealth and great political power, was no mean antagonist. For a few churchmen to declare war upon this Moloch seemed too much like David's sally against Goliath. This modern Goliath was willing to resort to any and all tactics. There are countless stories, many of them apparently authentic, of frame-ups, bribery, intimidation and violence against these Protestant Jesuits. The Anti-Saloon League exposed the corruption of the wets.  The wets, to be sure, were equally alert to detect corruption among the drys.

## An Early Judas

One of the first serious accusations was made by a certain Rev. U. G. Robinson of St. Louis — a former League superintendent.  In 1903 Robinson was in the employ of the League in Springfield, Missouri.  He had made many enemies and there had been several attempts to remove him.  When Dr. S. I. Lindsay became superintendent, in 1906, he retained Robinson notwithstanding complaints against him.  Two years later Lindsay resigned and Robinson was chosen to succeed him. The national organization had protested against his nomination and now refused to confirm his election.  Angered by this, Robinson began a guerilla warfare against the national headquarters committee.  The state committee, annoyed at this friction, sought to dismiss him, but before this could be done, Robinson had the Missouri League incorporated with himself as superintendent.  He notified National Superintendent Baker of what he had done and requested a conference to adjust their difficulties. This Baker refused and, at the request of the local committee, took active charge of the work in Missouri.  A letter of Baker's denouncing Robinson was widely published in church papers and soon put an end to the latter's influence and income. To recoup himself, he next offered to sell his corporation to the national League for $2150.  Baker opposed this deal, but on the advice of local church officials it was agreed to.

Robinson's wrath was not appeased by this piece of religious stock jobbery.  Continuing his attacks, he began the publication of a rival paper called the *National Issue*, founded, he declared, to " preserve, purify and protect the church " from the Anti-Saloon League.[1]  He entered into correspondence with the National Liquor League of New York, offering, for $300, to stir

[1] *American Issue*, Maryland Edition, Aug. 21, 1909.

up dissension in the Anti-Saloon League National Convention at Washington, D. C., in 1911. His plan was exposed by W. E. (" Pussyfoot ") Johnson and nothing came of it.[2]

Robinson charged the League officials with almost every crime from petty larceny to rape. Only two of the many, among the more serious charges, warrant discussion. These were:

1. That Russell and Baker were getting rich through the League and the American Issue Publishing Company.

To this charge the following answer was made, signed by Baker and E. H. Cherrington, general manager of the Publishing Company:

The American Issue Publishing Co. is operated under the direction of a board of trustees . . . under the control of the Anti-Saloon League of America. Under the laws of the State of Ohio . . . it is necessary for every trustee of a corporation to be a stockholder in such corporation. For the sole purpose of complying with this provision of the law, these five members of the *American Issue* board hold shares of stock in the concern, but not a single member of this board has ever received or can ever receive a single penny of the profits from the American Issue Publishing Company.

Rev. H. H. Russell, associate general superintendent of the Anti-Saloon League of America, is not a stockholder in the American Issue Publishing Company, is not a member of the board of trustees and has nothing to do with the management of the concern.[3]

Robinson published a picture of Baker's home, stating that it was a twelve-room house which, with its furnishings, cost twenty thousand dollars. As a matter of fact Baker's home was a six-room dwelling in Westerville, Ohio, and even at the

[2] *American Issue*, Maryland Edition, June 29, 1912; the letters between Robinson and the National League as well as the Liquor League's denial that the deal was consummated; also, July 27, 1912.

[3] During the hearings on campaign expenditures before the Senate committee, in 1926, Senator Reed asked Wheeler concerning the whereabouts of the trust agreement under which the directors of the American Issue Publishing Company hold that property for the Anti-Saloon League. Wheeler replied that he supposed it was at Westerville, to which Senator Reed replied that Cherrington had disclaimed knowledge of its whereabouts. *United States Daily*, July 3, 1926. The fact is that no such document exists.

present writing, despite enhanced realty values, is worth hardly half that sum.[4]

2. That Dr. Thoms, League superintendent in the state of Washington, stole the church collections and fled to Alaska.

This is the only one of Robinson's charges that can be proved. Thoms had been recommended as a minister in good standing and had been appointed superintendent in the state of Washington. Certain employees of the state League became convinced of Thoms' peculations and presented formal charges to the state headquarters committee. Without investigation the committee assumed the complaint to be a case of insubordination and reprimanded the employees. An appeal was then taken to the general superintendent, who started immediately for Seattle to investigate. Before he arrived, Thoms and his wife had left for Alaska. Suit was entered against him for recovery and a judgment of $3000 was obtained, which was never executed.

The League officials were frequently asked why they did not sue Robinson for libel. Two reasons were given. In the first place such a suit would have had to be brought in St. Louis, and chances of securing a conviction by a jury there were somewhat remote. Furthermore, since no reputable newspaper had published Robinson's charges, the League did not think it wise to institute proceedings and give occasion for their publication as news. As a matter of fact, a libel action had been brought against Robinson in Stone County, Missouri, in October, 1905, and a judgment of $4000 obtained against him for actual and punitive damages.[5]

[4] Robinson's charge was repeated in 1917 by Congressman Jeff McLemore (*Congressional Record*, 65th Congress, 1st Session, 1917, p. 6285.) Another prominent wet Congressman, from Massachusetts, at the time of Baker's death made an investigation of the wealth which he had frequently charged Baker with having amassed, and found (as he expressed it to the author) that " there was nothing in that — Baker died a relatively poor man."

[5] P. A. Baker, *A Statement — Refuting Falsehoods and Reciting Facts*, (pamphlet, Westerville, about 1908) p. 14.

*Michigan Mountebanks*

Congressman Jeff McLemore of Texas in 1917 accused the League of gross corruption:

It is an unspeakable fraud. Why? Because it has collected millions of dollars of sacred money from the churches and has squandered it among a lot of hypocritical grafters. I have in my possession the names of nineteen men who were workers for the Michigan Anti-Saloon League. Their records, taken from church and court records of Michigan are: Seventeen are preachers who have at one time or other been " run in " or " run out " for (1) mis-appropriation of Anti-Saloon League money, (2) licentious conduct, (3) adultery, (4) perjury, (5) assault on a small boy, (6) theft, (7) drunkenness, (8) bigamy, (9) seduction, (10) assaulting a negro girl, (11) blackmail, (12) undue intimacy with women of the congregation, (13) swindling.

Two were sent to prison, six were expelled from the church, three fled to escape arrest, three were convicted and paid their fines. The remainder wore their cases out.

From what I know these men are still Anti-Saloon League workers, for they understand their business and are good money getters. . . . If Congress would treat these lobbyists as they deserve, we would in the future hear but little of this bunch of religious grafters.[6]

Correspondence with Mr. McLemore has failed to reveal the source of his information beyond an article which appeared in his own newspaper, *State Topics*, on November 9, 1912.[7] The

---

[6] *Congressional Record*, 65th Congress, 1st Session, 1917, pp. 6283–87. On the hundreds of charges made against the League and its agents there is little reliable data obtainable. In 1917 McLemore declared " that certain mail-order whisky houses have in the past been heavy contributors to its game, in return for which the League was expected to close saloons in counties or states into which whisky could be shipped from outside." The author has been unable to get any verification for this either from McLemore personally or from other sources. The activity of the League in promoting the interstate liquor shipment legislation is certainly not consistent with such a charge.

[7] In August, 1912, McLemore wrote the president of the Texas Brewing Company as follows:

" Can't I prevail on you to take a little stock in *State Topics?* I organized some time ago with a capital of $5000 and shares of $100 each. I have among my stockholders H. B. Rice, Mayor of Houston; John H. Kirby; J. S. Cullinan of the Texas Company; M. M. Phinney of the Stone-Webster Company;

paper quotes as authority an undated issue of the *Knights of the Royal Arch Journal* of Oakland, California. This list included, *inter alia,* the following:

Rev. S. C. Strickland, the superintendent of the Kalamazoo district, is a swift one. He made the collectors and solicitors in his district turn all funds over to him. He in turn sent the state superintendent a statement of all money collected, but he kept the cash. Not one cent would he turn over.

Rev. R. G. Malone, superintendent of the Grand Traverse district, arrested for licentious conduct; fled the state; now in the employ of the Minnesota League.

Rev. George Kulp, League orator, Grand Rapids, arrested for adultery.

W. R. Bird, one of the League's most eloquent speakers in the Detroit district, convicted of drunkenness.

Rev. Stephen St. Johns, Pontiac member of the League's force of workers, serving a term for assaulting a colored girl.[8]

The charges made against these men are serious. Every effort to secure additional information from wet organizations produced nothing but a mere repetition of the above charges. The author, therefore, appealed to the responsible leaders of the Anti-Saloon League.

The Rev. H. H. Rood, editor of the Michigan edition of the *American Issue,* said that after checking the list very carefully he recognized only three of the men. Rood is conversant with affairs in Michigan, having been a student in college there, a pastor for five years, and an employee of the Anti-Saloon League for nine years. Concerning Strickland he writes:

H. Prince; R. L. Autrey; Jonathan Lane; A. M. McFadden, President Texas Cattle Raisers Association; and William Doherty, Assistant General Manager of the Frisco. I only ask each to take a little stock, as I want to get it distributed as much as possible, and now if I can get you to take at least three shares, it will assist me very materially in getting the paper on its feet. Texas needs such a paper as *State Topics* and I think our people ought to help it out." — *The Breweries and Texas Politics,* San Antonio, 1916, Vol. 1, p. 571.

[8] The author has been unable to learn anything concerning the other twelve. It is not even clear that they were ever employed by the League.

I knew Rev. S. C. Strickland very well. He was an employee of the Anti-Saloon League at the very beginning of its history in Michigan or in the very early years.

The League did not get on well financially in those early days and Mr. Strickland, not having received his salary, did retain pledges made for the League work as security for his salary. I do not know but this was the understanding between him and the then state superintendent. I have reason to believe it was. In after time the League was reorganized and George W. Morrow became superintendent. There was some controversy between Mr. Strickland and Morrow in regard to Strickland's back salary, but matters were so adjusted that Mr. Strickland went out to speak for the League from time to time while I was on the Michigan League force. . . . He was one of the most conscientious, honest men I ever knew. I don't believe he ever took a dollar or defrauded any man of a single cent knowingly. He occupied many pastorates in the Michigan Conference efficiently and was held in high esteem without, so far as I know, a single reflection upon his character, until he passed on some years ago.

Rev. George Kulp, who is designated as a League orator of Grand Rapids, is probably the Rev. George B. Kulp who at one time was pastor of the First Methodist Church at Battle Creek. I never knew or heard of his being connected with the Anti-Saloon League, though he may have, in the early days, given an occasional address. He was not, I am very certain, ever connected with the League force. . . . This Kulp, to whom I refer, was expelled from the Michigan Conference or withdrew because of immorality.

Rood further says that Malone was never in the service of the Anti-Saloon League except to make an occasional address. He was for a time engaged in organizing Good Templars lodges in Michigan. The Rev. R. N. Holsaple, the present superintendent of the Anti-Saloon League in Michigan, denies any knowledge of the men mentioned except Strickland and Malone. As for Malone, he wrote:

I do not think there was ever any charge of dishonesty sustained against him.

I understand that Mr. Malone was for a short time connected with

the League, but do not know whether he was ever arrested on such
a charge as is mentioned in this list. I do know that he went to South
Dakota in 1911, was president of the state Grange and very highly
respected. He worked under my direction in connection with the
South Dakota Anti-Saloon League during the state prohibition campaign in that state in the year 1916. He is now in this city [Detroit]
conducting a school of Americanization, giving instruction to aliens
in preparation for naturalization, and is doing wonderful work.

I know nothing about any of the other men mentioned and cannot
find that any of them were ever connected with the Anti-Saloon
League.

Dr. George W. Morrow, who was superintendent of the
Michigan League from 1905 to 1913, brands the charges " absolute falsehoods." He too remembers only Strickland and
Malone and says that they were honored and respected for their
honesty and " sacrificial social service."

It is highly probable that the charges made by *State Topics*
against some of these men are true. It is likewise highly improbable that they served for any length of time as Anti-
Saloon League Workers. While it is incredible that they are all
Elmer Gantrys, it is certain that his type is not entirely absent.
The fact that the charges against the men were not used ex-
tensively by the wets and were never quoted in a reputable
liquor journal leads one to suspect that even the enemies of
the League did not regard them as especially reliable. It is not
fair to damn an entire organization, employing thousands of
different individuals for occasional services, on the record of a
few renegades. Until more evidence is made available, the
foregoing does not by any means establish the truth of the
allegation that the League is composed of " conscienceless
scoundrels and grafters."

### A Man from Missouri

In March, 1923, the *Minute Man,* organ of the Association
Against the Prohibition Amendment in Missouri, devoted its

entire issue to an *exposé* of the Rev. Dr. W. C. Shupp, superintendent of the Missouri League. Shupp was charged with using his influence with enforcement officials to procure an alcohol withdrawal permit for the Druggists Coöperative Co., a concern in which he and his son were interested together with one H. W. Trippett. Because of Trippett's malodorous reputation with the enforcement officers, the permit was refused; Shupp appealed to higher authority and it was procured. It was charged that this concern operated in open violation of the Prohibition Law from August, 1922, to January, 1923. It was further charged that in order to expand the business, Trippett acquired an interest in the Ludwig Remedy Company and Shupp again used his influence to obtain permits. Shupp was alleged to have accepted $500 from one Arthur Wigand, paid to him in the offices of the Ludwig Company Dec. 23, 1922. The money had been furnished Wigand by the Association Against the Prohibition Amendment. C. F. Smith, who was to be general manager of the company, also represented the Association. Up to 1923, Shupp had sedulously concealed his connection with the Druggists Coöperative Company, but, learning that an investigation was pending, he issued a public statement that he had financed the company for his son and had employed Trippett as chemist. There was an additional charge that Shupp had accepted over $1000 from certain bootleggers to see that their competitors were raided and that, where such payments were not forthcoming, Shupp took no steps to enforce the law.[9]

Attorney General Barrett, on Jan. 10, 1923, instituted an investigation. The Association also sent these charges, supported by affidavits, to Prohibition Commissioner Haynes, who promised a thorough investigation. As a result, Trippett was

[9] Congressman Dyer of Missouri repeated these charges in the House of Representatives. (*Congressional Record*, 68th Congress, 1st Session, 1924, pp. 5290-91.)

arrested for violation of the Prohibition Law and Shupp resigned from the Missouri League because of " broken health." [10]

### A Black Sheep in New York

Of all the cases of alleged or actual corruption within the League the most famous — or infamous — is that of Superintendent Anderson of New York, who was found guilty of third degree forgery in 1924 and sentenced to two years in prison. Something of the history of this extraordinary man and of the facts leading up to his *dénouement* are necessary to a fair understanding of the case.

William H. Anderson was graduated from the University of Michigan in 1892 and, after teaching school for a few years, returned and took a law degree in 1896. He practiced law until 1900, when he became attorney for the Illinois League. He presently became state superintendent, serving until 1906, when he was transferred for a year to New York. Between 1907 and 1914 he was busy, as we have seen, in Maryland. His last promotion brought him again to New York.

Anderson was recognized from the beginning as one of the ablest and most vigorous soldiers in the League's legions. He was honored in its national councils and served for a time as national legislative superintendent. His vigorous methods, which he characterized as "using the meat ax," earned him enmity but also no little respect from the wets. From the beginning he was accused of using the temperance organization solely as a " good thing " for himself.

" Who is W. H. Anderson of the Anti-Saloon League? " asked

[10] The *Minute Man* of March, 1923, gives the complete story. (*Globe Democrat*, Feb. 18, 1923; *St. Louis Star*, Feb. 8 and 9, 1924; *Congressional Record*, 68th Congress, 1st Session, 1924, pp. 5290–91; letter dated Dec. 8, 1925, to author from the present superintendent.) Up to date the headquarters committee and the board of trustees persist in their refusal to believe that Mr. Shupp did anything off-color and insist that it was " an effort on the part of the liquor interests to discredit the Anti-Saloon League of Missouri by crushing Shupp."

an indignant reader of the *Baltimore News*,[11] " who is taking such an interest in the people's welfare? Is he working for glory or the dollar? Some gum-shoe lawyer or minister, who was a failure and is now working the church for his pocket's sake? " To which Anderson replied:

It would not be hard to find out. I will cheerfully refer any man, who has any good reason for wanting to know, to every place I have lived and done business and let him make an investigation.

For the present, I was invited to come to Maryland by the official representatives of the federated churches. I have brought my family, bought a home, declared my intention of becoming a citizen and become admitted to the Maryland bar. I am here to outstay the saloon. Since I work about fourteen hours a day, I plead guilty to drawing a reasonable salary, fixed by the headquarters committee, since it is against my principles to allow my family to starve. I am willing to rest the question as to whether I give value received upon the testimony of the opposition.[12]

His financial integrity was attacked; he was called " a dirty, lying scoundrel "; it was said that " no wild beast could possibly be as great a menace as the person now known as William H. Anderson." At other times he was pictured as a " pirate king," a " political black hand," " a squatter who was run out of Illinois " and a " chaser of moonbeams." [13] Anderson appeared to relish this, for he never failed to publish in the *American Issue* such choice bits as came to his attention.

In methods he was frankly opportunistic:

It is the policy of the League to use any legal weapon that will do the most execution against the beverage liquor traffic. We are always, locally, for the measures that the liquor people do not want. The gun that will get the game is the gun we want.[14]

" To my mind," said a prominent Democratic politician, " William H. Anderson is the most skillful politician in the

[11] Jan. 25, 1908.
[12] *American Issue*, Maryland Edition, Feb. 8, 1908.
[13] *Baltimore Sun*, Feb. 21, 1912, and July 19, 1908.
[14] *American Issue*, Maryland Edition, Sept. 26, 1908.

State of Maryland." [15]　Expressions of respect for his ability came from unexpected sources.　Early in 1912 Anderson had challenged the honesty and sincerity of Speaker Trippe of the Maryland house and had accused him of using his influence to defeat local option by appointing a confirmed wet as chairman of the temperance committee and attempting to oust dry Republicans.　Trippe thereupon declared Anderson to be an " enemy to the public good," and called him a liar and a coward. Commenting upon this incident in the *Evening Sun,* H. L. Mencken said:

> The satanic Anderson, camerlingo of the Anti-Saloon League, has emerged triumphant from one more roughhouse with a politician. This time it is the Hon. James McC. Trippe . . . who bears the marks of his teeth.　Trippe of course doesn't know it.　Carried away by the reverberations of his own roaring, he is convinced . . . that he has disposed of Anderson.　But the truth is that Anderson has put him exactly where he wanted to put him.　A week ago it was still possible for the Hon. Mr. Trippe to pretend to a lofty impartiality, a judicial calm.　Today any such pretension would make a horse laugh.　His number is plainly visible.　Anderson has achieved his goat.
>
> Personally I grieve to behold such doings for I am a violent and incurable friend of alcoholism . . . and nothing would please me more than to hear of the collapse of the Anti-Saloon League.　But as a connoisseur of sophistry and bellowing, I am forced to admit and admire the quite extraordinary virtuosity of the Hon. Mr. Anderson. . . .
>
> The easy superiority of the man is constantly shown by the manner in which his opponents engage him.　Instead of . . . meeting argument with argument . . . they . . . take alarm at his first salvo and thereafter confine themselves to calling names.　He is, I believe, the most denounced man in Baltimore.　I have heard him called every nasty thing under the sun from liar to caitiff . . . accused of every crime from forgery . . . to the throwing of bombs. More than once it has been solemnly proposed, usually by liquorish ward heelers, that he be run out of town.　He is the vampire and hobgoblin of every bartender's nightmare. . . .

[15] *Baltimore Sun* and *Baltimore News,* Aug. 15 and 16, 1911.

My own belief is that the Hon. Mr. Anderson is perfectly sincere.
. . . He delights in toying with his opponents, in first letting them
run away with the line, and then tearing out their gills. Thus with
the lamented Trippe. First he irritated the great statesman, scien-
tifically and diabolically, and then, when Trippe . . . began bawl-
ing like ten thousand lions and hopping up and down like a hen on
a stove lid, and so lost his diaphanous vestments of judicial impar-
tiality, and stood forth, as it were, in the political altogether, then
Anderson turned away from the scene and was shaken by his own
snickers.

An affecting spectacle! A clever fellow! My advice to the
saloon keepers is that they imitate the Anti-Saloon League and send
to distant climes for some super-Anderson.[16]

In striking contrast to the typical fanatic, Anderson was a
sportsman. In a fair and open fight he was a good loser; in
the tactics which he employed, involving bitter personal attacks,
there was little malice; and in his denunciation of opponents
his bark was usually more violent than his bite.

Anderson arrived to take charge in New York City on New
Year's Day, 1914. At six o'clock that afternoon representatives of six newspapers were in his room. The next morning each had a column account of the interview, and the New
York League, which had been painfully inconspicuous and
anemic for several years, found itself suddenly the object of
much attention and concern. As the *Baltimore Sun*[17] put it:

The Hon. William H. Anderson arrived in New York the middle
of yesterday afternoon carrying a toothbrush, a copy of Baxter's
*Saints' Rest* and a change of medicated flannels. This morning he
had six columns in the leading New York newspapers. Such is
science.

From the day he set foot in the metropolis, the liquor interests were on the defensive. As for the Anti-Saloon League, his
coming was like a cold shower or a shot of " high life," and
things began to happen. Publicity was the chief weapon in the

[16] *Baltimore Evening Sun,* Feb. 12, 1912.    [17] Jan. 2, 1914.

arsenal of the League, and Anderson had a capacity for getting it comparable to that of a movie star or a transatlantic aviator. "In the few short months since his arrival," said the *New York World*,[18] "he has changed the whole political line-up in New York State. Six months ago prohibition was about as much of an issue . . . as Mormonism, pragmatism or the fourth dimension." He was called the "White Hope of Temperance," the "Arch Foe of Demon Rum," the "Napoleonic Leader of the Anti-Saloon League." When his first local option bill was killed that spring, Anderson, with customary bluntness, declared that William Barnes of Albany had ordered the assembly judiciary committee to "sit on the bill until it becomes extinct." Proposing to smoke Barnes out, Anderson called his stenographer and said he wanted her to take a letter to William Barnes, "Boss of the Liquor End of the Republican Party." The literal-minded stenographer so addressed the letter, though that had not been Anderson's intention. The enraged Barnes declared that the League chief had violated the postal law and threatened to prosecute him unless he retracted. Anderson offered to retract, if Barnes proved any of his statements to be false and then appealed to him to "be game and prove his sincerity in a series of public debates." Barnes refused to debate and sued him for slander, but nothing came of it but publicity for Anderson.[19]

On another occasion he secured the introduction of a bill requiring all liquor to be labeled with a skull and crossbones and the words, "This preparation contains alcohol, which is a habit-forming, irritant, narcotic poison." The wets were in hysterics. "Only a sample of the foolish things this prohibitionist stands for. Every bottle of rock and rye would be marked just like laudanum and carbolic acid. People couldn't help making mistakes; they'd start out to cure a cold and wind up by committing hari-kari." It was only a publicity stunt, and

[18] June 14, 1914.  [19] *New York World*, June 14, 1914.

the secretary of the United States Brewers' Association admitted that it was the best ever put over on them. Step by step Anderson drove the saloon from a large section of New York state. When the Eighteenth Amendment was adopted he saw to it that New York ratified, and it was largely due to his skill and indefatigable efforts that the Mullan-Gage enforcement law was adopted.

The ratification of the Eighteenth Amendment did not lessen his activities. Violators of the Prohibition Law and advocates for light wines and beer were reviled as "a lot of unwashed, wild-eyed foreigners who have no comprehension of the spirit of America." Such language in a conclave of the Klan would no doubt have won him friends, but in New York City it was like a red rag to a bull. As though seeking to add insult to injury, he insisted that the Catholic leaders in New York were the worst enemies of prohibition and good government.[20]   In a city where seventy percent of all churchgoers were Catholics and thirty-six percent of all the people in 1920 were foreign born, the majority of whom were unnaturalized, such tactics could not fail to earn Anderson enemies. True, he insisted that he was not attacking the Catholic Church or aliens as such, but only those who opposed prohibition. These were not easy distinctions for the layman; and in condemning some, Anderson had to take the responsibility for condemning all. Apparently he realized this; he declared that his concern was for the state and not the city anyway. "If it were possible for New York City," he said, "to dribble to hell through a beer funnel without dragging anybody else down, there are plenty of people would say, 'Let her go!'"[21]

More fatal perhaps, to himself and his organization, was his attack on the newspapers:

[20] *American Issue*, New York Edition, Oct. 13, 1923; Oct. 6, 1923; *Current Opinion*, May, 1920; *New York Evening Post*, March 9, 1920; *New York World*, March 10, 1920; *News*, March 10, 1920.
[21] *New York Sun*, March 22, 1920.

Now in New York City many of the newspapers have openly incited to anarchy. Many newspapers during the war were suppressed for less dangerous offenses against the sovereignty of the United States than the *New York World,* for example. . . . These wet newspapers . . . have repeatedly, in the City of New York, incited to lawlessness.[22]

Later in an address at Burlington, Vt.,[23] he declared that " most of the newspapers in New York are dishonest on this question."

Having by his own " meat-ax methods " and incautious language alienated a large section of the people of the city and state, it was inevitable that there should be retaliation. Several efforts had been made to " get " Anderson and with him the League. In 1920, Assemblyman Cuvillier, later famous as the author of the repeal of the Mullan-Gage law, demanded a thorough investigation of the League, which the assembly authorized in March, by a vote of 61 to 52. The mouths of the wets watered at the prospect of treating the League to a Roman holiday. Two directors of the League and eleven ministers, it was said, were anxious to testify.[24] All of the millionaire contributors were to be quizzed, but no names were mentioned except that of Rockefeller.[25] It was suggested that the first session of the committee be held in the League offices to examine the financial records showing the support of four thousand churches and a hundred thousand contributors. Cuvillier promised to show that Anderson's agents, posing as friends of the brewers, fought Speaker Sweet with framed-up charges of brewery support and that Anderson had been accepting $15,000 a year from John D. Rockefeller and had kept this fact from the directors of the League.[26] Rockefeller, of course, denied

---

[22] *Hearings before Committee on Judiciary* on H. R. 5033, House of Representatives, 1921, p. 27.
[23] *New York Times,* Oct. 3, 1921.
[24] *Ibid.,* March 6, 1920.
[25] *New York World,* March 9, 1920.
[26] *Ibid.,* March 10, 1920, and *New York Post,* March 10, 1920.

the charge completely although admitting contributions to the League.

As for Anderson, he treated the whole affair with contempt. He defied the legislature and said he would welcome the opportunity of showing that bribery was rife at Albany, one legislator having received a $40,000 retainer from the wets. He declared that certain ex-service men in the legislature, of whom Cuvillier was spokesman, were tools of the brewers, and that William Barnes was a pro-brewery political boss.[27] " Most of the legislators . . . are in something like the frame of mind, respecting the investigation of the Anti-Saloon League, of the man who had the bear by the tail and wanted to let go." He warned the clergy that it was not safe to believe anything the New York City newspapers said, without independent corroboration.[28]

Although the assembly seemed dead in earnest, the senate refused to coöperate and the inquiry was dropped.[29] There is some indication that the legislature felt it was playing with fire and there was danger that some of the sparks might fall in politically flammable places. So far as the League was concerned, it did not, of course, want an investigation, but it was not intimidated by the threat of one. Anderson called the wets' bluff, as he had done so often, and found it composed chiefly of wind. On March 22, the assembly adopted by a unanimous vote a resolution to compel Anderson to appear and explain the charges he had made against Cuvillier and other members of the assembly. Anderson responded characteristically that he was ready to retract any statement which was proved false. He chided the politicians for being so sensitive. " This is no pink tea or parlor game for points, and the place for political sensitive plants is in the hothouse and not on the beer side of the assembly of New York." [30] He did not appear,

---

[27] *New York Times,* March 6 and 16, 1920.
[28] Circular sent to clergy, March 17, 1920; *Bronx Home News,* March 14, 1920.　　[29] *New York Times,* March 4, 1920.
[30] *New York Post,* March 23, 1920.

to explain or apologize, and Cuvillier's strident demand that he be cited and punished for contempt went unheeded.

The storm broke in the spring of 1923. The Mullan-Gage Law was repealed; the Anti-Saloon League was compelled by the court to report its campaign expenditures [31] and Anderson himself was indicted for larceny, extortion and third degree forgery, and subsequently sent to Sing Sing. A complete history of the facts involved in his indictment and conviction cannot be given here. Space permits only a summary of the facts established.[32]

In 1917 it was arranged between Anderson and one O. B. Phillips, employed as a special financial agent for the League, that Phillips' commissions in excess of ten thousand dollars should be shared with him. In 1918 the sum had been too small to divide, but the plan was carried out in 1919 and again in 1920.

It appeared that on July 7, 1920, Anderson had instructed the League's bookkeeper to draw a check for $2500 to Anderson's own order and charge it to Phillips' salary and commissions account, explaining that he had loaned Phillips $2500 which was being repaid in this way. He deposited the check to his personal account. On March 2, 1921, another check for $1375 was likewise charged to Phillips' account. He explained this time that it was a repayment of money advanced to Phillips. Early in March, to aid him in making out his income tax returns, Phillips was informed that the League books showed his salary and commissions during the preceding year to be $18,893. Phillips claimed that he had received approximately $4000 less than this and objected to paying a tax on money he had not received. Anderson thereupon instructed the bookkeeper to transfer $4400 from Phillips' salary account to his expense account, which was done. But, since the vouchers in

[31] See pp. 215–18.
[32] People *v.* Anderson, 122 Misc. 801; 210 App. Div. 59, 1924; affirmed without opinion, 239 N. Y. 534, 1924.

Phillips' expense account for that year had been only $57.40, it made it appear that the League still owed Phillips $4400 for expenses.

The somewhat technical nature of the forgery of which Anderson was accused appears in the following excerpt from the judge's charge to the jury:

> Under the *first* count of the indictment an intent to defraud someone or some corporation is essential, and the defendant's guilt cannot be established unless it appear from the facts and circumstances and the entries themselves or in some way that there was an intention on his part to defraud; that there was an intention when he made the alterations or directed that they be made; that there was an intention on his part to defraud someone or some corporation.
>
> To establish the defendant's guilt under the *second* count of the indictment it must appear that there was an intentional falsification or an unlawful or corrupt alteration of an account or book of accounts which false entry may be used — and I emphasize the words " may be " — used to prejudice the rights of the corporation, the owner of the account books — the corporation in this case — or bind such corporation, or is capable of being used as legal proof at some time, or in some way, or at some place, against such corporation.[33]

In explaining his dealings with Phillips and his use of the money thus obtained, Anderson said he did not turn the money over to the League but deposited it to his own account, crediting the League upon its indebtedness to him of some $24,700. The officials of the Anti-Saloon League admitted this indebtedness and approved this as one way of paying it. Anderson's story of the creation of this debt, the court summarized:

> On March 26, 1918, defendant for the first time represented to the board of directors of the League that from March 1, 1913, to December 30, 1914, he upon his own initiative had conducted a publicity campaign for the League . . . costing $24,700: that he financed it out of his own funds by mortgaging his home, hypothecating his life insurance policies and borrowing from friends on his personal notes.

[33] 122 Misc. 801. Forgery in the third degree is defined in Sec. 889 of the Penal Law, Chapter 41, Consolidated Laws.

Anderson claimed that he could not give names and vouchers to show how these expenditures were made because he had given his word of honor that he would not reveal their identity. The board of directors, believing him, authorized payment with interest at six percent, as funds became available, and at the time of the trial approximately $11,000 had been paid. This narration the court characterized as " demonstrably " false in view of the fact that at the trial Anderson testified that the money advanced by him was paid out of funds aggregating approximately $25,000, given to him in 1912 and 1913 by one John T. King. He admitted that he never knew King personally or where he lived or did business. The identity of another person, named Mann, whom Anderson claimed to have been his disbursing agent in his publicity campaign, was not revealed. Anderson said that he gave Mann large sums of money in the Pennsylvania terminal but that he had not seen him since 1914. In spite of vigorous objections of the defendant's counsel, ex-Governor Whitman, the trial court admitted this evidence. Of the King story the court said, bluntly, " It is not possible otherwise to characterize the narration except to say that it had every earmark of being a fictitious concoction and one which it was almost impossible for even the most gullible to credit." [34] There is small doubt that the explanations Anderson offered had as much to do with his conviction as the technical forgery.[35]

From information which the author has reason to believe, it seems that the preposterous King story had its elements of

[34] 122 Misc. 801, 815.

[35] Anderson declared that a combination of politics, the press, and disgruntled former League employees led to his indictment and conviction. He quoted District Attorney Banton as having said, " If I put Anderson out of business, it will make me governor." As for the wets, he said their efforts " to destroy me are perfectly legitimate." Before the trial he had asserted that Phillips and former employees of the League who had been dismissed for peculation had offered to sell " revelations " to the *New York World.* But it was decided to have the story first appear in the *Evening Mail,* a paper friendly to prohibition, whose editor, H. L. Stoddard, had intimated that if Anderson would resign the story would not appear. — *American Issue,* New York Edition, Feb. 3 and July 21, 1923; *New York Times,* Jan. 30 and July 17, 1923.

truth. The story runs that while Anderson was superintendent
in Maryland, John T. King, prominent Connecticut Republican, approached him on behalf of Senator Penrose of Pennsylvania, requesting his coöperation in putting over a certain political deal. Anderson agreed to help, and King gave him some
$20,000 as a personal gift.[36] The ethics of such tactics are
questionable enough, but we are here concerned with Anderson's veracity, not his ethics.

His story to the board of directors that the carrying on of his
publicity campaign necessitated the mortgaging of his home
was a shade less accurate. He had intended to use the King
money to pay for his home in Yonkers. Because of the necessity for cash to put the Anti-Saloon League of New York on
the map, he used this money for publicity. As a consequence
he was able to make but a small payment on his home and gave
a mortgage for the remainder. There is, however, no explanation of the manner in which the money was spent beyond that
which Anderson gave to the jury. The Mann incident certainly reads like romance.

There are certain other misconceptions concerning this case
that fairness requires be corrected. The impression has been
that Anderson invented the story of the publicity campaign
in order to shake down the League for $25,000. As a matter of
fact, when he was invited to take charge of the New York
League he was told by the directors that since the income of
the organization was small (it was then barely $30,000 a year)
he must assume responsibility in getting publicity. In 1918,
having more than quadrupled the League's income, Anderson
submitted a statement of his personal expenditures. After investigation the directors agreed to repay him. Realizing, however, that the payment of so large a sum at one time would
cripple the League, it authorized any member of the staff,

[36] Letter to the author from O. S. Poland, counsel to New York League,
Nov. 15, 1927. Mr. Poland says he believes the story to be true.

not engaged exclusively in collecting funds, to add to his salary
by soliciting subscriptions outside the churches on a five percent commission basis. No employee of the League ever took
advantage of this ruling, but Anderson used it to justify his
private agreement with Phillips.[37]

Anderson had reaped the harvest of the vituperative whirl-
wind he had sown. The wets in New York and not a few of
the local drys were glad to be rid of him. The drys outside
of the city, however, filled the columns of the *American Issue*
for almost a year with letters expressing unshakable faith in
him. Most of the directors and officers of the League stood
by him as did most of the church press of the country.[38] Unfortunately for Anderson, he had to fight his battle in New
York, not Kansas.

## Crabbe of Kansas

The New York *Nation*, February 24, 1926, published an
article by one W. G. Clugston, a staff writer on the Topeka
*State Journal*, bearing the intriguing title, " The Anti-Saloon
League's Lost Virtue." According to this writer the Kansas
League had been exposed and thoroughly discredited by Dr.
J. G. Schaibly, a Methodist minister. Dr. C. M. Sheldon,
editor of the *Christian Herald*, this writer claimed, was so
appalled by the disclosures that he urged the churches of Kansas to close their doors to the League. According to Clugston,
there were three villains and one hero in the piece. The three
were F. L. Crabbe, for five years League superintendent, Attorney General C. B. Griffith, and Supreme Court Justice R. J. Hopkins. Dr. Schaibly was the hero.

Stripped of rhetoric, the facts as given by Clugston were as
follows: So many complaints of the tactics employed by
Crabbe poured into the League that the headquarters

[37] *American Issue,* New York Edition, Feb. 17, March 24, April 14 and
July 28, 1923; *New York Times,* Jan. 30 and Feb. 10 and 16, 1923.
[38] *American Issue,* New York Edition, May 5, 1923.

THE FEET OF CLAY

*Courtesy of the New York World*

"In New York City many of the newspapers have openly incited to anarchy. Many newspapers during the war were suppressed for less dangerous offenses against the sovereignty of the United States than the *New York World.*"

— Anderson.

committee was forced to make an investigation and dismiss him. Dr. Schaibly, who was chosen to succeed Crabbe, demanded a public accounting and a thorough house cleaning. When the headquarters committee refused this, says Clugston, and asked Schaibly to keep quiet or get out, he chose the latter course. But before doing so, he photographed some canceled checks showing that Griffith and Hopkins had been paid $3000 and $1200 respectively by the League while drawing their regular salaries from the state. Crabbe in turn drew money from the state treasury for law enforcement work. At the same time, representing himself as an assistant attorney general, he organized enforcement campaigns in over thirty communities and ran off with the funds collected. These activities of Crabbe were carried on without the knowledge or sanction of the League, and none of the money so collected was turned into the League treasury.

Clugston does not accuse the League of being directly involved in Crabbe's peccadillos. But he does accuse it of having become an accomplice " after the fact " by issuing a statement " whitewashing " these transactions after they became known. " But in Kansas as in New York," he writes, " the Anti-Saloon League as an organization sought to cover up rather than clear up illegal acts of its agents and has done everything in its power to keep the facts from the public."

The charge that the League " whitewashed " the whole matter and kept the facts from the public is simply not true. In January, 1926, the League, through its headquarters committee, made a careful investigation and made public a statement signed by an independent auditor giving in much greater detail every important disclosure which Clugston gives. Crabbe was roundly denounced, his methods angrily repudiated and he himself summarily dismissed.[39] He was forced to return $2500 to

---

[39] *Topeka Daily Capital*, Jan. 22, 1926. Among the members of the special committee of investigation were W. R. Stubbs, a former governor of Kansas, and E. H. Lindley, chancellor of the state university.

the League, which, with $2000 due him as salary, was paid to his victims.

The League took exception to the charges against Griffith and Hopkins. It is not an unheard-of thing for public officials to have sources of income outside their official salaries. Nor was it so much as suggested that either of these men was less zealous or sincere in the performance of his public duties. Their payments from the League covered a period of five or six years, and averaged annually about $350 each. This money was paid to cover expenses. Justice Hopkins delivered 125 addresses in all parts of the state, and received barely seven dollars per meeting.[40]

As for Dr. Schaibly, he had never been state superintendent, but served for a time as acting superintendent in the fall of 1925 when the Crabbe investigation was in progress. He was dismissed when it was learned that he had taken private correspondence from the League files and turned it over to the newspapers.[41]

The intimation that the Kansas churches, at Dr. Sheldon's warning, closed their doors to the League is likewise more than an exaggeration. In March, 1926, a church conference, attended by over four hundred ministers representing a membership of over 88,000, endorsed the Kansas League and elected representatives to serve on its board of trustees.[42]

With all the smoke that has been raised concerning corruption within the League, it is surprising to learn that there is so little fire. " I recognize," said Frank Kent of the *Baltimore Sun,* " that to concede that the Anti-Saloon League is anything but a ' bunch of crooks ' will cause a good many wets around here severe pain. . . . What I have said about the character

[40] *Topeka Daily Capital,* Jan. 22, 1926.

[41] Letter from J. A. McClellan, the present superintendent of the Kansas League, 1927.

[42] *Ottawa Herald,* Kansas, March 6, 1926.

of these men is a fundamental fact which it seems to me ought to be understood. They are not only honest but the real leaders are amazingly astute, incredibly efficient, practical to a point and with an ability to see ahead about eight times as far as the average political party leader."

# CHAPTER IX

## " HIGH POLITICS "

The fanaticism of the temperance reformers has been a favorite theme for newspaper columnists, cartoonists and wags. In the welter of conflicting propaganda about prohibition and prohibitionists there is danger of forgetting that these crusaders were not fighting a figment, but were engaged in battle with a most powerful enemy. " We must not overlook the fact," said the *American Issue,* " that we confront a foe that has ill-gotten wealth without limit and no conscience in the spending of it. Love for country, human character, domestic happiness, personal reputation, have no place in its code of warfare. . . . Bribery is one of the mildest of its methods for accomplishing its purpose." [1] " Falsehood, bribery, cupidity, terrorism and slander, are their weapons," said Purley Baker. " I have been hounded by detectives and harassed by defectives and waylaid by harlots . . . but I have not been honored beyond many of my brethren. Many of them wear on their bodies the marks of honorable warfare. . . . I have had the sergeant-at-arms in the legislature of my native state . . . escort me to the door . . . while the big well-fed and well-drunk brewery lobbyist would stand in front of the speaker's desk thumbing his vest and smiling at my discomfort. . . . But all this has not stayed the hand of retributive justice that reaches for the throat of an American, and, please God, what is soon to be a world, outlaw." [2] Nor should it be assumed that this was merely rhetoric, although it has become the fashion so to regard it. Senator Reed of Mis-

[1] Maryland Edition, Jan. 16, 1912.
[2] *Proceedings of the Nineteenth Convention of the Anti-Saloon League,* 1919, p. 31.

souri, during his examination of Wheeler, charged that the Anti-Saloon League itself had forced the liquor trade into politics.[3] The fact is that Congress, in July, 1862, included a tax of one dollar per barrel on beer in its domestic liquors taxes, and within four months the United States Brewers' Association was formed. " Patriotism," we are told, " ready to sacrifice self-interest, was the most patent motive of those who organized this body and those who joined it." [4]

Besides being patriotic, they were also practical business men who realized that self-sacrifice had its limitations. The preamble to their constitution said:

> Coöperation is necessary. Owners of breweries, separately, are unable to exercise a proper influence in the legislative and public administration. It appears especially necessary for the brewing trade that its interests be vigorously and energetically prosecuted before the legislative and executive departments, as this branch of business is of considerable political and financial importance, exerting a direct as well as an indirect influence on political and social relations.[5]

Early in October, 1863, after almost daily correspondence with government officers, the brewers succeeded in having the tax reduced to sixty cents a barrel. When the Federal Excise Tax Law was revised in 1866, the brewers had a large part in its preparation.[6]

[3] *Report of the Senate Committee on Campaign Expenditures,* June, 1926, Senate Report 1197, 69th Congress, 1st Session, p. 1374.

[4] *Year Book of the United States Brewers' Association,* 1909, p. 11.

[5] See *Proceedings of the Ninth Brewers' Congress,* 1869, p. 13.

[6] " When the 1865 Congress created a Special Revenue Commission with a view to perfecting the system, the United States Brewers' Association again volunteered its assistance, and at its own expense sent a committee to Europe for the purpose of studying the excise methods in the various beer-producing countries.

" Under special instruction from the Treasury Department, the Special Revenue Commissioner attended the brewers' convention at which this committee reported. So deeply was this officer impressed with the report, its remarkable wealth of economic and statistical information, and the sound conclusions based upon it as to our country, that he recommended its transmission to Congress in its original form.

" . . . Congress adopted the system which was proposed by the brewers and which in its essential features remains in force to the present day." — *Year*

The National Brewers' Congress in 1867 declared: " We will sustain no candidate of whatever party, in any election, who is in any way disposed toward the total abstinence cause." The following year its president said that the New York brewers endeavored " to secure candidates for the legislature who would, without regard to political party, promote and protect the brewing interest. Neither means nor money were spared. The entire German population was enlisted. Editorials were published in sixty different newspapers: 30,000 campaign circulars were distributed." [7]

When the Democrats in 1872 nominated Horace Greeley for the presidency, the Republicans countered with a famous plank against sumptuary legislation. At the convention of the Brewers' Association the president announced: [8]

The Democrats have placed at the head of their ticket a man whose antecedents will warrant him a pliant tool in the hands of the temperance party, and none of you gentlemen can support him. It is necessary for you to make an issue at this election throughout the entire country, and although I have belonged to the Democratic party ever since I had a vote, I would sooner vote for the Republican ticket than cast my vote for such a candidate.

The next year he expressed his satisfaction at the outcome of the election:

The last presidential election has shown us what unity among us can do. Let our vote and work in the future be heard from in every direction.

The brewers were familiar with the methods of pressure politics ten years before the Anti-Saloon League was born. The New York State Brewers' and Maltsters' Association on March

*Book of the United States Brewers' Association,* 1909, p. 13. See *Bonfort's Wine and Spirit Circular,* Oct. 10, 1890, for an account of the influence of the brewers in Congress.

[7] *Proceedings of the Seventh Brewers' Congress,* 1867, pp. 3–10; also, *Eighth Brewers' Congress,* 1868, p. 4.

[8] *Proceedings of the Twelfth Brewers' Congress,* 1872, p. 6.

20, 1883, declared that it was an anti-prohibition association, pure and simple, and that it would not affiliate with any political party; that it would quiz all candidates for public office concerning their stand on temperance legislation; that when candidates of both or all parties answered satisfactorily, members were to be free to vote as they deemed best, but where candidates failed to answer at all or sent unsatisfactory replies, their election was to be fought with vigor; and that if no candidate answered favorably, an independent nomination would be considered.[9]

The organ of the wholesale liquor dealers boasted of the success of these methods.

Do you deny that the liquor vote controls the situation in this state? What defeated Warner Miller and elected Governor Hill? What gave the Democratic party its present majority in the Assembly? What elected the Tammany ticket in this last year? Was it not the united strength of the liquor vote? [10]

Though the League could scarcely be accused of driving the liquor trade into politics, the entry of the League into the field after 1893 required the liquor dealers to redouble their political efforts. While the booming guns of state-wide prohibition parties were disconcerting, they were easily located and soon silenced, so that up to 1895 the field looked promising for the trade. The local option campaign of the Anti-Saloon League, however, was like sniping from behind trees and stone fences, and the liquor people realized it was to be a battle to the death.

### The Saloon in Action

Where the League used the Protestant churches as the basis for political power, the liquor interests used the saloon. Lo-

[9] *The Voice,* Sept. 24, 1885.
[10] *Wine and Spirit Gazette,* April 28, 1891, quoted in H. F. Gosnell, *Boss Platt and His New York Machine,* Chicago, 1924, p. 41.

cally the saloon became the political center for anti-temperance agitation. The supervision of liquor selling by the local authorities made the saloon keeper desirous of controlling the situation for his own protection. Originally a defensive instrument, politics tended to become a primary function of the saloon. The " Boodle " Board of Aldermen in New York, 1884, included twelve saloon keepers and four saloon-controlled politicians in a total membership of twenty-four. In the same year, of 1002 conventions and primaries of the Republican and Democratic parties, 633 were held in saloons and 96 in places next door to saloons.[11] Eleven of the twenty-four aldermen elected in 1890 were saloon keepers. As for Tammany itself, the membership of the General Committee in 1890 was 4562, and of this number 681 were liquor dealers.[12] At this time there were nine saloon keepers on the Board of Aldermen in Chicago, an equal number in Detroit, and four in Omaha.[13]

## Allied Machines

In New York City alone there were over 8600 saloons in 1912; Chicago boasted more than 7000.[14] But the liquor traffic did not limit its political activities to the saloon. Personal Liberty Leagues, Model License Leagues, Manufacturers' and Dealers' Associations, and thousands of other local organizations were formed to stay the wave of temperance reform.

[11] Robert Graham, *New York and Its Masters*, New York, 1887, pp. 38, 39; W. M. Ivins, *Machine Politics and Money in Elections in New York City*, New York, 1887, pp. 21, 125.

[12] *New York Evening Post*, Oct. 1-14, 1890. *New York Daily Tribune*, Oct. 9, 12, 1890.

[13] *The Voice*, Sept. 26, 1889, gives a list of offices held by liquor dealers in thirty-three cities. An editorial in *McClure's Magazine*, October, 1908, said: " The case of Tammany Hall . . . is most familiar. Its politicians for half a century have graduated into public affairs through the common school of the saloon. . . . The same condition exists in nearly every one of the larger cities of the country. An analysis of the membership of the boards of aldermen in these cities for the past few decades shows a percentage of saloon keepers which is astounding." See *McClure's*, Sept., 1907, for a description of saloon control in San Francisco.

[14] *World Almanac*, 1914, p. 249.

There were, in 1908, 1747 breweries, 1200 distilleries and over 100,000 saloons, whose employees, numbering more than a million, were directly interested in the protection of the trade from the onslaught of the dry hosts. Hotels with bars, cafés that served liquor, farmers who raised hops and grapes, and many other allied industries swelled the wet ranks. The manufacturers' and dealers' associations were estimated to have 70,000 members.[15]

The methods employed were essentially the same as those used by other pressure groups: publicity, organization of voters, and lobbying. Fancy-priced publicity agents prepared their literature; clever lobbyists secured favorable legislation, which high-salaried attorneys drafted and later defended before the courts.

## THE TEXAS BREWERS

In 1916, seven Texas breweries were fined a total of $281,000 for violating certain laws respecting poll taxes, political contributions and political activities of corporations. Their charters were forfeited and their successors were permanently enjoined from such activities.[16]

As early as May 14, 1903, the following agreement had been made:

The undersigned hereby agree to pay an assessment of 20 (twenty) cents per barrel on their sales of keg beer in Texas, and 1 (one) cent per dozen of bottle beer, from the 1st day of June, 1903, to the 1st day of June, 1904. The money to be spent by a committee to be appointed by and under the direction of subscribers for the purpose of promoting anti-prohibition matters in Texas.

[15] Hampton's *New Broadway Magazine*, Aug., 1908.
[16] *Biennial Report of the Attorney General,* 1914–16, pp. 22, 23. Attorney General B. F. Looney instituted the proceedings in the case of the State of Texas *v.* Dallas Brewery *et al.* in the district court of Hopkins County in 1915. The various defendants pleaded *nolle contendere,* but the attorney general refused to accept this settlement until his evidence be read in open court and placed on public record. Two volumes containing " practically all of the evidence introduced " were privately printed in 1916. — *The Breweries and Texas Politics,* San Antonio, 1916, 2 vols., 1605 pp.

The money to be paid from time to time as needed, and called for by the committee.

> Galveston Brewing Co., by B. Adoue, Pres.
> Texas Brewing Co., Zane Cetti, Pres.
> San Antonio Brewing Ass'n, O. Koehler, Pres.
> Dallas Brewery, S. T. Morgan, Pres.
> Houston Ice and Brewing Co., H. Hamilton, Pres.
> American Brewing Ass'n, H. Prince, Sec'y and Treas.
> Lone Star Brewing Co., B. Adoue, Vice-Pres.
> Anheuser-Busch Brewing Ass'n, E. S. Clauss.
> Wm. J. Levy Brewing Co., B. Adoue, Vice-Pres.

The attorney general's petition, filed January 9, 1915, alleged that:

The foregoing contract was carried out by the parties thereto and the money derived thereunder was used for the purpose of attempting to influence, affect and control . . . legislation and the result of elections in Texas, and for the purpose of securing the payment of poll taxes to qualify persons known to such parties to have views on the subject matter of such elections favorable to the legalizing of the sale of intoxicating liquors.[17]

Dissatisfied with the funds thus provided and large sums contributed by the United States Brewers' Association, a plan was adopted in 1908 to enlist all dealers and manufacturers who sold goods to Texas brewers. The following letter [18] was addressed to these allied industries:

Houston, Texas, June 23, 1908.

Dear Sirs:

We have a state-wide prohibition fight on our hands and it is fast and furious.

The fight is before the state Democratic primary, to be held July 25. The result of the Texas Democratic primary is equivalent to an election, therefore, the result at the primary is for a purpose final.

We need money and are appealing to all merchants, manufacturers, persons and corporations from whom each of the breweries in Texas

[17] *The Breweries and Texas Politics*, Vol. 1, p. 15.
[18] *Ibid.*, Vol. 1, p. 124.

bought goods in the year 1907, to give us 1 percent of the amount of the bill bought and paid for.

On this basis we assess you the sum of $ .

Kindly send us your check at once, making it payable to the writer individually. This donation from you will be bread cast upon the water.

> Yours very truly,
> Texas Brewers' Association,
> B. Adoue, President

Under this veiled threat more than ten thousand dollars was collected from 116 firms and corporations throughout the United States.[19]

It is not possible to discover the total raised for political purposes. Some idea may be gained from a statement, May 31, 1911, of the vice-president and general manager of the San Antonio Brewing Association, that " We are now in the midst of a campaign which will cost the breweries of this state the sum of $500,000." The Galveston Brewing Company claimed that between 1905 and 1907 the Texas Brewers' Association spent over $300,000 to fight prohibition.[20] Perhaps the best testimony is that of the head of the Texas Association:

> Over one-half million dollars have been spent during the past five years to fight vicious legislation and to resist local option elections; in fact, we can say that one million dollars has been spent for protection of the brewing industry in Texas since 1900, or an average of over $100,000 per annum.[21]

The manner in which this money was spent is described in great detail. Propaganda on a large scale was undertaken. An

[19] *Ibid.*, Vol. 1, pp. 128–30. Among those contributing were: American Steel Package Co., American Cork Co., American Hominy Co., Brunswick-Balke-Collender Co., Liquid Carbonic Co., Sprague Electric Co. The names of sixty-four of these concerns who did not at first respond were passed along for the information of the trade. They included: American Car and Foundry Co., American Car and Equipment Co., Corn Products Refining Co., Fairbanks, Morse and Co., Krebs Brothers (of Salem, Oregon), General Electric Co., Western Electric Co. [20] *Ibid.*, Vol. 1, pp. 150, 549.
[21] Letter of March 2, 1911, *Ibid.*, Vol. 1, p. 332.

educational bureau was established and maintained. As early as 1902 the manager of the Texas Brewers' Association wrote the San Antonio Brewing Association: " It is very important that we get the newspapers under our influence." During the single month of January, 1909, over a quarter of a million handbills were distributed. One member put out between fifty and sixty thousand and " of the 700 wholesalers and retailers nearly every one took from 100 to 5000." Advertisements were placed in every colored newspaper in the state. " Boiler plate " was furnished from time to time to the country newspapers. One such article appeared in 650 publications in 1914. Through judicious advertising the brewers in 1911 boasted that " every daily newspaper in the State of Texas of any consequence . . . is on our side." The complete control which they exercised over a portion, at least, of the press is reflected in a letter of the president of the San Antonio Association: " I have written out a statement for our newspaper editors to be guided by . . . and [they] will govern themselves accordingly." They controlled most of the labor journals.[22]

They were zealous in organizing and getting out the wet vote. Negro ministers were found effective in looking after the negro votes in local option elections. They organized the Mexican vote, but in this they encountered difficulties similar to those met in organizing the negroes — namely, Mexicans did not pay their poll taxes.[23] Brewery employees were informed that the management would not tolerate failure to pay poll taxes and vote. The German voters were mobilized through the Grand Lodge of The Sons of Hermann. Catholic priests were induced

[22] *The Breweries and Texas Politics,* Vol. 2, p. 666; Vol. 1, pp. 214, 278, 110–112, 155, 164. For further details of these publicity activities see Vol. 1, pp. 184, 347, 418, 432–33, 483–85, 571–72; Vol. 2, pp. 67, 587, 743–44, 785, 1151–57, 1474–77.

[23] " All our votes are Mexicans," said an organizer in one county, " but we need money to work it. Very near all are good voters but they do not pay their poll taxes, unless someone does it. For that reason we have to have money to attend to that part, and also money for the day of the election. . . ." — *Ibid.,* Vol. I, pp. 55, 301; Vol. 2, p. 959.

to speak against prohibition, and every effort was made to marshal the Catholic vote. The Citizens' Forward Movement,
Young Men's Business League, Liberty Leagues, etc., received
the brewers' blessing and financial aid. The San Antonio
Brewing Company, Jan. 11, 1906, sent the following notice to
all agents: " Of prime importance to us . . . is proper organization. Call in your friends, the business men especially that are
in sympathy with our cause, and see that the proper organization is effected at once." In all local option elections the saloon vote was marched to the polls.[24]

## Controlling the Legislature

" We have arranged with the ruling political party," said an
agent of the San Antonio Brewing Association, " to allow us to
name a senator and representative to the legislature. We are
trying to get Judge Dean to run as senator, and believe he will
go if paid for his time while away from his business. I feel
quite sure it will take at least $3000 to pay him while away
from his practice here, but he would be a valuable man in the
legislature at this time [1908]. I think we can get Judge
Burns, who is also a good one, without paying him anything.
Burns has been speaker of the house in New Mexico and knows
how to do things." [25]

Members of the Association were kept informed as to who

[24] *Ibid.*, Vol. 1, p. 308; Vol. 2, p. 668; Vol. 1, pp. 447, 80–88, 359, 241; Vol.
2, pp. 577, 1137.

[25] *Ibid.*, Vol. 1, p. 258. Frequently their agents appeared to be working at
cross purposes. Consider the alarm of one such at the too obvious tactics of a
fellow-Warwick. " Paget of Galveston," he wrote, " is in this building, closeted
with Mr. Hayes Shannon and others, as I understand for the purpose of decid-
ing upon a candidate for the legislature. . . . It looks like every time we begin
to quietly arrange matters for the future, some fellow will step in and disarrange
everything we try to do! If this fellow would stay in Galveston, we would be
much better off. His presence here is generally heralded by some of our . . .
friends, and the pros [drys] know what is going on, and make considerable capital out of it. If we were let alone, think we could get a good conservative man
of our kind nominated to the legislature." Paget was campaign manager for
the Texas Brewers' Association and frequently was heard to compare himself
to " the great von Moltke." — *Breweries and Texas Politics,* Vol. 1, p. 390; Vol.
2, p. 885.

their friends in the legislature were. When legislation dealing with liquor was pending, they were appealed to in a variety of ways. Large sums were sometimes spent on entertainments. In one case $4800 was spent on a single party. At these functions it was always made plain who the host was and what he wanted. Lobbyists talked with the governor, with senators and representatives and " perfected combinations and consolidations and arrangements " to insure the passage of friendly legislation and to defeat that which was unfriendly. Complete records were kept of all legislative candidates and their attitude toward the liquor question. Those favorable received help in many ways. Lobbyists were given blanket instructions to do what was necessary " regardless of the expense." As to what was necessary, there is plenty of evidence; $295 was paid to a member for " his attendance on the legislature." Legislators who were fortunate enough to own newspapers received numerous checks for advertising. There was no mincing of words in explaining why this was paid; it was admitted that in one case, at least, advertising space was purchased " only because the publisher of that paper was a member of the legislature." One member made no bones about it. In seeking a renewal of an advertising contract, he based his claim on the fact that " as a member of the liquor committee I accomplished the defeat of a bill designed to teach prohibition in the public schools of the state." The ready use of money may be inferred from the description given of a certain bit of difficult lobbying in which the brewers' agent said, " This work has to be done very quietly and through people that cannot be approached in a financial way." [26]

## Local Option Elections

The election laws were not permitted to hinder these activities. The law forbade the furnishing of conveyances to carry

[26] *The Breweries and Texas Politics*, Vol. 1, pp. 142, 186, 205, 373, 459, 479; also, pp. 346, 355, 375, 484, 495, 428.

people to the polls, " but," said Paget, the brewers' agent, " we do it all the same, as there are more ways than one of choking a cat." The brewers frequently depended upon the impelling motive of saloon graft to induce office-holders to fight against curtailment of it. Although willing to have these corrupt officials fight their battles, they did not hesitate to use the knowledge of this corruption to upset election returns. Concerning the Grimes County local option election in 1906, Paget wrote, " I had information . . . that the officials were in the lead of graft, getting money from the joints now openly run in the county, I knew they would not give up the plant without a struggle." In spite of this the drys won and Paget proposed to contest the result, assuring his chief, " We will get the decision all right as soon as we can get the courts." The dry victory in Robertson County, 1910, was successfully contested and rescinded for reasons which Paget said " are best not written about." In the local option election in Liberty County, 1907, apparently the election judges on both sides had been fixed, for he wrote: " The election will be absolutely illegal, void, no matter which way it goes." He is cautious about explaining, " as it might get one of the judges of election into trouble, and as he is a good friend of ours, that would be a very poor return for his kindness. I do not mind explaining it to you *viva voce*, but it would not be advisable to put it on paper." But in Henderson County, where the prohibitionists had won, it was found, when the ballot boxes were opened, that " our friends had made an error in their calculations and there were more illegal anti [wet] votes than pros [dry] and consequently the contest failed." [27]

These political methods were not confined to the state of Texas. In 1896 the New York liquor dealers set about defeating the Raines excise bill. To that end a slush fund was

[27] *Ibid.*, Vol. 2, pp. 751–52, 784, 1007, 858, 805. On the use of money in elections, see Vol. 1, pp. 385–89, 326–28; Vol. 2, p. 1077.

raised " big enough to buy all the men in the senate who are purchasable." Boss Platt, who wanted the bill passed, threatened the liquor people with a " lot of criminal prosecutions " if the measure was defeated. As a consequence the money was sent back and the deal was not consummated! In the fight for prohibition in the Florida legislature in 1908, one of the drys, it was said, was offered thirty thousand dollars to vote against the measure. In the Maryland legislature of 1912 there were rumors of bribery and corruption by the liquor interests on a large scale.[28]

## THE SENATE LIFTS THE LID

Another *exposé,* more thorough and more damning, of the brewers' political activities, took place in Pennsylvania in 1914. Indictments were returned against approximately one hundred corporations and associations for violation of the conspiracy section of the Federal criminal code. Practically all entered pleas of *nolle contendere* and were fined. The evidence collected at that investigation was later subpœnaed by the United States Senate Judiciary Committee in September, 1919, at the instance of Wheeler.[29]

In its report to the Senate the committee said:

With regard to the conduct and activities of the brewing and liquor interests, the committee is of the opinion that the record clearly establishes the following facts:

(a) That they have furnished large sums of money for the purpose of secretly controlling newspapers and periodicals.

---

[28] Gosnell, *Boss Platt and His New York Machine,* Chicago, 1924, p. 164, quoting *New York Tribune* for Feb. 29, 1896; Platt's *Autobiography,* p. 472; *Proceedings of the Thirteenth Convention of the Anti-Saloon League,* 1909; *Baltimore News,* Jan. 2, 1912.

[29] *Congressional Record,* 65th Congress, 2d Session, 1919, p. 5187. The proceedings were instituted by E. L. Humes, U. S. District Attorney. At their conclusion he continued in possession of the records. When the Senate investigation began, Humes, now in the service, was detailed by the Secretary of War to aid the committee. (Letter to the author from Major Humes, Feb. 18, 1926.)

(b) That they have undertaken to and have frequently succeeded in controlling primaries, elections and political organizations.

(c) That they have contributed enormous sums of money to political campaigns in violation of the Federal statutes and the statutes of several of the states.

(d) That they have exacted pledges from candidates for public office prior to the election.

(e) That . . . they have attempted and partly succeeded in subsidizing the public press.

(f) That to suppress and coerce persons hostile to and to compel support for them they have resorted to an extensive system of boycotting unfriendly American manufacturing and mercantile concerns.

(g) That they have created their own political organization in many states and in smaller political units for the purpose of carrying into effect their own political will and have financed the same with large contributions and assessments.

(h) That with a view of using it for their own political purposes they have contributed large sums of money to the German-American Alliance. . . .

(i) That they organized clubs, leagues and corporations of various kinds for the purpose of secretly carrying on their political activities without having their interest known to the public.

(j) That they improperly treated the funds expended for political purposes as a proper expenditure of their business and consequently failed to return the same for taxation under the revenue laws of the United States.

(k) That they undertook through a cunningly conceived plan of advertising and subsidation to control and dominate the foreign language press of the United States.

(l) That they have subsidized authors of recognized standing in literary circles to write articles of their selection for many standard publications.

(m) That for many years a working agreement existed between the brewing and distilling interests of the country by the terms of which the brewing interests contributed two-thirds and the distilling interests one-third of the political expenditures made by the joint interests.[30]

[30] *Brewing and Liquor Interests and German and Bolshevik Propaganda,* Senate Doc. 62, 66th Congress, 1st Session, 1919, Vol. 1, pp. 1385.

It is not proposed to enter in any detailed manner into the
mass of documentary and testamentary evidence that was submitted in support of these charges. The merest summary is
possible.

### Finances

The basis for financing the activities of the United States
Brewers' Association was a barrelage tax imposed on all members. Beginning at one-quarter of a cent, by 1913 the tax was
three cents, which, levied on more than 25,000,000 barrels,
yielded annually for a period of five years over $750,000.
Checks and stubs were systematically destroyed. In the single
year 1915 there was deposited in the central treasury $1,049,-
091, or $1,400,000; it is not certain which amount. During
the period 1913–18, exclusive of 1916, the sum paid into the
central treasury was $4,457,941. The state associations levied
as high as twenty cents to fifty cents a barrel. In four years
the Pennsylvania Association raised $922,000. In 1914 $300,-
000 was deposited to the credit of the Pennsylvania state association. These sums do not by any means represent the total
collected or spent. Large sums were raised and disbursed by
individuals or under other auspices. In 1917 an advertising
fund of $535,000 was collected in this way, though less than
half of the six hundred members of the national association
contributed.[31]

The national association maintained an organization bureau
whose work it was to conduct political campaigns, rally the
voters, and to see that the drys were kept in their place. In
1915 the bureau reported that the brewers had taken an active
part, and in many cases a leading part, in the direction of the
following campaigns: Colorado, Connecticut, Florida, Georgia,
Idaho, Illinois, Indiana, Kentucky, Louisiana, Maine, Massa-

[31] *Brewing and Liquor Interests and German and Bolshevik Propaganda,*
Senate Doc. 62, 66th Congress, 1st Session, 1919, Vol. I, pp. 85, 342, 401, 77, 96,
346, 417, 425.

chusetts, Michigan, Minnesota, Missouri, Nebraska, New Jersey, North Carolina, Ohio, Pennsylvania, Rhode Island, South Dakota, Tennessee, Texas, Utah, West Virginia and Wisconsin.[32] The efficiency with which this bureau worked has been colorfully told in its own reports:

## Iowa [33]

Early in June, 1913, the brewers of Iowa requested you to outline a plan of campaign for the State and expressed a willingness to follow the details of such a plan when they were perfected. The Brewers of Iowa stated that they were confronted with complete annihilation unless it were possible to so educate the people of the State that a majority in either branch of their Legislature would oppose state-wide prohibition and favor some constructive form of legislation that would result in option elections instead of the present petition system. Following your instructions, your organization department had a complete survey of the State made to ascertain the actual conditions existing in the State, and upon this survey an analysis of those conditions was made, and a general plan of campaign outlined. The first fight in connection with that campaign occurred at the primaries held in Iowa, June 1st, 1914. Previous to that time the Indianapolis German-American Alliance Bureau, at your direction, sent several of its very best men into the State to awaken the Germans to a realization of the detriments that state-wide prohibition would bring to Iowa. Correspondence resulting in the enlistment of the liberal clergy throughout the State in an aggressive campaign against the fanatical dry element, and through the work of these and other men, the German-American Alliance was made a strong and effective ally in the fight. At the same time that the men from the Indianapolis bureau entered the State your organization department sent labor organizers into Iowa, whose duty it was to arouse as far as possible the labor element of the State, and in this direction excellent work was also accomplished. Perhaps the most gratifying condition found to exist in Iowa was the complete willingness of the brewers of that State, and their counsel, Mr. Henry Thuenen, of Davenport, to follow out the plans of campaign suggested by you.

[32] *Ibid.*, p. 1021.  [33] *Ibid.*, p. 458.

## Ohio [34]

Undoubtedly the greatest success which has to be recorded at the recent elections was the result in Ohio. . . . At a conference held with those interested in the industry in that State, your advice and counsel was asked as to the advisability of submitting a constitutional amendment which would have the effect of repealing the County Option Law, and inhibiting future Legislatures from passing statutory state-wide prohibition. It was pointed out in that meeting that should such action be taken, the Anti-Saloon League might retaliate with a constitutional amendment providing for state-wide prohibition. . . .

At the meeting referred to, in Cincinnati, when it was decided to initiate a Home Rule Amendment providing for the repeal of the County Option Law, your instructions issued to this department to throw as many available men into the State to assist in the circulation of the petitions was immediately complied with, and the whole force which had been engaged in the survey work in other States, was immediately placed at the disposal of Mr. Hunt to arrange for the circulation of the petitions. As a result of the efforts put forth by this force, augmenting the force already at the disposal of the Ohio campaign manager, 304,062 voters of Ohio affixed their signatures to the petitions for the amendment in less than thirty days' time, and this mammoth petition was filed with the Secretary of State on August 4th. True to the prediction made at the meeting in Cincinnati in June, the Anti-Saloon League, upon the announcement that the liberals would petition for the repeal of County Option, began the circulation of petitions providing for constitutional prohibition, and filed on August 4th, with the Secretary of State, 175,000 signatures, or 129,000 less than those signing the liberal petition. . . . Your organization department put all of its available men in Ohio and kept them there from early September until the election was held. . . . .

One of the remarkable features of the campaign came as a result of the excellent work performed by the United Brewery Workers and through them by all liberal elements of organized labor. . . . Your plans of campaign were strictly followed in Ohio with the result that prohibition was defeated by approximately 85,000 votes, and strictly local option is written into the constitution of the State, with an

[34] *Ibid.*, Vol. 1, p. 461.

inhibition against statutory state-wide prohibition by a majority approximating 15,000.

The brewers, like the League, exacted pledges from candidates for public office. The latter were quick to respond, especially where there was need for financial aid. Myer J. Stein, candidate for the Republican nomination for United States Senator from Illinois in 1914, wrote to the agent of the brewers:

I am enclosing you those parts of my platform pertaining to the subject of personal liberty and to the malt liquor industry. I want to circulate one million of these pamphlets as well as to wage an educational campaign through the state, if I can get the required assistance. I do not wish any individual subscriptions to exceed $25, and if consistent with your principles, I would appreciate your aid.[35]

Information relative to candidates and the general political situation in hundreds of communities was carefully gathered. The thoroughgoing nature of these inquiries may be illustrated by the card which they kept for each candidate: [36]

[35] *Ibid.*, p. 1001.
[36] *Ibid.*, p. 1263. The community surveys were equally penetrating, as is indicated by the following items culled from the one hundred and six questions on their community score card (*ibid.*, pp. 1256–59):
  15. How many justices of the peace in the county?
  19. How many school districts?
  23. Percentage of inhabitants church members?
  24. What religion predominates?
  27. Lodge members and location?
  28. Political activity?
  29. Officers of various lodges?
  30. Membership of Eagles? Elks? Owls? Moose? etc.
  54. German population?
  60. What is situation as to organized labor?
  61. What industries employ most men?
  62. Name unions in town.
  64. Officers of each local union and membership?
  71. Give all the active leaders in Democratic party in county and their attitude on the liquor question?
  88. Give the name of the newspapers in the county, their politics and attitude upon the liquor question?
  89. Names of foreign newspapers in county; nationality of each; circulation of each, name and address of publisher of each?

1. Full name?
2. Age?
3. Married or Single?
4. If married, does wife exercise any undue influence in regard to his business or political affairs?
5. Politics?
6. Is he popular or unpopular in his community?
7. Schooling?
8. Business?
9. Financial standing?
10. Where is his banking business, commercial and private, transacted?
11. What position does the bank (or banks) assume on the wet and dry questions?
12. Is candidate known as a liberal or dry man?
13. Was he ever a candidate for any political office?
14. Elected or defeated?
15. Elected by how many?
16. Defeated by how many?
17. Number of votes in the city?
18. Number of votes in the county?
19. Religion?
20. To what fraternal organizations does he belong?
21. Recreation?
22. Name some of his closest associates?
General remarks.

## Propaganda

The propaganda output of the Association was formidable. Its monthly magazine, *The Hearthstone,* was established and had a circulation of 301,000 in 1915, chiefly in the small communities. The " news bureau " sent its weekly news service to 5300 of the 12,000 weekly papers in the country. Circulation of these papers was estimated at 1000 each, so that altogether the bureau reached about 5,300,000 subscribers. In 1914 they reported that " personal liberty " articles were being published in 683 newspapers, representing twenty-nine different languages, with a combined circulation of 7,500,000. It was esti-

mated that 431,600,000 actual pieces of literature were sent out
by the brewers or the foreign language press in 1915.[37]  The
board of trustees of the Association reported their expenditures
for propaganda in 1915 as:

Foreign Language Press .......... $ 70,000
German-American Alliance ........    30,000
Newspapers and News Bureau ....    30,000
Publicity (general) .............    20,000
_____
Total ......... $150,000

Advertising for frankly political purposes was carried on,
and special writers were paid to write articles for such leading
magazines as *The Medical Record, Journal of Medical Association, Survey, Outlook, National Municipal Review,* and even
the *American Undertaker.*  " Boiler-plate " material was furnished to hundreds of small newspapers throughout the country because such material could not be altered by the editorial
staff.[38]

Mr. Charles H. Allen in 1915 purchased the *Montgomery
Advertiser,* of Alabama, with $100,000 advanced by the brew-
ers.  Christian Feigenspan, Newark brewer, advanced some
$150,000 from time to time to finance the *Newark Ledger.*  In
1917 he collected $260,000, from fifteen brewers and the Asso-
ciation, to enable Arthur Brisbane to purchase the *Washington
Times.*  It was felt that " public welfare and our own industry
— because of your [Brisbane's] well-known convictions —
would be benefited by your personal ownership of a daily newspaper."  In all, $375,000 was so advanced without interest, to
be paid back only as the profits from the paper made repayment possible.  The only evidence of this debt was a note of

[37] A play, *The Passing of Hans Dippel,* presenting the story of a German
saloon keeper, a good man and true, gradually ruined by the fanatical drys, was
presented in eight cities in Ohio and Missouri. — *Ibid.,* p. 1253.

[38] *Ibid.,* pp. 1252–54, 60, 780, 456, 476, 478, 533, 996, 473.

the Growing Circulation Corporation, a concern owned by Brisbane. In July, 1918, Feigenspan testified that he had received nothing toward its liquidation.[39]

The salaries paid by the brewers for political and educational work compare favorably with those of the Anti-Saloon League. Robert Crain, as Washington representative, received over $2,000 a month; Hugh Fox, its secretary, received $1,250 per month. The numerous workers received from $200 to $600 per month, and the incomparable Percy Andreae was paid $40,000 a year for his work with the National Association of Commerce and Labor.[40]

## The Brewers' Blacklist

Not only did the brewers appeal to allied industries for funds; they insisted that business men from whom they purchased goods should have no other god than John Barleycorn.

[39] *Ibid.*, pp. 38–52, 70–73, 658, 754–55, 9, 40–41. Feigenspan wrote to Brisbane June 29, 1917, in part, as follows: "We agreed to supply you with a capital of five hundred thousand dollars ($500,000) for the purchase and establishment of a newspaper by you. We have, at this time, supplied two hundred and ninety-five thousand dollars ($295,000), although I do not enter into any legal obligation to do so, on behalf of myself or others. The understanding of myself and my friends with you, of which understanding this is a memorandum, is as follows:

"The money, which we gladly contribute to your enterprise, is to be disposed of, absolutely at your discretion for the purchase, maintenance and establishment of a daily newspaper.

"It is understood, that, after a period of five years, you will repay to me and my associates, at your discretion and convenience, on account of the principal, so much of the profits as may be derived from such newspaper as may, in your judgment, be taken out of the business without interfering with its proper operation and development; and that you shall be under no liability whatsoever for repayment of the sums contributed other than out of such profits. It is understood that no interest shall be paid upon this money, our claim to be satisfied in full upon the repayment of the principal without interest."

On July 30, 1918, he wrote (*ibid.*):

"The only evidence of the foregoing indebtedness which I hold is a note of the Growing Circulation Corporation, dated June 21, 1917, for $300,000 upon which there was advanced the sum of $275,000 only, and a memorandum, dated at Newark, N. J., on June 21, 1917, signed by Mr. Arthur Brisbane. Up to the present date I have received no payment on account of the foregoing indebtedness."

[Signed] C. W. Feigenspan

[40] *Ibid.*, pp. 811, 870 and 451.

Manufacturers and dealers who failed to respond or who committed the heinous offense of contributing to the Anti-Saloon League were placed on an " unfriendly " list and members of the Association were advised not to patronize them. Such a blacklist sent out in April, 1915, contained the names of forty-nine firms, among them: The Pennsylvania Railroad Company; United States Steel Corporation; Pittsburgh Coal Company; John Wanamaker's; Western Union Telegraph Company; Hershey Chocolate Company; Goodyear Rubber Company; Reo Auto Company; S. S. Kresge Company; J. N. Gamble, of Proctor and Gamble; H. J. Heinz, of H. J. Heinz Company; S. S. Marvin, of the National Biscuit Company. B. F. Goodrich Company " claimed to be friendly, but two officers contributed to the Anti-Saloon League." Detectives were employed to investigate alleged contributions to dry organizations.[41]

Contributing to the drys and failure to contribute to the wets were not the sole reasons for proscription. The Liggett Drug Stores were considered unfriendly because they refused to sell liquor; the Blackstone Hotel in Chicago, because it observed and advocated the general observance of the Sunday closing law. The grievance against H. J. Heinz seems to be that he was president of a Sabbath school association which adopted a resolution favoring prohibition. The Delaware, Lackawanna and Western Railroad was listed because it forbade employees to drink; the Maryland Casualty Company, because its president favored local option.[42]

[41] *Ibid.*, pp. 117–18.

[42] *Ibid.*, pp. 117, 134–44, 215, 289. The League's position was less strategic for enforcing a boycott, but there is reason to believe it would not have hesitated to use that weapon if it could, and perhaps on occasion the weapon was used. Superintendent Baker warned a League convention: " The Temperance people must learn to quit spending money where it is used against their principles. To oppose a candidate for office because he stands for bad policies and at the same time support the men who support him is not consistent. To work and vote against the saloons in a community and then buy goods from those who work and vote for saloons is to be a half supporter of the saloons. If temper-

Because of the malodorous reputation of the liquor traffic, the brewers sought to veil their activities in sweet-sounding names: " Civic Liberty Leagues," " Manufacturing and Business Associations," " Manufacturers and Dealers Clubs," " Liberty Leagues," were some of the names under which they masqueraded. " The National Association of Commerce and Labor," organized in October, 1913, was designed to unite industries allied to the brewing business.[43] " The American Hotel Protective Association " was financed in part by the brewers.

The tactics employed by the brewers were certainly not peculiar to them. Defending what to them was a legitimate business, they had to meet the attacks of a well-organized and determined foe. If the brewers were in politics, so were the churches; if the liquor interests boycotted, the League was not guiltless; if the wets hid their political activities behind fancy names, other manufacturers and business men, wrapped in the ample folds of the Protestant Church, fought for sober and efficient workmen by driving the liquor traffic into the sea.

---

ance people and especially temperance women will withdraw their support from business men who espouse the cause of the saloon, and give that support to business men who oppose the saloon, it will not take long to get rid of the saloon." — *Proceedings of the Fourteenth Convention of the Anti-Saloon League,* 1911; see, also, *American Issue,* Ohio Edition, Feb. 5, 1910; Maryland Edition, Jan. 8, 1908; Oct. 24, 1908; and March 14, 1909.

[43] *Ibid.,* pp. 833–38, 314, 317. The name itself was adopted because of its official sound. — *Ibid.,* pp. 95, 369–400.

## WHO'S TO BLAME

A favorite Anti-Saloon League cartoon, frequently called "Passing the Buck."
The League unhesitatingly placed the blame upon the voter.

## APPENDIX A

### HOUSE VOTE ON HOBSON RESOLUTION, DEC. 22, 1914

| | Affirmative | | | Negative | | | Not Voting | | |
|---|---|---|---|---|---|---|---|---|---|
| | Dem. | Rep. | Other | Dem. | Rep. | Other | Dem. | Rep. | Other |
| Maine................... | ... | 2 | ... | 1 | ... | ... | ... | 1 | ... |
| New Hampshire.............. | ... | ... | ... | 2 | ... | ... | ... | ... | ... |
| Vermont................. | ... | 1 | ... | ... | 1 | ... | ... | ... | ... |
| Massachusetts.............. | 1 | ... | ... | 5 | 8 | ... | ... | ... | ... |
| Rhode Island.............. | ... | ... | ... | 2 | 1 | ... | ... | ... | ... |
| Connecticut................ | ... | ... | ... | 5 | ... | ... | ... | ... | ... |
| TOTAL NEW ENGLAND........ | 1 | 3 | ... | 15 | 10 | ... | ... | 1 | ... |
| New York.................. | ... | 3 | ... | 26 | 6 | 1 | 5 | 2 | ... |
| New Jersey................. | 1 | ... | ... | 7 | 2 | ... | 1 | ... | ... |
| Pennsylvania............... | 10 | 9 | ... | 6 | 5 | ... | 2 | 4 | ... |
| Delaware.................. | ... | ... | ... | 1 | ... | ... | ... | ... | ... |
| Maryland.................. | 2 | ... | ... | 4 | ... | ... | ... | ... | ... |
| TOTAL ATLANTIC............. | 13 | 12 | ... | 44 | 13 | 1 | 8 | 6 | ... |
| Ohio...................... | 3 | 3 | ... | 10 | ... | ... | 5 | ... | ... |
| Indiana................... | ... | ... | ... | 13 | ... | ... | ... | ... | ... |
| Illinois................... | 9 | 2 | ... | 10 | 3 | ... | 2 | ... | ... |
| Michigan.................. | ... | 9 | 2 | 2 | ... | ... | ... | ... | ... |
| Wisconsin................. | ... | 1 | ... | 2 | 7 | ... | 1 | ... | ... |
| Minnesota................. | ... | 4 | ... | 1 | 5 | ... | ... | ... | ... |
| Iowa...................... | 1 | 7 | ... | 1 | 1 | ... | 1 | ... | ... |
| TOTAL MID-WEST............. | 13 | 26 | 2 | 39 | 16 | ... | 9 | ... | ... |
| North Dakota............... | ... | 3 | ... | ... | ... | ... | ... | ... | ... |
| South Dakota............... | ... | 2 | ... | ... | ... | ... | ... | 1 | ... |
| Nebraska.................. | ... | 3 | ... | 3 | ... | ... | ... | ... | ... |
| Montana................... | 2 | ... | ... | ... | ... | ... | ... | ... | ... |
| Wyoming.................. | ... | 1 | ... | ... | ... | ... | ... | ... | ... |
| Idaho..................... | ... | 2 | ... | ... | ... | ... | ... | ... | ... |
| TOTAL NORTHWEST........... | 2 | 11 | ... | 3 | ... | ... | ... | 1 | ... |
| Kansas.................... | 2 | 4 | ... | ... | ... | ... | 1 | ... | 1 |
| Colorado.................. | 4 | ... | ... | ... | ... | ... | ... | ... | ... |
| Utah...................... | ... | ... | ... | ... | 2 | ... | ... | ... | ... |
| Nevada.................... | ... | ... | ... | ... | 1 | ... | ... | ... | ... |
| Arizona................... | 1 | ... | ... | ... | ... | ... | ... | ... | ... |
| New Mexico................ | 1 | ... | ... | ... | ... | ... | ... | ... | ... |
| TOTAL SOUTHWEST........... | 8 | 4 | ... | ... | 3 | ... | 1 | ... | ... |
| California................. | 1 | 2 | ... | 2 | 4 | 1 | 1 | ... | ... |
| Washington................ | ... | 3 | 2 | ... | ... | ... | ... | ... | ... |
| Oregon.................... | ... | 3 | ... | ... | ... | ... | ... | ... | ... |
| TOTAL PACIFIC............. | 1 | 8 | 2 | 2 | 4 | 1 | 1 | ... | ... |
| West Virginia.............. | 1 | 3 | ... | ... | ... | ... | 1 | 1 | ... |
| Kentucky.................. | 5 | 2 | ... | 4 | ... | ... | ... | ... | ... |
| Tennessee................. | 7 | 2 | ... | ... | ... | ... | 1 | ... | ... |
| Missouri.................. | 11 | ... | ... | 3 | 1 | ... | 1 | ... | ... |
| Oklahoma................. | 5 | 1 | ... | ... | ... | ... | 1 | 1 | ... |
| TOTAL BORDER.............. | 29 | 8 | ... | 7 | 1 | ... | 4 | 2 | ... |
| Virginia................... | 7 | 1 | ... | 2 | ... | ... | ... | ... | ... |
| North Carolina............. | 7 | ... | ... | 1 | ... | ... | 2 | ... | ... |
| South Carolina............. | 7 | ... | ... | ... | ... | ... | ... | ... | ... |
| Georgia................... | 8 | ... | ... | 3 | ... | ... | 1 | ... | ... |
| Florida................... | 2 | ... | ... | ... | ... | ... | 2 | ... | ... |
| Alabama.................. | 4 | ... | ... | 5 | ... | ... | 1 | ... | ... |
| Mississippi................ | 7 | ... | ... | 1 | ... | ... | ... | ... | ... |
| Louisiana................. | 1 | ... | ... | 6 | ... | ... | 1 | ... | ... |
| Arkansas.................. | 7 | ... | ... | ... | ... | ... | ... | ... | ... |
| Texas..................... | 3 | ... | ... | 13 | ... | ... | 2 | ... | ... |
| TOTAL SOUTH............... | 53 | 1 | ... | 31 | ... | ... | 8 | ... | ... |
| GRAND TOTAL............ | 120 | 73 | 4 | 141 | 47 | 2 | 32 | 10 | 1 |

## APPENDIX B
HOUSE VOTE ON DISTRICT OF COLUMBIA PROHIBITION BILL
Feb. 28, 1917

| | AFFIRMATIVE | | | NEGATIVE | | | NOT VOTING | | |
|---|---|---|---|---|---|---|---|---|---|
| | Dem. | Rep. | Other | Dem. | Rep. | Other | Dem. | Rep. | Other |
| Maine...................... | ... | 3 | ... | 1 | ... | ... | ... | ... | ... |
| New Hampshire............... | ... | 2 | ... | ... | ... | ... | ... | ... | ... |
| Vermont.................... | ... | 1 | ... | ... | 1 | ... | ... | ... | ... |
| Massachusetts............... | ... | 6 | ... | 4 | 6 | ... | ... | ... | ... |
| Rhode Island............... | ... | ... | ... | ... | 2 | ... | 1 | ... | ... |
| Connecticut................ | ... | ... | ... | ... | 4 | ... | ... | 1 | ... |
| TOTAL NEW ENGLAND......... | ... | 12 | ... | 5 | 13 | ... | 1 | 1 | ... |
| New York................... | ... | 11 | ... | 13 | 12 | ... | 5 | 1 | 1 |
| New Jersey................. | ... | 1 | ... | 4 | 7 | ... | ... | ... | ... |
| Pennsylvania............... | ... | 12 | ... | 6 | 17 | ... | ... | 1 | ... |
| Delaware................... | ... | 1 | ... | ... | ... | ... | ... | ... | ... |
| Maryland................... | 2 | ... | ... | 3 | 1 | ... | ... | ... | ... |
| TOTAL ATLANTIC.............. | 2 | 25 | ... | 26 | 37 | ... | 5 | 2 | 1 |
| Ohio....................... | 1 | 11 | ... | 8 | 1 | ... | ... | 1 | ... |
| Indiana.................... | 11 | 2 | ... | ... | ... | ... | ... | ... | ... |
| Illinois................... | 5 | 12 | ... | 5 | 5 | ... | ... | ... | ... |
| Michigan................... | ... | 9 | ... | 1 | 2 | ... | 1 | ... | ... |
| Wisconsin.................. | ... | 6 | ... | 3 | 2 | ... | ... | ... | ... |
| Minnesota.................. | ... | 6 | 1 | 1 | 2 | ... | ... | ... | ... |
| Iowa....................... | 1 | 9 | ... | ... | 1 | ... | ... | ... | ... |
| TOTAL MID-WEST............. | 18 | 55 | 1 | 18 | 13 | ... | 1 | 1 | ... |
| North Dakota............... | ... | 3 | ... | ... | ... | ... | ... | ... | ... |
| South Dakota............... | 1 | 2 | ... | ... | ... | ... | ... | ... | ... |
| Nebraska................... | 2 | 3 | ... | 1 | ... | ... | ... | ... | ... |
| Montana.................... | 2 | ... | ... | ... | ... | ... | ... | ... | ... |
| Wyoming.................... | ... | 1 | ... | ... | ... | ... | ... | ... | ... |
| Idaho...................... | ... | 2 | ... | ... | ... | ... | ... | ... | ... |
| TOTAL NORTHWEST............. | 5 | 11 | ... | 1 | ... | ... | ... | ... | ... |
| Kansas..................... | 6 | 2 | ... | ... | ... | ... | ... | ... | ... |
| Colorado................... | 3 | 1 | ... | ... | ... | ... | ... | ... | ... |
| Utah....................... | 1 | 1 | ... | ... | ... | ... | ... | ... | ... |
| Nevada..................... | ... | ... | ... | ... | 1 | ... | ... | ... | ... |
| Arizona.................... | 1 | ... | ... | ... | ... | ... | ... | ... | ... |
| New Mexico................. | ... | 1 | ... | ... | ... | ... | ... | ... | ... |
| TOTAL SOUTHWEST............. | 11 | 5 | ... | ... | 1 | ... | ... | ... | ... |
| California................. | 4 | 1 | 2 | ... | 1 | 1 | ... | 2 | ... |
| Washington................. | 1 | 3 | ... | ... | ... | ... | ... | 1 | ... |
| Oregon..................... | ... | 2 | ... | ... | 1 | ... | ... | ... | ... |
| TOTAL PACIFIC............... | 5 | 6 | 2 | ... | 2 | 1 | 1 | 3 | ... |
| West Virginia.............. | 2 | 4 | ... | ... | ... | ... | ... | ... | 9... |
| Kentucky................... | 5 | 2 | ... | 4 | ... | ... | ... | ... | ... |
| Tennessee.................. | 8 | 2 | ... | ... | ... | ... | ... | ... | ... |
| Missouri................... | 10 | ... | ... | 1 | 2 | ... | 2 | ... | ... |
| Oklahoma................... | 6 | 1 | ... | ... | ... | ... | 1 | ... | ... |
| TOTAL BORDER............... | 31 | 9 | ... | 5 | 2 | ... | 3 | ... | ... |
| Virginia................... | 9 | 1 | ... | ... | ... | ... | ... | ... | ... |
| North Carolina............. | 8 | 1 | ... | 1 | ... | ... | ... | ... | ... |
| South Carolina............. | 6 | ... | ... | ... | ... | ... | 1 | ... | ... |
| Georgia.................... | 12 | ... | ... | 1 | ... | ... | 1 | ... | ... |
| Florida.................... | 2 | ... | ... | ... | ... | ... | ... | ... | ... |
| Alabama.................... | 8 | ... | ... | 2 | ... | ... | ... | ... | ... |
| Mississippi................ | 8 | ... | ... | ... | ... | ... | ... | ... | ... |
| Louisiana.................. | 5 | ... | ... | 2 | ... | 1 | ... | ... | ... |
| Arkansas................... | 6 | ... | ... | ... | ... | ... | 1 | ... | ... |
| Texas...................... | 10 | ... | ... | 7 | ... | ... | 1 | ... | ... |
| TOTAL SOUTH................. | 74 | 2 | ... | 13 | ... | 1 | 4 | ... | ... |
| GRAND TOTAL............ | 146 | 125 | 3 | 68 | 68 | 2 | 15 | 7 | 1 |

## APPENDIX C

HOUSE VOTE ON PROHIBITION AMENDMENT, DEC. 17, 1917

| | Affirmative | | | Negative | | | Not Voting | | | Gain over vote on Hobson resolution of 1914 | | |
|---|---|---|---|---|---|---|---|---|---|---|---|---|
| | Dem. | Rep. | Other | Dem. | Rep. | Other | Dem. | Rep. | Other | Dem. | Rep. | Other |
| Maine | | 4 | | | | | | | | | 2 | |
| New Hampshire | | 2 | | | | | | | | | 2 | |
| Vermont | | 1 | | | 1 | | | | | | | |
| Massachusetts | 1 | 4 | 1 | 1 | 5 | | 2 | 2 | | | 4 | 1 |
| Rhode Island | | 1 | | 1 | 1 | | | | | | 1 | |
| Connecticut | | | | 1 | 4 | | | | | | | |
| Total New England | 1 | 12 | 1 | 3 | 11 | | 2 | 2 | | | 9 | 1 |
| New York | 1 | 12 | | 15 | 11 | 1 | | 3 | | 1 | 9 | |
| New Jersey | | 2 | | 2 | 6 | | 1 | 1 | | −1 | 2 | |
| Pennsylvania | 4 | 14 | | 4 | 14 | | | | | −6 | 5 | |
| Delaware | 1 | | | | | | | | | 1 | | |
| Maryland | 1 | 1 | | 3 | 1 | | | | | −1 | 1 | |
| Total Atlantic | 7 | 29 | | 24 | 32 | 1 | 1 | 4 | | −6 | 17 | |
| Ohio | 5 | 7 | | 7 | 1 | | 1 | 1 | | 2 | 4 | |
| Indiana | 4 | 9 | | | | | | | | 4 | 9 | |
| Illinois | 2 | 15 | | 3 | 4 | 1 | | 2 | | −7 | 13 | |
| Michigan | | 10 | | 1 | 1 | | | 1 | | | 1 | −2 |
| Wisconsin | | 6 | | | 5 | | | | | | 5 | |
| Minnesota | | 8 | 1 | 1 | | | | | | | 4 | 1 |
| Iowa | | 10 | | | 1 | | | | | −1 | 3 | |
| Total Mid-West | 11 | 65 | 1 | 12 | 12 | 1 | 1 | 4 | | −2 | 39 | −1 |
| North Dakota | | 2 | 1 | | | | | | | | | |
| South Dakota | 1 | 2 | | | | | | | | | | |
| Nebraska | 2 | 3 | | | | | 1 | | | 2 | | |
| Montana | 1 | 1 | | | | | | | | 1 | | |
| Wyoming | | 1 | | | | | | | | | | |
| Idaho | | 2 | | | | | | | | | | |
| Total Northwest | 4 | 11 | 1 | | | | 1 | | | 3 | | |
| Kansas | 5 | 3 | | | | | | | | 3 | −1 | |
| Colorado | 2 | 1 | | | | | 1 | | | −2 | 1 | |
| Utah | 2 | | | | | | | | | 2 | | |
| Nevada | | | | | 1 | | | | | | | |
| Arizona | 1 | | | | | | | | | | | |
| New Mexico | 1 | | | | | | | | | | | |
| Total Southwest | 11 | 4 | | | 1 | | 1 | | | 3 | | |
| California | 2 | 2 | 1 | 2 | 2 | | | 2 | | 1 | | 1 |
| Washington | 1 | 3 | | | | | | 1 | | 1 | | −2 |
| Oregon | | 2 | | | 1 | | | | | | −1 | |
| Total Pacific | 3 | 7 | 1 | 2 | 3 | | | 3 | | 2 | −1 | −1 |
| West Virginia | 1 | 4 | | | | | 1 | | | | 1 | |
| Kentucky | 6 | 2 | | 3 | | | | | | 1 | | |
| Tennessee | 8 | 2 | | | | | | | | 1 | | |
| Missouri | 12 | | | 1 | 2 | | 1 | | | 1 | | |
| Oklahoma | 6 | 1 | | | | | | 1 | | 1 | | |
| Total Border | 33 | 9 | | 4 | 2 | | 2 | 1 | | 4 | 1 | |
| Virginia | 9 | 1 | | | | | | | | 2 | | |
| North Carolina | 8 | | | 2 | | | | | | 1 | | |
| South Carolina | 6 | | | 1 | | | | | | −1 | | |
| Georgia | 12 | | | | | | | | | 4 | | |
| Florida | 4 | | | | | | | | | 2 | | |
| Alabama | 5 | | | | | | | | | 1 | | |
| Mississippi | 8 | | | 5 | | | | | | 1 | | |
| Louisiana | 4 | | | 3 | 1 | | | | | 3 | | |
| Arkansas | 6 | | | | | | 1 | | | −1 | | |
| Texas | 8 | | | 8 | | | 2 | | | 5 | | |
| Total South | 70 | 1 | | 19 | 1 | | 3 | | | 17 | | |
| GRAND TOTAL | 140 | 138 | 4 | 64 | 62 | 2 | 11 | 14 | | 21 | 65 | −1 |

## APPENDIX D

The following list of the larger contributors to the National Anti-Saloon League was submitted to the Senate Committee on Campaign Expenditures, 1926. (Senate Report 1197, 69th Congress, 2d Session.)

### SOME IMPORTANT CONTRIBUTORS TO THE ANTI-SALOON LEAGUE

| | | |
|---|---|---:|
| **1924** Balance | ...................................................... | $322,350 |
| Oct. 13 — Joseph Boyer | ........................................ | 1,250 |
| Oct. 21 — H. L. Mason, Jr. | ................................... | 1,000 |
| **1925** | | |
| Jan. 12 — H. M. Austin | ...................................... | 1,000 |
| Feb. 5 — Joseph Boyer | ........................................ | 5,000 |
| Feb. 5 — P. A. Peterson | ...................................... | 250 |
| Mar. 3 — " | ...................................... | 500 |
| Apr. 6 — " | ...................................... | 250 |
| Apr. 11 — J. D. Rockefeller, Jr. and Sr. | ....................... | 20,000 |
| Apr. 15 — North Woodward M. E. Church, S. S. Kresge | .......... | 5,000 |
| June 9 — A friend of W. H. Russell [Probably H. H. Russell] | ..... | 600 |
| July 9 — H. G. Pounsford | .................................... | 500 |
| July 29 — P. A. Peterson | ..................................... | 250 |
| Aug. 10 — Joseph Boyer | ....................................... | 1,000 |
| Sept. 18 — P. A. Peterson | .................................... | 500 |
| Dec. 4 — The Misses Colvin | .................................. | 1,000 |
| Dec. 23 — H. G. Pounsford | ................................... | 500 |
| **1926** | | |
| Jan. 11 — H. M. Austin | ...................................... | 1,000 |
| Feb. 26 — P. A. Peterson | ..................................... | 1,000 |
| Feb. 24 — Joseph Boyer | ....................................... | 2,500 |
| Mar. 6 — Thomas G. Long | .................................... | 600 |
| Apr. 1 — A. E. Laitner ......................................... (North Woodward M. E. Church for S. S. Kresge) .. | | 2,500 |
| Apr. 1 — J. H. Baker, Frederick, Md. | ........................ | 500 |
| Apr. 1 — Charles M. Cox, Dedham, Mass. | ...................... | 500 |
| Apr. 10 — A. E. Laitner, Treasurer, North Woodward M. E. Church | | 2,500 |
| Apr. 10 — Rufus Bates, Treasurer, First Congregational Church, Weymouth, Mass. | ............................... | 1,000 |
| Apr. 10 — Wm. G. Harbison, Pittsburgh | ....................... | 250 |
| Apr. 30 — James S. McKee, Muscatine, Iowa | ................... | 1,000 |
| May 5 — H. G. Pounsford | .................................... | 500 |
| May 10 — C. O. Blood, Lynn, Mass. | ........................... | 1,000 |
| May 3 — P. A. Peterson | ...................................... | 3,000 |
| May 10 — Charles L. Huston, Coatsville, Pa. | .................... | 500 |

May 17 — Joseph Boyer, Detroit .............................. 2,500
May 17 — E. Jameson, New York City ......................... 500
May 21 — Clarence H. Howard, St. Louis ...................... 500
May 24 — Hugh Strange, Menosha, Wis. ....................... 500
May 24 — Paul Strange, Menosha, Wis. ........................ 500
June  2 — A lifetime friend of H. H. Russell ..................... 600

To this list of League contributors may be added the following supplied by the United States Brewers' Association:

Officers of Rogers Peet and Co., of New York
United States Steel Corporation
James Horton, Horton's Ice Cream Co.
A. L. Garford (formerly of Garford Motor Co.)
J. L. Hudson, Hudson Motor Car Co., Detroit
Henry M. Leland, manager, Cadillac Motor Car Co.
John Wanamaker, Philadelphia
Joseph Boyer, Burroughs Adding Machine Co., Detroit
John T. Stone, president, Maryland Casualty Co.
R. E. Olds, president, Reo Motor Car Co.
R. H. Scott, manager, Reo Motor Car Co.
S. S. Marvin, manager, National Biscuit Co.

(*U. S. Senate Document No. 62,* 66th Congress, 1st Session, 1919, pp. 117 ff.)

APPENDIX

SUMMARY OF FINANCES OF STATE AND

1911–1919 and

Based on questionnaire sent

| STATE | METHODS | | SOURCES | | |
|---|---|---|---|---|---|
| | 1911–19 | 1920–25 | Individuals | Churches | Corporations |
| Arkansas..... | No record | Churches | Less than 5% | 95% | None |
| Connecticut | None | 1922–24 † | 30% | 70% | None |
| Illinois....... | No record | No record | .... | .... | ..... |
| Kansas....... | Organized 1917 | Public meetings | 15% | 85% | None |
| Louisiana..... | Three-year pledge system * | .... | .... | .... | ..... |
| Mississippi | Organized 1916* | .... | 6% | 94% | None |
| Nevada...... | Organized 1917 | Churches and individuals | 10% | 90% | None |
| New Jersey | ............. | .... | 19% | 80% | Less than 1% |
| North Carolina | Offerings in public meetings | Same | 85% ‡ | 5% § | 10% |
| Oklahoma.... | Subscriptions and cash at meetings | .... | ...... | .... | .... |
| Pennsylvania.. | Churches | Churches | About 6% | 94% | None |
| South Carolina | Public meeting, gifts, pledges | .... | 4% | 95% | 1% |
| South Dakota. | Subscriptions and cash at meetings | Same | 100% ¶ | .... | .... |
| Virginia...... | Churches of 14 denominations | .... | 18–20% | 80–82% | None |
| National Anti-Saloon League | Individuals and churches | }.....{ | 1911–19, 20% | 80% | .... |
| | | | 1919–25, 8% | 92% | Less than 1% |

* Received financial aid from National League.
† During this period the Connecticut league was administered by the National League.

# E

## NATIONAL ANTI-SALOON LEAGUES

1920–1925

to superintendents in 1926

| RECEIPTS | | EXPENDITURES | | CONTRIBUTORS |
| Peak Year | Total | Peak Year | Total | |
| 1911–25 | 1911–19 | 1911–25 | 1911–19 | |
|---|---|---|---|---|
| $6,500 | Records lost in fire | About $6,500 | ...... | ...... |
| 1925  8,000 | ...... | 1925  14,000 | ...... | ...... |
| 239,000 | $1,149,000 | ...... | ...... | No record |
| 1922  52,559 | ...... | 51,899 | ...... | 15,000 |
| ...... | ...... | ...... | ...... | 1,000 |
| Over  7,000 | 32,000 | 7,000 | 28,800 | ...... |
| 2,716 | 1918–19  3,927 | 2,515 | 1918–19  3,800 | 1,200 |
| 85,291 | 462,046 | 84,841 | 462,046 | 12,633 |
| 1920  29,246 | 62,307 | 1920  29,038 | 60,000 | 4,000 |
| 1914  10,439 | 65,687 | 1914  9,351 | 63,835 | ...... |
| 1920  187,617 | 770,041 | 1920  187,742 | 757,671 | About  115,000 |
| 3,500 | 18,000 | 7,000 | 22,500 | 3,000 |
| 40,706 | 126,714 | 45,897 | 60,000 | 7,000 |
| ...... | ...... | ...... | ...... | ...... |
| 1914  84,074 | 326,548 | 1914  84,450 | 325,311 | 1920–24  22,000 |
| 1918–19  820,359 | 2,282,650 | 1918–19  820,359 | 2,282,650 | 1919  135,000 |

‡ Represents the amount furnished by the National League, which is incorporated.
§ Given by the church as a body.
¶ Includes individuals in church meetings.

# APPENDIX F

## FEES PAID TO SPECIAL SPEAKERS EMPLOYED BY THE NATIONAL ANTI-SALOON LEAGUE, 1914–'25

| | 1914 | 1915 | 1916 | 1917 | 1918 | 1919 | 1920 | 1921 | 1922 | 1923 | 1924 | 1925 | TOTAL |
|---|---|---|---|---|---|---|---|---|---|---|---|---|---|
| Bale, F. G. | | | | 734 | | 559 | | | | | | | 1,293 |
| Banks, L. A. | 1,700 | 5,028 | 4,800 | 5,522 | 5,672 | 6,059 | 6,597 | 5,918 | 4,943 | 4,550 | 3,950 | | 54,739 |
| Barton, A. J. | | 555 | | | | | | | | | | | 555 |
| Bitler, J. S. | 1,075 | 603 | | | | | | | | | | | 1,678 |
| Bryan, W. J. | | | | | | 11,000 | | | | | | | 11,000 |
| Cairns, T. A. | 1,650 | 300 | | | | 250 | | | | | | | 2,200 |
| Camp, J. G. | | | | | | 1,186 | 1,371 | | | | | | 2,557 |
| Cochran, E. R. | | | | | | 265 | | | | | | | 265 |
| Cotton, M. E. | | | | | | | | 450 | | 589 | | | 1,039 |
| Ebbetts, F. B. | | | 171 | | | | | | | | | | 171 |
| Finch, A. J. | | | | 268 | | | | | | | | | 268 |
| Geisel, C. E. | | | 985 | 2,770 | | | | | | | | | 3,755 |
| Gibson, H. C. | | | | | | | | | 151 | | | | 151 |
| Glenn, R. B. | | | 1,590 | 700 | | | | | | | | | 2,290 |
| Green, Ida. | | | | | | | 300 | 900 | | | | | 1,200 |
| Hammond, G. M. | | | | | | 1,600 | 3,000 | 3,000 | 1,072 | | | | 8,672 |
| Henry, G. A. | | | | | | | 600 | 975 | | | | | 1,575 |
| Herwig, W. J. | | | | | | | | | | 679 | | | 679 |
| High, F. A. | | | | 405 | | | | | | | | | 405 |
| Hobson, R. P. | 400 | 10,625 | 12,450 | 17,275 | 18,737 | 31,038 | 32,800 | 29,600 | 18,325 | | | | 171,250 |
| Holloway, G. A. | | | | 650 | | | | | | | | | 650 |
| Holsaple, R. N. | | | | 113 | | | | | | | | | 113 |
| Horton, L. R. | | | | | | | | | 1,125 | 2,876 | 3,064 | 1,004 | 8,069 |
| Hutton, R. P. | | | 506 | | | | | | | | | | 506 |
| Johnson, W. E. | | | | 2,700 | 1,438 | 2,700 | 3,300 | 3,600 | 4,186 | | | 883† | 18,807 |
| Kramer, J. F. | | | | | | | | | 625 | | | | 625 |
| Landis, F. | | 150 | 2,550 | | | | | | | | | | 2,700 |

| Name | 1 | 2 | 3 | 4 | 5 | 6 | 7 | 8 | 9 | 10 | 11 | 12 | Total |
|---|---|---|---|---|---|---|---|---|---|---|---|---|---|
| Landrith, I. | | | 740 | | 1,260 | 7,763 | 4,260 | 4,880 | 4,377 | 5,625 | 5,036 | | 33,941 |
| McBride, F. S. | | | | | | 78 | | | | | | | 78 |
| Mills, B. F. | | 750 | | | | | | | | | | | 750 |
| Morrow, G. W. | 4,234* | 2,667 | 2,785 | 2,876 | 2,981 | 4,271 | 4,661 | 4,694 | 5,118 | 5,400 | 3,471 | 536 | 43,694 |
| Nolan, J. Q. | | | | | | 343 | | | | | | | 343 |
| Patterson, M. R. | 5,420 | 8,000 | 6,250 | 5,000 | 5,487 | 7,750 | | 4,304 | | | | | 42,211 |
| Patterson, R. J. | | | 900 | | | | | | | | | | 900 |
| Peters, J. S. | | | | | | | 1,045 | 3,911 | | | | | 4,956 |
| Phifer, W. D. | | | | 1,017 | | 407 | | | | | | | 1,424 |
| Poling, D. A. | 200 | | | | | | | | | | | | 200 |
| Pool, W. C. | | | | | | | 480 | 697 | | | | | 1,177 |
| Rankin, A. C. | | | | | | −426 | | | | | | | 426 |
| Richardson, E. J. | | | | 1,225 | 200 | | | | | | | | 1,425 |
| Saleeby, C. W. | | | | | | | 22,185 | 2,178 | | | | | 24,363 |
| Small, S. W. | 5,588 | 5,551 | 6,833 | 6,467 | 566 | | | | | | 5,450 | 2,200 | 32,655 |
| Smith, D. M. | 3,666 | | 5,483 | 687 | | 9,536 | 13,963 | 12,220 | 15,730 | 14,363 | 8,820 | 9,543 | 94,011 |
| Sterns, E. I. | 1,000 | | 3,000 | 3,000 | 250 | | | | | | | | 7,250 |
| Steele, S. A. | | | | | 175 | | | | | | | | 175 |
| Stuart, G. R. | | | 3,250 | 2,000 | 900 | 749 | 750 | | | | | | 7,649 |
| Swadener, M. | 1,771 | | 2,567 | 2,396 | 2,218 | 2,407 | 2,646 | 2,042 | | | | | 16,047 |
| Swift, C. F. | | | | | | | 3,187 | 2,694 | | | | | 5,881 |
| Upshaw, W. D. | | | | 1,050 | | 1,621 | | | | 50 | 25 | 35 | 2,781 |
| Wallace, M. | | | | 1,156 | 1,725 | 1,575 | | | | | | | 4,456 |
| Willis, F. B. | | | | | | 1,200 | | | | | | | 1,200 |
| Wright, S. | 800 | | 50 | | | | | | | | | | 850 |
| Woolley, W. G. | 601 | 3,200 | 4,750 | 5,400 | 5,267 | 6,727 | 4,971 | 2,742 | | | | | 33,658 |
| Ebbert, F. B. | | | | | | | | | | | 3,067 | 3,125† | 6,192 |
| TOTAL | 19,556 | 45,375 | 60,263 | 63,410 | 46,876 | 99,510 | 106,116 | 84,805 | 55,652 | 34,132 | 32,883 | 17,326 | 665,905 |

From *Report of the Senate Committee on Campaign Expenditures*, 1926, p. 1406, Exhibit No. 183.

* Both 1913 and 1914.  † 1926.

# INDEX

Abstinence, League does not require, of candidates, 87

Advertising, by brewers for political purposes, 252, 254; fund of $535,000 for U. S. Brewers' Association, 258, 263

Alcohol, deaths caused by, 40; assignation and anarchy (League propaganda), 45; *Ledger in Industry* (pamphlet), 56; insanity from, 56

Aldrich, George W., Republican boss, aids Anti-Saloon League, 179

Aliens, Anti-Saloon League suspicious of, 31; League demands deportation of, 34; Anderson insults, 233

Allen, Charles H., purchases *Montgomery Advertiser* with brewers' money, 263

Alvord, Anti-Saloon League lobbyist, quoted by Cannon, 137

*America,* Catholic paper, denounces Anti-Saloon League as tyranny, 28, note

*American Advance,* Prohibition Party paper, attacks League as Methodist machine, 19

American Federation of Labor, attitude of, toward liquor, 53

*American Issue,* summarizes status of liquor trade, 49; Publishing Company, 73; circulation of, 74 ff.; report of job department of publishing company, 75; describes liquor traffic, 243

A. P. A. (American Protective Association), and Anti-Saloon League, 24; League and aliens, 31. *See* Oglesby

American Temperance Society, pledges complete abstinence, 37

Anderson, William H., promotion of, 14, note; author of *Church in Action Against the Saloon,* 16, note; reports strength of New York League, 21 ff.; denounces Catholic

opposition to prohibition, 25; characterized by Hayes, 26; replies to Hayes, 26; defended by Hess, 27; calls Republican platform a cowardly falsehood, 82, note; fights Speaker Sweet of New York, 96; activities as lobbyist in Illinois and Maryland, 107–13; denounced as pariah, 111–12; interviews Speaker Cannon, 137; leads ratification fight in New York, 177–79; collections on commission basis, 193, note; convicted, 228; history of case, 228–40. *See* Anti-Rat Society

Andreae, Percy, says League is Protestant oligarchy, 18; paid $40,000 a year by U. S. Brewers' Association, 264

Annapolis, Maryland, Anti-Saloon League lobbying in, 107 ff.

Anti-Corn-Law League, methods similar to Anti-Saloon League, 79, 80, note

*Anti-Prohibition Manual,* describes methods and admits effectiveness of League tactics, 125

Anti-Rat Society, Anderson satirizes campaign of, in *Baltimore Sun,* 51, note

Anti-Saloon League, a pressure group, Preface and 83; J. M. Ellis, first lobbyist, 2; founded at Oberlin College, 2, 4; similar organizations preceding, 5, footnote; national organization founded, 6; Rev. Hiram Price, first national president, 6; nature of organization, 8 ff.; board of directors, 10; executive committee, 10, 11; general supt., 11, 12; financial sec., 12; Publishing Co., 12 and note; centralized control, 15; League machine, 15; plan of organization, 15; a political organization for Church, 16, note; non-partizan nature, 17, 81; reason for the name, 38; of Maryland, 44; attitude

200–207; purposes of (table), 201, 204 ff.; League must file political, 236; of brewers in Texas politics, 249–56.

Exposé of Anderson by Sweet, 97

"Face on the Barroom Floor," poem by H. D'Arcy, 67, note

Fairchild, James H., president of Oberlin College, head of Temperance Alliance, 2

Fanaticism, of Anti-Saloon League, 24; of League leaders, 29; Anderson not typical, 231; a favorite theme, 243

Farmers, organized by Anti-Saloon League, 124

Feigenspan, Christian, Newark brewer, subsidizes *Newark Ledger*, 263; subsidizes Arthur Brisbane, 263–64 and note

Fess, Simeon, of Ohio, speaks for League, 206

"Field Days," Anti-Saloon League finance system, 191

Finances, of Anti-Saloon League, early years, 181; Rockefeller aids, 182–84; brewers explain sources, 185, note; names of contributors kept secret, 185 and note; Wheeler explains sources, 188; the "widow's mite," 188–89; sources of, 189; size of contributions, 190–91; pledge plan to increase, 190–93; small, numerous donations, 193; collections on commission basis, 193, note; of national League, 194–200; budget system in churches, 194; special funds, contributors to, 198 and note; of American Issue Publishing Co., 199; salaries paid by League, 203–7; League and Corrupt Practices Acts, 207–18; corruption in Michigan League, 223–26; Anderson case, 228–40; crooked finances in Kansas, 240–43; of brewers in Texas, 249–51; of U. S. Brewers' Association, 258. *See* Dyer; "Field Days"

Financial secretary, 12

*Flag, The Stainless,* a League pamphlet, 63

Fleischmann Distilling Company, supports M. T. Herrick in Ohio, 90

Florida, Anti-Saloon League lobbying in, 114, note. *See* Bribery

Food, waste of, by liquor traffic, 69; food control bill, Lever, 166–71

Foreign language press, subsidized by brewers, 262–63

Forgery, Anderson convicted of, 228, 236–40

Fox, Hugh, sec. of U. S. Brewers' Association, salary of, 264

Frame-up, Anderson accused of "framing" Speaker Sweet, 96 ff.

Franking privilege, League's use of, accused of abuse, 134

Franklin, W., pres. of Kentucky Distillers' Co., 57

Frear, Congressman, of Wisconsin, endorsed by League, 94

Gehlke, C. E., studies relation of woman suffrage to temperance, 86, note

General superintendent, 11, 12; salary of, 207

German-American Alliance denounces politics in the pulpit, 34; Congress revokes charter of, 72; protests Local Option Law, 110; aids brewers in Iowa, 259; financed by brewers, 263

German, names of brewers, a target for League propaganda, 70; brewers denounced as pro-German, 157, 166; population appealed to by brewers, 246; voters organized by Texas brewers, 252–53; voters organized by brewers in Iowa, 259. *See* Hexamer

Germany, Congress declares war on, 163

Gibbons, Cardinal, opposes ratification of Eighteenth Amendment, 27; sends personal representative to attend League meeting, 108; favors local option, 119

Gilmore, T. M., president of Model License League, recognizes power of Anti-Saloon League, 22; "the saloon is doomed," 158; League a corporation-controlled lobby, 182

Goethe, cited as advocate of prohibition, 60

Graft, Texas brewers rely on, 255

Grant, U. S., cited as advocate of prohibition, 60